Published by:

Wiley Publishing, Inc.

111 River St.
Hoboken, NJ 07030-5774

ISBN: 978-0-470-63233-8 (paper); 978-0-470-94626-8 (ebk);
978-0-470-94625-1 (ebk); 978-0-470-94624-4 (ebk)

Editor: Cate Latting
Production Editor: Jonathan Scott
Photo Editor: Richard Fox
Cartographer: Roberta Stockwell
Production by Wiley Indianapolis Composition Services

For information on our other products and services or to obtain technical
support, please contact our Customer Care Department within the U.S.
at 877/762-2974, outside the U.S. at 317/572-3993 or fax 317/572-4002.

Wiley also publishes its books in a variety of electronic formats. Some
content that appears in print may not be available in electronic formats.

Manufactured in China

5   4   3   2   1

A Note from the Publisher

Organizing your time. That's what this guide is all about.

Other guides give you long lists of things to see and do and then expect you to fit the pieces together. The Day by Day guides are different. They tell you the best of everything, and then show you how to see it *in the smartest, most time-efficient way*. Our authors have designed detailed itineraries for you, organized by time, neighborhood, or special interest. Each tour comes with a bulleted map that takes you from stop to stop.

Hoping to pay your respects at the Pearl Harbor memorials, snorkel through schools of rainbow-colored fish, or hike to the top of Diamond Head? Planning a leisurely walk through Chinatown, or a whirlwind tour of the very best Oahu has to offer? Whatever your interest or schedule, the Day by Days give you the smartest routes to follow. Not only do we take you to the top attractions, hotels, and restaurants, but we also help you access those special moments that locals get to experience—those "finds" that turn tourists into travelers.

The Day by Days are also your top choice if you're looking for one complete guide for all your travel needs. The best hotels and restaurants for every budget, the greatest shopping values, the wildest nightlife—it's all here.

Why should you trust our judgment? Because our authors personally visit each place they write about. They're an independent lot who say what they think and would never include places they wouldn't recommend to their best friends. They're also open to suggestions from readers. If you'd like to contact them, please send your comments my way at feedback@wiley.com, and I'll pass them on.

Enjoy your Day by Day guide—the most helpful travel companion you can buy. And have the trip of a lifetime.

Warm regards,

Kelly Regan

Kelly Regan, Editorial Director
Frommer's Travel Guides

About the Author

A resident of the Big Island, **Jeanette Foster** has skied the slopes of Mauna Kea—during a Fourth of July ski meet, no less—and gone scuba diving with manta rays off the Kona Coast. A prolific writer widely published in travel, sports, and adventure magazines, she's also a contributing editor to *Hawaii* magazine, the editor of *Zagat's Survey to Hawaii's Top Restaurants,* and the Hawaii chapter author of *1,000 Places to See in the U.S.A. and Canada Before You Die.* In addition to writing this guide, Jeanette is the author of *Frommer's Hawaii 2011; Frommer's Maui 2011; Frommer's Kauai; Frommer's Hawaii with Kids; Frommer's Honolulu, Waikiki & Oahu; Frommer's Hawaii Day by Day; and Frommer's Maui Day by Day.*

Acknowledgments

Special thanks to Priscilla Life, the best researcher in Hawaii.

An Additional Note

Please be advised that travel information is subject to change at any time— and this is especially true of prices. We therefore suggest that you write or call ahead for confirmation when making your travel plans. The authors, editors, and publisher cannot be held responsible for the experiences of readers while traveling. Your safety is important to us, however, so we encourage you to stay alert and be aware of your surroundings.

Star Ratings, Icons & Abbreviations

Every hotel, restaurant, and attraction listing in this guide has been ranked for quality, value, service, amenities, and special features using a **star-rating system.** Hotels, restaurants, attractions, shopping, and nightlife are rated on a scale of zero stars (recommended) to three stars (exceptional). In addition to the star-rating system, we also use a **kids** icon to point out the best bets for families. Within each tour, we recommend cafes, bars, or restaurants where you can take a break. Each of these stops appears in a shaded box marked with a coffee-cup-shaped bullet ☕.

The following **abbreviations** are used for credit cards:

AE	American Express	DISC	Discover	V	Visa
DC	Diners Club	MC	MasterCard		

Travel Resources at Frommers.com

Frommer's travel resources don't end with this guide. Frommer's website, **www.frommers.com,** has travel information on more than 4,000 destinations. We update features regularly, giving you access to the most current trip-planning information and the best airfare, lodging, and car-rental bargains. You can also listen to podcasts, connect with other Frommers.com members through our active-reader forums, share your travel photos, read blogs from guidebook editors and fellow travelers, and much more.

A Note on Prices

In the "Take a Break" and "Best Bets" sections of this book, we have used a system of dollar signs to show a range of costs for 1 night in a hotel (the price of a double-occupancy room) or the cost of an entree at a restaurant. Use the following table to decipher the dollar signs:

Cost	Hotels	Restaurants
$	under $130	under $15
$$	$130–$200	$15–$30
$$$	$200–$300	$30–$40
$$$$	$300–$395	$40–$50
$$$$$	over $395	over $50

How to Contact Us

In researching this book, we discovered many wonderful places—hotels, restaurants, shops, and more. We're sure you'll find others. Please tell us about them, so we can share the information with your fellow travelers in upcoming editions. If you were disappointed with a recommendation, we'd love to know that, too. Please write to:

Frommer's Honolulu & Oahu Day by Day, 2nd Edition
Wiley Publishing, Inc. • 111 River St. • Hoboken, NJ 07030-5774

16 Favorite **Moments**

16 Favorite Moments

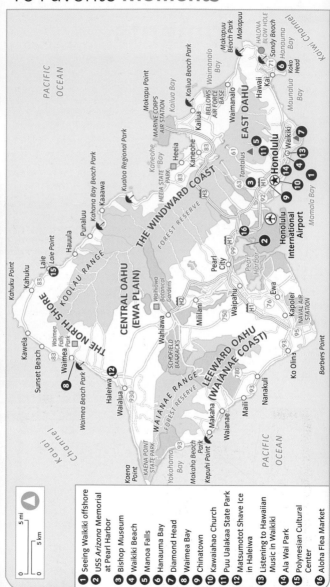

Previous page: Kualoa Regional Park at sunset.

Honolulu is filled with so many magic moments: the orange glow as the sun rises behind the outline of Diamond Head, the silvery reflection of the moon on the inky black waters of Waikiki at night, the intoxicating smell of plumeria flowers in the air, or the quiet whisper of bamboo dancing in the breeze. I hope this chapter will help you find a few favorite moments of your own.

1 Seeing Waikiki offshore. If you think Waikiki is beautiful, wait until you see it from a boat. I strongly urge you to either take a boat cruise during the day or, for the more romantically inclined, take a sunset cruise and watch the sun go down and the lights of Waikiki and Honolulu come up. If you are prone to seasickness, try the *Navatek* cruise; a high-tech stabilizing device eliminates any bobbing around in the water. See p 182.

2 Experiencing a turning point in America's history: the bombing of Pearl Harbor. I guarantee that you will never forget your reaction when you step on the deck of the USS *Arizona* Memorial at Pearl Harbor, and look down at the dark oil oozing like dripping blood from the ship underneath. December 7, 1941, the day when the 608-foot (185m) *Arizona* sank in just 9 minutes after being bombed during the Japanese air raid, will no longer seem like something from a book—it will be very real. The 1,177 men onboard plunged to a fiery death—and the United States went to war. *My tip:* Go early; you'll wait 2 to 3 hours if you visit at midday. You must wear closed-toe shoes. See p 41.

3 Walking back in history by exploring Bishop Museum. People always ask me: "Where do I see the 'real' Hawaii?" I always send them to the Bishop Museum. Don't think dreary rooms with stuff crowded into cases—think living history, as in experiencing goose bumps as a deep booming voice breaks into Hawaiian chant when you enter the Hawaiian Hall, or excitement as you watch live performances of traditional hula. Created by a Hawaiian princess in 1899, it not only is the foremost repository for Hawaiian cultural artifacts, but also has a new Science Center, where you can step into the interior of an erupting volcano. See p 41.

4 Getting a tan on Waikiki Beach. I've soaked up rays all over the globe, but nothing compares to the special experience of being kissed by the sun and serenaded by the sound of the tumbling surf while you lie on the soft sand of this world-famous beach. My favorite place to put my beach mat is directly in front of the big, pink Royal Hawaiian Hotel (where the angle of the beach is perfect for sunning). It's also a great spot for

USS Arizona *Memorial.*

Explore Oahu's underwater world at calm, shallow Hanauma Bay.

people-watching. I recommend arriving early; by midday (when the rays are at their peak), it's towel-to-towel out there. *See p 161.*

⑤ **Venturing into a rainforest just 15 minutes from Waikiki.** Don't miss my favorite magical experience on Oahu: immersing yourself in the misty sunbeams, where colorful birds flit among giant ferns and hanging vines, while towering tropical trees form a thick canopy that shelters all below in cool shadows. The emerald world of the Manoa Falls trail is a true Eden, and it's also a very short hike (less than a mile) to a freshwater pool and waterfall. *See p 167.*

⑥ **Snorkeling among the rainbow-colored fish in the warm waters of Hanauma Bay.** I love this underwater park, once a volcanic crater, because it's teeming with tropical fish and bordered by a 2,000-foot (610m) gold-sand beach. Plus, the bay's shallow water (10 ft./3m in places) is perfect for neophyte snorkelers. Arrive early to beat the crowds—and be aware that the bay is closed on Tuesday, when the fish have the day off. *See p 177.*

⑦ **Hiking to the top of Diamond Head for the perfect view of the island.** See Waikiki and Honolulu from the top of Hawaii's most famous landmark. Nearly everyone can handle this 1.4-mile (2.3km) round-trip hike, which goes up to the top of the 750-foot (229m) volcanic cone, where you have a 360-degree view of Oahu. Allow an hour for the trip up and back, bring $1 for the entry fee, and don't forget your camera. *See p 165.*

⑧ **Watching the North Shore's big waves.** When monstrous waves—some 30 feet (9.1m) tall—steamroll into Waimea Bay (Nov–Mar), I head out to the North Shore. Not only is it an amazing show, watching the best surfers in the world paddle out to challenge these freight trains, but it's also shocking to see how small they appear in the lip of the giant waves. My favorite part is feeling those waves when they break on the shore—the ground actually shakes and everyone on the beach is covered with salt-spray mist. And this unforgettable experience won't cost you a dime. *See p 136.*

⑨ **Buying a lei in Chinatown.** I love dipping into the cultural sights and exotic experiences to be had in Honolulu's Chinatown. Wander through this several-square-block area with its jumble of Asian shops offering herbs, Chinese groceries, and acupuncture services. Be sure to check out the lei sellers on Maunakea Street (near N. Hotel St.), where Hawaii's finest leis go for as little as $5. *See p 120.*

10 **Attending a Hawaiian-language church service.** On Sunday, I head over to the historic Kawaiahao Church, built in 1842, for the service (which is in Hawaiian) and the Hawaiian music. You can practically feel the presence of the Hawaiian monarchy, many of whom were crowned in this very building. Admission is free—let your conscience be your guide as to a donation. *See p 23.*

11 **Basking in the best sunset you'll ever see.** Anyone can stand on the beach and watch the sun set, but my favorite viewing point for saying *aloha-oe* to Sol is driving up a 1,048-foot (320m) hill named after a sweet potato. Actually, it's more romantic than it sounds. Puu Ualakaa State Park, at the end of Round Hill Drive, translates into "rolling sweet potato hill" (the name describes how early Hawaiians harvested the crop). This majestic view of the sunset is not to be missed. *See p 21.*

12 **Ordering a shave ice in a tropical flavor you can hardly pronounce.** I think you can actually taste the islands by slurping shave

You'll find leis of every color and description for sale in Chinatown.

ice. It's not quite a snow cone, but similar: Ice is shaved and then an exotic flavor is poured over it. My favorite is *li hing mui* (lee hing moo-ee), or dried plum, with sweet Japanese adzuki beans hidden inside. This taste of tropical paradise goes for less than $1.50 at Matsumoto Shave Ice in Haleiwa. *See p 16.*

13 **Listening to the soothing sounds of Hawaiian music.** Just before sunset, I head for the huge banyan tree at the Moana Surfrider's Banyan Veranda in Waikiki, order a libation, and sway to live Hawaiian music. Another quintessential sunset oasis is the Halekulani's House Without a Key, a sophisticated oceanfront lounge with wonderful hula and steel guitar music, a great view of Diamond Head, and the best mai tais on the island. *See p 131.*

14 **Discovering the ancient Hawaiian sport of canoe paddling.** For something you most likely will see only in Hawaii, find a comfortable spot at Ala Wai Park, next to the canal, and watch hundreds of canoe paddlers re-create this centuries-old sport of taking traditional Hawaiian canoes out to sea. Or try it yourself off Waikiki Beach. *See p 36.*

15 **Immersing yourself at the Polynesian Cultural Center.** Even though I have traveled throughout the Pacific, I still love spending a day (yes, plan for the entire day) at the Polynesian Cultural Center, a kind of living museum of Polynesia. Here you can see firsthand the lifestyles, songs, dance, costumes, and architecture of seven Pacific islands or archipelagos—Fiji, New Zealand, Marquesas, Samoa, Tahiti, Tonga, and Hawaii—in the re-created villages scattered throughout a 42-acre (17-hectare) lagoon park. *See p 17.*

House Without a Key is one of my favorite places to listen to music and sip a mai tai.

16 Finding a Bargain at the Aloha Flea Market. I'm not sure whether to categorize this as shopping or entertainment, but 50¢ will get you into this all-day show at the Aloha Stadium parking lot, where more than 1,000 vendors sell everything from junk to jewels. Half the fun is talking to the vendors and listening to their stories. Serious shoppers should go early for the best deals. Open Wednesday, Saturday, and Sunday from 6am to 3pm. *See p 29.* ●

Finding Your Way Around, Oahu-Style

Mainlanders sometimes find the directions given by locals a bit confusing. Seldom will you hear the terms east, west, north, and south; instead, islanders refer to directions as either ***makai*** (ma-kae), meaning toward the sea, or ***mauka*** (*mow*-kah), toward the mountains. In Honolulu, people use **Diamond Head** as a direction meaning to the east (in the direction of the world-famous crater called Diamond Head), and **Ewa** as a direction meaning to the west (toward the town called Ewa, on the other side of Pearl Harbor).

So, if you ask a local for directions, this is what you're likely to hear: "Drive 2 blocks *makai* (toward the sea), then turn Diamond Head (east) at the stoplight. Go 1 block, and turn *mauka* (toward the mountains). It's on the Ewa (western) side of the street."

1 Strategies for Seeing **Oahu**

Strategies for Seeing **Oahu**

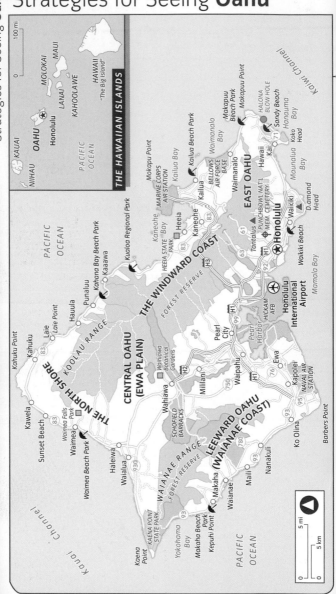

THE HAWAIIAN ISLANDS

0 [____] 100 mi

KAUAI
NIIHAU

OAHU
Honolulu

MOLOKAI
LANAI
KAHOOLAWE

MAUI

HAWAII
"The Big Island"

PACIFIC
OCEAN

Previous page: Waimea Canyon.

Oahu may be an island, but it's a good-size island, and your vacation time is precious. There really is just one cardinal rule: Relax. Don't run yourself ragged trying to see absolutely every thing—take the time to experience the magic of the island. In this chapter, I have several suggestions for making the most out of your time.

Rule #1. Go in the off season.

Not only will you save a bundle, but there will be fewer people, you'll get better service, the beaches will be less crowded, and you'll be able to get into your favorite restaurants. The "off season," September 1 to mid-December and March to June 1, is also when the weather is at its best (not too hot, not too rainy).

Rule #2. To get the best deals, do some research.

In this book, I give you my favorite picks of hotels, restaurants, activities, and airlines, but use that as a starting point. Go online and check out airfares, hotels, and package deals (airfare plus accommodations and sometimes car rental). Find out what prices are being offered before you book.

Rule #3. Think about how you want to spend your vacation.

Is this a lie-on-the-beach vacation or a get-up-early-and-do-an-adventure-every-day vacation? Or a combination? Whether you are traveling with your sweetie or you're bringing your family, make sure that everyone gets in on the planning—it makes for a vacation that everyone can enjoy.

Rule #4. Don't overschedule.

Don't make your days jampacked from the time you get up until you drop off to sleep at night. This is Hawaii: Stop and smell the plumeria. Allow time to just relax. And don't forget that you will most likely arrive

Stop and smell the plumeria.

jet-lagged, so ease into your vacation. Exposure to sunlight can help reset your internal clock, so hit the beach on your first day (and bring your suntan lotion).

Rule #5. Allow plenty of time to get around the island.

If you glance at a map, Oahu looks deceptively small—like you could just zip from one side of the island to the other. But you have to take traffic into consideration; from 6 to 9am and 3 to 6pm the main roads will be bumper-to-bumper with rush-hour traffic. Plan accordingly: Sleep late and get on the road after the traffic has cleared out.

I highly recommend that you rent a car, but don't just "view" the island from the car window. Plan to get out as much as possible to breathe in the tropical aroma, fill up on those views, and listen to the sounds of the tropics.

A relaxed drive along a winding coastal road may be a highlight of your trip.

Rule #6. If your visit is short, stay in one place.

Most places on Oahu are within easy driving distance of each other, and checking in and out of several hotels can get old fast. There's the schlepping of the luggage, the waiting in line to check in, the unpacking, and more . . . only to repeat the entire process a few days later. Your vacation time is too dear.

Rule #7. Pick the key activity of the day and plan accordingly.

To maximize your time, decide what you really want to do that day, and then plan all other activities in the same geographical area. That way you won't have to track back and forth across the island.

Rule #8. Remember you are on the island of aloha.

Honolulu is not the U.S. mainland. The islanders' way of life is very different. Slow down. Smile and say "aloha"; it's what the local residents do. Ask them: "Howzit?" (the local expression for "How are you?"). When they ask you tell 'em "Couldn't be better—I'm in Hawaii!" Wave at everyone. Laugh a lot, even if things aren't going as planned (hey, you're in paradise; how bad can it be?).

Rule #9. Use this book as a reference, not a concrete plan.

You will not hurt my feelings if you don't follow every single tour and do absolutely everything I suggest in the itinerary. Pick and choose according to your interests—don't feel like you have to follow my suggestions to the letter. ●

Attending a Hula competition is a great way to experience Hawaiian culture.

The Best of Oahu in Three Days

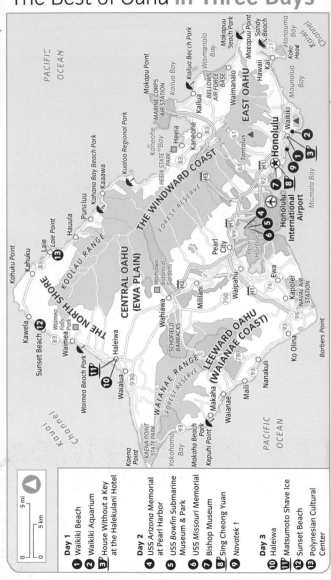

Day 1
1. Waikiki Beach
2. Waikiki Aquarium
3. House Without a Key at the Halekulani Hotel

Day 2
4. USS Arizona Memorial at Pearl Harbor
5. USS Bowfin Submarine Museum & Park
6. USS Missouri Memorial
7. Bishop Museum
8. Sing Cheong Yuan
9. Navatek 1

Day 3
10. Haleiwa
11. Matsumoto Shave Ice
12. Sunset Beach
13. Polynesian Cultural Center

Previous page: Statues at Polynesian Cultural Center.

You could spend weeks on Oahu without running out of things to do, but it's possible to see the highlights of this romantic isle in just 3 days. Following this tour will let you see the best of Oahu, from Waikiki to the North Shore. You'll definitely need to rent a car, so remember to plan for that cost. Each day begins and ends in Waikiki, which, like most urban cities, has traffic congestion, so allow plenty of travel time, especially during rush hour.
START: Waikiki. Trip Length: 109-mile (175km) loop.

Day 1

1 ★★★ kids Waikiki Beach. You'll never forget your first steps onto the powdery sands of this world-famous beach. If you're just off the plane, plan to spread your towel on the beach, take in the smell of the salt air, feel the warm breeze on your skin, and relax; you're in Hawaii. See p 161.

Walk down Waikiki Beach toward Diamond Head. Bus: 20.

2 ★★ kids Waikiki Aquarium. Explore Hawaii's underwater world without getting wet. This small but fabulous aquarium houses some 2,500 animals representing more than 420 species. You'll find everything from translucent jellyfish to lumbering turtles to

Chambered nautilus.

endangered Hawaiian monk seals—and even sharks. My favorite things to see are the chambered nautilus (nature's submarine and inspiration for Jules Verne's *20,000 Leagues Under the Sea*), the Edge of the Reef exhibit (where you see reef fish up close and personal), and the Mahimahi Hatchery (where these delicious eating fish are raised from egg to adult). ⏱ 2½ hr.; get there early on weekends before the crowds come. 2777 Kalakaua Ave. (across from Kapiolani Park). ☎ 808/923-9741. www.waquarium.org. Admission $9 adults; $6 active military, seniors, and college students; $4 children 13–17; $2 children 5–12; free for children 4 and under. Daily 9am–5pm (last tickets sold at 4:30pm).

Waikiki Beach. Spending some time in the sun is a great way to combat jet lag.

Retrace your steps down Waikiki Beach to Halekulani Hotel, or take bus no. 42.

3 ★★★ **House Without a Key at the Halekulani Hotel.** As the sun sinks toward the horizon, take a break with a libation at one of the most beautiful hotels on Waikiki Beach. You can watch the former Miss Hawaii, Kanoelehua Miller, dance hula to the riffs of Hawaiian steel guitar under a century-old kiawe tree. With the sunset and ocean glowing behind her, and Diamond Head visible in the distance, the scene is straight out of a storybook romantic, evocative, nostalgic. *2199 Kalia Rd. (Diamond Head side of Lewers St.).* ☎ *808/923-2311. $$$.*

Day 2

Get an early start to beat the crowds at Pearl Harbor. Drive west on H-1 past the airport to the USS *Arizona* Memorial exit, then follow the green-and-white signs; there's ample free parking. Or take the *Arizona* Memorial Shuttle Bus VIP (☎ 808/839-0911), which picks up at Waikiki hotels 6:50am–1pm ($9 per person round-trip). Bus: 20.

4 ★★★ **kids** USS *Arizona* **Memorial at Pearl Harbor.** The top attraction on Oahu is this unforgettable memorial. On December 7, 1941, the Japanese launched an air raid on Pearl Harbor that plunged the U.S. into World War II. This 608-foot (185m) battleship sank in 9 minutes without firing a shot, taking 1,177 sailors and Marines to their deaths. The deck of the *Arizona* lies 6 feet (1.8m) below the surface of the sea, with oil slowly oozing up from the engine room and staining the harbor's calm, blue water. Some say the ship still weeps for its lost crew. The excellent, 2½-hour ★★★ **Audio Tour** will make the trip even more meaningful—it's like having your own personal park ranger as a guide. The fee is $5 and worth every nickel. **Note:** Due to increased security measures, visitors cannot carry purses, handbags, fanny packs, backpacks, camera bags, diaper bags, or other items that offer concealment on the boat. Storage is available for a fee. ⏱ *3 hr.; go first thing in the morning to avoid the huge crowds; waits of 1–3 hr. are common. Pearl Harbor.* ☎ *808/422-0561 (recorded info), or 808/422-2771. www.nps.gov/usar. Free admission. Daily 7:30am–5pm (programs run 7:45am–3pm). Shirts and*

Observation deck at the USS Arizona *Memorial.*

closed-toe shoes required; no swimsuits or flip-flops allowed. Wheelchairs gladly accommodated.

If you're a real nautical history buff, stop in at the next few museums, which are described in the "Wartime Honolulu" tour starting on p 46. Otherwise, head directly to the Bishop Museum.

5 ★ kids **USS *Bowfin* Submarine Museum & Park.** *See p 47, bullet* **2**.

6 ★ kids **USS *Missouri* Memorial.** *See p 47, bullet* **3**.

From Arizona Memorial Dr. turn right on Kamehameha Hwy. (Hwy. 99). Take the ramp onto H-1 East toward Honolulu. Take Exit 20A (Likelike Hwy. exit). Turn left on Kalihi St. (Hwy. 63) to Bernice St. and turn right. Bus: 40, then transfer to the B City Express.

7 ★★★ kids **Bishop Museum.** If you are the least bit curious about what ancient Hawaii was like, this museum is a must-see. This multi-building museum has the world's greatest collection of natural and cultural artifacts from Hawaii and the Pacific. Another highlight is the terrific new 16,500-square-foot (1,533-sq.-m) Science Adventure Center, specializing in volcanology (one exhibit lets you walk inside an erupting volcano) and oceanography. In the Hawaiian Hall, you can venture back in history and see what Hawaiian culture was like before Westerners arrived. Don't miss my faves: the **Hula performances ★,** Monday to Friday at 11am and 2pm, and the terrific show in the planetarium, **Explorers of Polynesia,** 3:30pm daily. 🕐 *3–4 hr. 1525 Bernice St., just off Kalihi St. (aka Likelike Hwy.).* ☎ *808/847-3511. www.bishopmuseum.org. Admission $18 adults, $15 children 4–12 and seniors. Daily 9am–5pm.*

The Bishop Museum is a great rainy-day activity, but it's worth a visit even if it's not raining.

Turn right from the Bishop Museum parking lot onto Bernice St., right again on Houghtailing St., then left on Olomea St. (which becomes Vineyard Blvd.). Turn right on Maunakea St. Bus: 2.

8 ★ kids **Sing Cheong Yuan.** Venture into Chinatown for delicious Asian pastries, such as moon cakes and almond cookies, all at very reasonable prices. The shop also has a wide selection of dried and sugared candies (ginger, pineapple, lotus root) that make great gifts for friends back home. *1027 Maunakea St. (near King St.).* ☎ *808/531-6688. $.*

Continue down Maunakea St., turn left on N. King St., then right on Nuuanu Ave. Make a slight left on Nimitz Hwy. (Hwy. 92). Look for the sign for Pier 6 just after Aloha Tower, and turn right. Bus: 56.

9 ★ kids ***Navatek I.*** Wrap up your second day on Oahu with a sunset dinner cruise aboard a 140-foot-long (43m) SWATH (Small Waterplane Area Twin Hull) vessel.

This unique ship's superstructure—the part you ride on—rests on twin torpedo-like hulls that cut through the water so you don't bob like a cork and spill your mai tai; it also cuts down greatly on sea-sickness. Highlights of the cruise include gazing at the horizon as the sun sinks into the Pacific, then watching Waikiki light up as darkness descends. If you go between January and April, you might be lucky enough to see a humpback whale. ⏱ *2 hr. Aloha Tower Marketplace, Pier 6.* ☎ *808/973-1311. Lunch cruises $74 adults, $38 children 2–11. Dinner cruises $80 adults, $48 children 2–11.*

Take a right on Ala Moana Blvd. and follow it into Waikiki. Bus: 19 or 20.

Day 3
Spend your third day on Oahu on the North Shore. Take H-1 west out of Waikiki, then take the H-2 north exit (Exit 8A) toward Mililani/Wahiawa. After 7 miles

This colorful sign welcomes visitors to Haleiwa.

(11km), H-2 becomes Kamehameha Hwy. (Hwy. 80). Look for the turnoff to Haleiwa town. Bus: 19, then transfer to 52.

10 ★★★ kids **Haleiwa.** Start your day exploring this famous North Shore surfing town. *See p 138, bullet* ❹.

11 ★ kids **Matsumoto Shave Ice.** For a tropical taste of the islands, stop at this nearly 50-year-old shop where Hawaii's rendition of a snow cone is served: Instead of crushed ice, the ice is actually shaved and has a unique texture. My favorite of the rainbow of flavors available is the li hing mui (pronounced lee hing moo-ee), which is a preserved plum with a mixture of Chinese spices, sugar, and salt. *66–087 Kamehameha Hwy., Haleiwa.* ☎ *808/637-4827. $.*

Continue down Kamehameha Hwy. for about 6½ miles (10km). Bus: 52.

12 ★★★ kids **Sunset Beach.** Swim in the summer or just sit and watch the big wave surfers in winter. *See p 161.*

Even die-hard landlubbers can enjoy a cruise on the stable Navatek.

Try to catch one of the performances at the Polynesian Cultural Center.

Drive another 12 miles (19km) down Kamehameha Hwy. to the town of Laie. Bus: 52 to Turtle Bay Resort, then 55.

⑬ ★★ kids **Polynesian Cultural Center.** This "living museum" of Polynesia features the lifestyles, songs, dance, costumes, and architecture of seven Pacific islands or archipelagos—Fiji, New Zealand, Marquesas, Samoa, Tahiti, Tonga, and Hawaii—in the re-created villages scattered throughout the 42-acre (17-hectare) lagoon park. I recommend traveling through this museum via canoe on a man-made freshwater lagoon. Each village is "inhabited" by native students from Polynesia who attend Hawaii's Brigham Young University. The park, which is operated by the Mormon Church, also features a variety of stage shows celebrating the music, dance, history, and culture of Polynesia. Stay for the show, but skip the luau. ⏱ *4–6 hr.; get there when the doors open to avoid the crowds. 55–370 Kamehameha Hwy., Laie.* ☎ *800/367-7060, 808/293-3333, or 808/923-2911. www.polynesia.com. Admission: Various packages available for $45–$225 adults, $35–$175 children 3–11; see website for details. Mon–Sat 12:30–9:30pm.*

To get back to Waikiki, just continue along Kamehameha Hwy. (Hwy. 83), which follows the windward coastline for about 22 miles (35km). Look for the sign for the Likelike Hwy. (Hwy. 63). From Likelike Hwy. take the Kalihi St./H-1 exit. Take H-1 to Waikiki. Bus: 55, then transfer to 19 or 20.

It's Sure Not New York City

Unfortunately, Honolulu does not have convenient public transportation, which is why I strongly recommend that you rent a car. In case that's not possible, I've added information on how to get around using Honolulu's public bus system (called TheBus), which costs $2.25 per ride. But TheBus is set up for Hawaii residents, not tourists carrying coolers, beach toys, or suitcases (all carry-ons must fit under the bus seat). Some trips may be extremely complicated, requiring several bus transfers, or TheBus may not stop right in front of your destination, forcing you to walk several blocks. Before you set out, always call **TheBus** (☎ **808/848-5555,** or 808/296-1818 for recorded information) or check out **www.thebus.org** to get information on your route.

The Best of Oahu in One Week

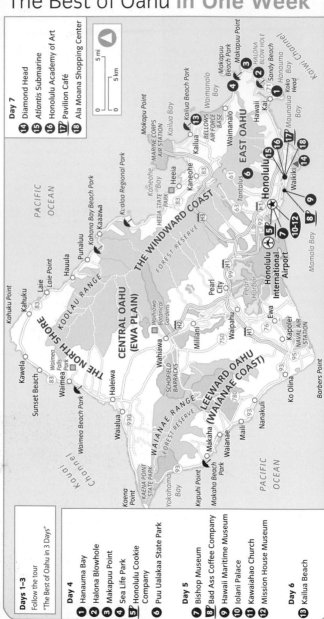

Day 7

14 Diamond Head
15 Atlantis Submarine
16 Honolulu Academy of Art
17 Pavilion Café
18 Ala Moana Shopping Center

Days 1–3

Follow the tour
"The Best of Oahu in 3 Days"

Day 4

1 Hanauma Bay
2 Halona Blowhole
3 Makapuu Point
4 Sea Life Park
5 Honolulu Cookie Company
6 Puu Ualakaa State Park

Day 5

7 Bishop Museum
8 Bad Ass Coffee Company
9 Hawaii Maritime Museum
10 Iolani Palace
11 Kawaiahao Church
12 Mission House Museum

Day 6

13 Kailua Beach

If possible, stay on Oahu for at least 1 week so that you can take in the sights at a slow, leisurely, island-style pace. You'll have time to see all the sights I recommended in the 3 day tour, plus explore the enchanting underwater world at Hanauma Bay and Sea Life Park, delve into Hawaiian history and culture, visit the art world, do some shopping, and spend more time at the beach. **START: Waikiki. Trip Length: 223 miles (359km).**

Days 1–3

For your first 3 days on Oahu, follow the itinerary for "The Best of Oahu in Three Days," starting on p 12, with one exception:

Spend a relaxing morning swimming with the turtles at Hanauma Bay.

On day 2, instead of visiting the Bishop Museum (don't worry—you'll see it later on this tour), spend the afternoon exploring Chinatown (see my tour of this exotic neighborhood on p 72) before the *Navatek* dinner cruise.

Day 4

From Waikiki, take H-1 East, which becomes the Kalanianaole Hwy. Look for the Koko Head Regional Park on the left; the beach is on the right (ocean side). Avoid the crowds by going early, about 8am, on a weekday; once the parking lot's full, you're out of luck. The Hanauma Bay Shuttle Bus runs from Waikiki to Hanauma Bay every half-hour from 8:45am to 1pm. You can catch it at any city bus stop in Waikiki. It returns every hour from noon to 4pm.

1 ★★★ **kids** **Hanauma Bay.**
Spend the morning at Oahu's best snorkeling beach. **Note:** The beach is closed on Tuesdays. *See p 177.*

Continue to drive east on Kalanianaole Hwy. Stop at mile marker 11.

2 **kids** **Halona Blowhole.**
See p 143, bullet **3**.

Continue to drive east on Kalanianaole Hwy. Look for the Makapuu Point sign.

3 **kids** **Makapuu Point.** *See p 144, bullet* **6**.

Continue east on Kalanianaole Hwy. Bus: 58.

4 ★ **kids** **Sea Life Park.** This 62-acre (25-hectare) ocean theme park, located in East Oahu, is one of the island's top attractions. You can swim with dolphins, get up close to the sea lions, or just relax and watch the marine mammal shows. My favorite stops are the stingray lagoon (where you can get a good

The Halona Blowhole shoots water up to 30 ft (9.1m) in the air

You can swim with the dolphins at Sea Life Park.

look at these normally shy creatures) and the sea turtle lagoon (which also doubles as a breeding sanctuary for the endangered Hawaiian green sea turtle). There's also a Hawaiian reef tank full of tropical fish; a "touch" pool, where you can touch a real sea cucumber (commonly found in tide pools); and a bird sanctuary, where you can see birds like the red-footed booby and the frigate bird. The chief curiosity, though, is the world's only "wholphin"—a cross between a false killer whale and an Atlantic bottle-nosed dolphin. On-site, marine biologists operate a recovery center for endangered marine life; during your visit, you may be able to see rehabilitated Hawaiian monk seals and seabirds. ⏱ *If you have kids allow 3 hr.; if not, 1 hr. 41–202 Kalanianaole Hwy. (at Makapuu Point), Honolulu. ☎ 808/259-7933. www.sealife parkhawaii.com. Admission $31 adults, $21 children 4–12. Daily 10:30am–5pm. Parking $5. Shuttle buses from Waikiki $20 per person. Bus: 22 or 58.*

Tour Honolulu from a Trolley Car

Hop on a 34-seat, open-air, motorized Waikiki Trolley for a fun way to get around the island. The Honolulu City Line loops around Waikiki and downtown Honolulu, stopping every 40 minutes at 12 key places (such as Iolani Palace, Chinatown, the State Capitol, the Aloha Tower, and Restaurant Row). The driver provides commentary along the way. Stops on the new 3-hour, fully narrated Ocean Coast Line on the southeast side of Oahu include Sea Life Park, Diamond Head, and Waikiki Beach. A 1-day trolley pass—which costs $30 for adults, $20 for seniors over 62, and $13 for kids ages 4 to 11—allows you to jump on and off all day long (8:30am–11:35pm). Four-day passes cost $52 for adults, $31 for seniors, and $20 for kids 4 to 11. Call ☎ **800/824-8804** or 808/593-2822 for more information, or go online (www.waikikitrolley.com).

Continue on Kalanianaole Hwy. (Hwy. 72), turn left on Pali Hwy. (Hwy. 61), then take H-1 east to Waikiki. Bus: 58.

5 kids **Honolulu Cookie Company.** So many exotic cookies, so little time . . . my fave is the dark-chocolate lilikoi (zingy lilikoi shortbread cookie, dipped in sweet dark chocolate). Absolutely yummy. *Waikiki Beach Walk, 227 Lewers St. (at Kalia St.).* ☎ *808/924-6651. $.*

From Waikiki, take Ala Wai Blvd. to McCully St., turn right, and drive *mauka* (inland) beyond the H-1 on-ramps to Wilder St. Turn left and go to Makiki St. Turn right and continue onward and upward about 3 miles (4.8km).

6 ★ **Puu Ualakaa State Park.** My favorite sunset view of Honolulu is from a 1,048-foot-high (319m) hill named for sweet potatoes. The poetic Hawaiian name means "rolling sweet potato hill," which describes how early planters used gravity to harvest their crop. On a clear day (which is almost always), the majestic, sweeping views stretch from Diamond Head to the Waianae Range—almost the length of Oahu. At night, several scenic overlooks provide romantic spots for young lovers to smooch under the stars with the city lights at their feet. It's a top-of-the-world experience—the view, that is. ⏲ *15–20 min. At the end of Round Top Dr. Daily 7am–6:45pm (to 7:45pm in summer). No bus service.*

Day 5

Take Ala Wai Blvd. out of Waikiki. Turn right at Kalakaua Ave., then left on S. Beretania St. and right at Piikoi St. Make a left onto Lunalilo St., and bear left onto H-1 West. Take Exit 20B, which puts you on Haloma St. Turn right at Houghtailing St., and then left onto Bernice St. Bus: 2.

7 ★★★ kids **Bishop Museum.** This entrancing museum may be the highlight of your trip. *See p 15, bullet* **7**.

Turn right out of the parking lot onto Bernice St., left at Kapalama Ave., and right again on N. School St. Make a right on Liliha St., a left on N King St., and right on River St. Turn left on Nimitz Hwy. and then right at Aloha Tower Dr. Bus: A (City Express A).

The Bishop Museum was founded by a Hawaiian princess, Bernice Pauahi, and her husband, Charles Reed Bishop.

8 Bad Ass Coffee Company.
Take a break at this gourmet Hawaiian coffee shop. My favorite is the delicious Kona coffee, but they also offer java from Molokai, Kauai, and Maui. *Aloha Tower Marketplace, 1 Aloha Tower Dr.* ☎ *808/524-0888. www.badasscoffee.com. $.*

Walk toward Diamond Head along the waterfront.

9 ★★ kids Hawaii Maritime Center. As we went to press, Bishop Museum, owner of the Hawaii Maritime Center, "temporarily" closed operations here "due to adverse economic conditions." Please call the Bishop Museum (☎ 808/847-3511) to see if the Hawaii Maritime Center has reopened. If it has, it is well worth a couple of hours of your time to wander around and learn the story of Hawaii's rich maritime past, from the ancient journey of Polynesian voyagers to the nostalgic days of the *Lurline,* which once brought tourists from San Francisco on 4-day cruises. Inside the Hawaii Maritime Center's Kalakaua Boathouse, patterned after His Majesty King David Kalakaua's own canoe house, are more than 30 exhibits, including Matson cruise

Bad Ass is a great place to stop for a cup of 100% Kona.

ships (which brought the first tourists to Waikiki), flying boats that delivered the mail, and the skeleton of a Pacific humpback whale that beached on Kahoolawe. Outside, the *Hokulea,* a double-hulled sailing canoe that in 1976 reenacted the Polynesian voyage of discovery, is moored next to the *Falls of Clyde,* a four-masted schooner that once ran tea from China to the west coast of the U.S. mainland. ⏱ *2 hr. Pier 7 (next to Aloha Tower).* ☎ *808/536-6373. www.bishopmuseum.org/exhibits/ hmc/hmc.html. Admission $8.50 adults, $7 seniors, $5.50 children 4–12. Daily 9am–5pm.*

Walk *mauka* up Bishop St., right on S. King, and left on Richards St.

10 ★ kids Iolani Palace. Once the site of a *heiau* (temple), Iolani Palace took 3 years and $350,000 to complete in 1882, with all the modern conveniences for its time (electric lights were installed here 4 years before they were in the White House). It was also in this palace that Queen Liliuokalani was overthrown and placed under house arrest for 9 months. The territorial and then the state government used the palace until 1968. At that point, the palace was in shambles and has since undergone a $7-million overhaul to restore it to its former glory. Admission options include the Grand Tour, a 90-minute docent-led tour that covers the state apartments, private quarters, and basement galleries; the 50-minute Audio Tour, which covers the same areas as the Grand Tour, but is self-guided; or the Galleries Tour, a self-guided tour of the basement galleries only, where you'll see the crown jewels, ancient feathered cloaks, royal china, and more. ⏱ *1–2 hr. At S. King and Richards sts.* ☎ *808/522-0832. Grand Tour $20 adults, $5 children 5–12; Audio Tour $13 adults, $5 children; Gallery*

Iolani Palace, the only royal palace in the U.S.

Tour $6 adults, $3 children, free for children 4 and under, but only allowed in the basement galleries. Tues–Sat 8:30am–2pm.

Continue to walk toward Diamond Head on S. King St. to Punchbowl St.

⓫ ★ **Kawaiahao Church.** When the missionaries came to Hawaii, the first thing they did was build churches. Four thatched grass churches had been built on this site before Rev. Hiram Bingham began building what he considered a "real" church—a New England–style congregational structure with Gothic influences. Between 1837 and 1842, the building of the church required some 14,000 giant coral slabs (some weighing more than 1,000 lb.). Hawaiian divers raped the reefs, digging out huge chunks of coral and causing irreparable environmental damage. Kawaiahao, Hawaii's oldest church, has been the site of numerous historical events, such as a speech made by King Kamehameha III in 1843, an excerpt of which became Hawaii's state motto (*"Ua mau ke ea o ka aina i ka pono,"* which translates as "The life of the land is preserved in righteousness"). The clock tower in the church, which was donated by King Kamehameha III and installed in 1850, continues to tick today. Don't sit in the pews in the back, marked with kahili feathers and velvet cushions; they are still reserved for the descendants of royalty. *957 Punchbowl St. (at King St.).* ☎ *808/522-1333. Free admission (donations appreciated). Mon–Fri 8am–4pm; Sun services in Hawaiian 9am.*

Continue in the Diamond Head direction on S. King St.

⓬ **Mission Houses Museum.** The original buildings of the Sandwich Islands Mission Headquarters still stand, and tours are often led by descendants of the original missionaries to Hawaii. The missionaries

I highly recommend attending a Hawaiian-language service at Kawaiahao Church.

A trek to the top of Diamond Head is rewarded with spectacular views.

brought their own prefab houses along with them when they came around Cape Horn from Boston in 1819. The Frame House was designed for New England winters and had small windows. (It must have been stiflingly hot inside.) Finished in 1921, it is Hawaii's oldest wooden structure. The missionaries believed that the best way to spread the Lord's message to the Hawaiians was to learn their language, and then to print literature for them to read. So it was the missionaries who gave the Hawaiians a written language. 🕐 *1 hr. 553 S. King St. (at Kawaiahao St.).* 📞 *808/531-0481. www.mission houses.org. $10 adults, $8 seniors, $6*

Gauguin's Two Tahitian Women on the Beach, *at the Honolulu Academy of Arts.*

students (age 6–college). Tues–Sat 10am–4pm.

To get back to Waikiki, pick up your car at Aloha Tower Marketplace and turn right on Nimitz Hwy., which becomes Ala Moana Blvd. and leads into Waikiki. Bus: 13.

Day 6

Take H-1 west to Exit 21 B (Pali Hwy. north). The Pali Hwy. (Hwy. 61) becomes the Kalanianaole Hwy., which becomes Kailua Rd. Veer to the right onto Kuulei Rd., then turn right on Kalahelo Ave., which becomes Kawailoa Rd., and follow it to the beach. Take TheBus 8 or 19 and transfer to TheBus 57.

⑬ ★★★ kids Kailua Beach. Spend the entire day on the windward side of Oahu at one of the island's most fabulous beaches. *See p 156.*

Day 7

Drive to the intersection of Diamond Head Rd. and 18th Ave. Follow the road through the tunnel (which is closed 6pm–6am) and park in the lot. Bus: 58 (from the Ala Moana Shopping Center).

⑭ ★ kids Diamond Head. On your last day on Oahu, get a bird's-eye view of the island from atop this 760-foot (232m) extinct volcano. *See p 165.*

Retrace your steps back to Waikiki.

Hawaii's Early History

Paddling outrigger sailing canoes, the first ancestors of today's Hawaiians followed the stars, waves, and birds across the sea to Hawaii, which they called "the land of raging fire." Those first settlers were part of the great Polynesian migration that settled the vast triangle of islands stretching among New Zealand, Easter Island, and Hawaii. No one is sure when they arrived in Hawaii from Tahiti and the Marquesas Islands, some 2,500 miles to the south, but recent archaeological digs at the Maluuluolele Park in Lahaina date back to A.D. 700 to 900.

All we have today are some archaeological finds, some scientific data, and ancient chants to tell the story of Hawaii's past. The chants, especially the *Kumulipo,* which is the chant of creation and the litany of genealogy of the *alii* (high-ranking chiefs) who ruled the islands, discuss the comings and goings between Hawaii and the islands of the south, presumed to be Tahiti. In fact, the channel between Maui, Kahoolawe, and Lanai is called *Kealaikahiki* or "the pathway to Tahiti."

Around 1300, the transoceanic voyages stopped for some reason, and Hawaii began to develop its own culture in earnest. The settlers built temples, fishponds, and aqueducts to irrigate taro plantations. Each island was a separate kingdom, and the *alii* created a caste system and established taboos. Violators were strangled, and high priests asked the gods Lono and Ku for divine guidance. Ritual human sacrifices were common.

---

⑮ ★★★ kids *Atlantis* Submarine. Now that you've seen Oahu from the top, plunge beneath the waves and see it underwater in this high-tech submarine. *See p 184.*

Take Ala Moana Blvd. in the Ewa direction, right on Ward Ave., and another right on Kinau St. to the parking lot. Bus: 2.

⑯ ★★★ kids Honolulu Academy of Arts. After feasting on the beauty of the island in the morning, feed your soul with an incredible art and cultural collection, located at one of Hawaii's most prestigious galleries. I recommend taking a guided tour. *See p 63, bullet ③.*

⑰ ★★ Pavilion Café. Take a break at this intimate cafe, which is shaded by a 70-year-old monkeypod tree and faces a landscaped garden with a rushing waterfall and sculptures by Jun Kaneko. Sip a glass of merlot or enjoy a chocolate walnut tart with a cup of green tea. *Honolulu Academy of Art, 900 Beretania St.* ☎ *808/532-8734. $$.*

Turn left, toward the ocean, on Ward Ave., then make a left on Ala Moana Blvd. Bus: 3.

⑱ ★★ Ala Moana Shopping Center. Spend your last few hours on the island wandering through Hawaii's largest shopping center. It's the perfect place to find souvenirs and gifts for your friends and relatives back home. *See p 123.*

The Best of Oahu in Two Weeks

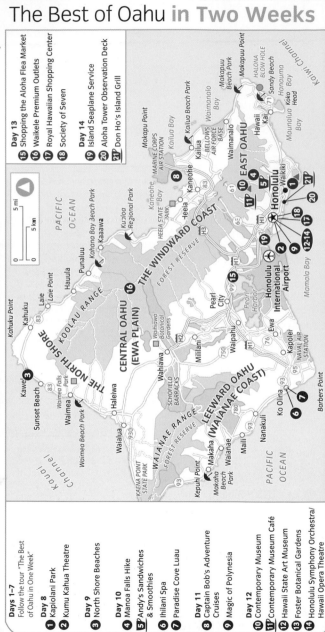

Days 1–7
Follow the tour "The Best of Oahu in One Week"

Day 8
1 Kapiolani Park
2 Kumu Kahua Theatre

Day 9
3 North Shore Beaches

Day 10
4 Manoa Falls Hike
5 Andy's Sandwiches & Smoothies
6 Ihilani Spa
7 Paradise Cove Luau

Day 11
8 Captain Bob's Adventure Cruises
9 Magic of Polynesia

Day 12
10 Contemporary Museum
11 Contemporary Museum Café
12 Hawaii State Art Museum
13 Foster Botanical Gardens
14 Honolulu Symphony Orchestra/ Hawaii Opera Theatre

Day 13
15 Shopping the Aloha Flea Market
16 Waikele Premium Outlets
17 Royal Hawaiian Shopping Center
18 Society of Seven

Day 14
19 Island Seaplane Service
20 Aloha Tower Observation Deck
21 Don Ho's Island Grill

wo weeks on Oahu is perfect: It gives you enough time to see all the sites and experience the true flavor of Hawaii with plenty of time left to relax and really enjoy your vacation. For the first week, follow my "The Best of Oahu in One Week" tour, which starts on p 18. On the second week of your holiday, you can explore a tropical rainforest, see more incredible beaches, sail on the windward side, have a day of retail therapy, discover Hawaii's nightlife, and even take in a luau. START: **Waikiki. Trip Length: 467 miles (752km).**

Day 8

Walk in the Diamond Head direction down Kalakaua Ave. Bus: 20.

❶ ★★ kids Kapiolani Park.
Spend a lazy day just a coconut's throw from the high-rise concrete jungle of Waikiki in this 133-acre (54-hectare) grassy park. You'll find plenty of open space, jogging paths, tennis courts, soccer and cricket fields, and even an archery range. For more information, see my "Kapiolani Park" tour starting on p 86

Head Ewa (west) on Ala Moana Blvd., which becomes Nimitz Hwy. Right on Bethal St. and left on Merchant St. Bus: B (City Express B).

❷ ★ Kumu Kahua Theatre.
Shows here offer an intriguing glimpse at island life. *See p 134.*

Local musicians perform at Kapiolani Park's bandstand.

Day 9

Take H-1 west out of Waikiki, then take the H-2 north exit (Exit 8A) toward Mililani/Wahiawa. After 7 miles (11km) H-2 becomes Kamehameha Hwy. (Hwy. 80). Look for the turnoff to Haleiwa town. Bus: 19, then transfer to 52.

❸ ★★★ kids North Shore Beaches. Spend the day beaching. Start with breakfast in Haleiwa with stops at North Shore's best beaches: Waimea, Pupukea, Sunset, and Bonsai/Pipeline. They're all reviewed in chapter 6, "The Best Beaches."

Retrace your route back to Waikiki.

Day 10

Take Manoa Rd. past Lyon Arboretum and park in the residential area below Paradise Park. Bus: 5.

❹ ★ kids Manoa Falls Hike.
Just 15 minutes from Waikiki you can lose yourself in a tropical rainforest. *See p 167.*

Retrace your route back down Manoa Rd., turn left on Oahu Ave., then left again on E. Manoa Rd.

❺ ★ kids Andy's Sandwiches & Smoothies. This neighborhood fixture is a terrific place to stop for a smoothie and a healthy snack (try the mango muffins) after your hike. *2904 E. Manoa Rd., opposite Manoa Marketplace.* ☎ *808/988-6161. $.*

My favorite luau on Oahu is the one at Paradise Cove.

From Manoa Rd. drive toward the ocean and get on the H-1 West. Stay on H-1 until it ends and becomes Farrington Hwy. Take the Ko Olina Exit and turn left on Aliinui Dr., then turn right on Olani St. No bus service.

6 ★★★ **Ihilani Spa.** Spend the rest of the day being pampered in this luxury spa. For details on the sensuous options to choose from, see the box "Pampering in Paradise" on p 107.

Retrace your route to Aliinui Dr.

7 **Paradise Cove Luau.** While you're out in Ko Olina, experience a luau. Don't expect an intimate affair—Paradise Cove generally has some 600 to 800 guests a night. In fact, the small thatched village feels a bit like a Hawaiian theme park. But you're getting more than just a luau: Paradise Cove provides an entire cultural experience, with Hawaiian games, craft demonstrations, and a beautiful shoreline looking out over what is usually a storybook sunset. Tahitian dancing and both ancient and modern hula make this a fun-filled evening for those spirited enough to join in. The food is not breathtaking: You'll find typical luau

cuisine (Hawaiian kalua pig, lomi salmon, poi, and coconut pudding and cake) and basic American fare (salads, rice, pineapple, chicken, and so on). ⏱ *3½ hr. Aliinui Dr., Ko Olina.* ☎ *808/842-5911. www.paradise covehawaii.com. Packages: $80–$137 for adults, free–$112 children (12 and under). Nightly 5–8:30pm.*

Retrace your route back to H-1, then take H-1 into Waikiki.

Day 11
Take Captain Bob's shuttle from Waikiki (it's included in the price of the following cruise).

8 ★ **kids** **Captain Bob's Adventure Cruises.** Spend the day on the water seeing the majestic Windward Coast the way it should be seen—from a boat. Captain Bob will take you on a 4-hour, lazy-day sail of Kaneohe Bay aboard his 42-foot (13m) catamaran. You'll skim across the almost-always-calm water above the shallow coral reef; land at the disappearing sandbar Ahu o Laka; and cruise past two small islands to snorkel spots full of tropical fish and, sometimes, turtles. ⏱ *All day (9am pickup, return 4pm). Kaneohe Bay.* ☎ *808/942-5077. $88 adults, $73 children 3–14, free for children 2 and under. Rates include all-you-can-eat barbecue lunch and transportation from Waikiki hotels. No cruises Sun or holidays.*

9 ★ *The Magic of Polynesia.* End your day by taking in this enthralling show. *See p 133.*

Day 12
For directions to today's stops, see the "Oahu's Best Gardens" tour on p 58 and "Honolulu for Art Lovers" on p 62.

10 ★★ **kids** **Contemporary Museum.** Start your day of culture and the arts at this incredible

It's worth visiting the Contemporary Museum just to stroll the grounds and take in the views.

museum that was once an elegant home. It features cutting-edge art and inspiring views of Honolulu and Waikiki. *See p 62, bullet* **1**.

11 ★ **Contemporary Museum Café.** After you've nourished your soul, nourish your body at this relaxing, intimate cafe. I recommend the crostini of the day (a toasted baguette with a savory topping) or the sinfully delicious flourless chocolate cake. Pair your choice with a just-brewed latte or some fresh lemonade. *Contemporary Museum, 2411 Makiki Heights Dr.* ☎ *808/523-3362. www.tcmhi.org. $$.*

12 ★★ **Hawaii State Art Museum.** Don't miss this art center, which displays works by artists

Heliconia, one of many native plants you can see in the Foster Botanical Gardens.

living in Hawaii. It's housed in the original Royal Hawaiian Hotel. *See p 63, bullet* **4**.

13 **Foster Botanical Garden.** In Hawaii, art can also be made by Mother Nature, and this historical garden is one of her best displays. *See p 59, bullet* **4**.

Take Ala Moana Blvd. to Ward Ave. and turn right. Turn left on King St. for entrance to the parking lot. Bus: 2 or 13.

14 **Honolulu Symphony Orchestra/Hawaii Opera Theatre.** Complete your day of culture with either a visit to the Symphony, which performs from September to May, or the Opera, which takes to the stage from January to March. *Honolulu Symphony Orchestra, Neal Blaisdell Concert Hall, 444 Ward Ave.* ☎ *808/524-0815. www.honolulu symphony.com or hawaiiopera.org. Symphony tickets start at $15; opera tickets start at $27.*

Day 13
For maps covering all the shopping areas below, see p 2, 26, and 113.

15 **kids Shopping the Aloha Flea Market.** More than just bargain shopping, this giant outdoor bazaar is an adventure full of strange food, odd goods, and incredible bargains. Nobody ever

You can find all kinds of Hawaiian trinkets at the Aloha Flea Market.

leaves this place empty-handed—or without having had lots of fun.

⑯ Waikele Premium Outlets. The second stop on your bargain-hunting day is at these discount outlet shops. This is retail therapy at frugal prices. Just say the word *Waikele* and my eyes glaze over. So many shops, so little time!

⑰ Royal Hawaiian Shopping Center. After you've seen the bargains, it's time to wander in luxury at the newly renovated 293,000-square-foot (27,220-sq.-m) open-air mall (17,000 sq. ft./1,580 sq. m larger than before). There are more than 100 stores and restaurants spread across four levels. Go bananas. *See p 125.*

⑱ ★ Society of Seven. This nightclub act, which is a blend of skits, Broadway hits, popular music, and costumed musical acts, is so popular it has been playing for more than 3 decades in a town where most shows barely make it 1 year. It's a great way to spend your last evening in paradise. ⏱ 1½ hr.–2½ hr. *Outrigger Waikiki on the Beach, 2335 Kalakaua Ave.* ☎ 808/922-6408.

Wed–Sat, dinner $75 (7pm); cocktail seating $43 (8pm).

Day 14
I suggest taking Island Seaplane's complimentary van from your hotel in Waikiki. They will even drop you at the Aloha Tower on your way back.

⑲ ★★ kids Island Seaplane Service. Spend your last day seeing why Oahu was the island of kings—and the only way to do it is from the air. You'll never forget the slapping sound of the waves as the seaplane skims across the water and then effortlessly lifts off into the air. I recommend taking the full hour tour and seeing the entire island. ⏱ 1 hr. 85 Lagoon Dr., Keehi Lagoon. ☎ 808/836-6273. www.islandseaplane.com. $135 ½-hr. tour, $250 1-hr. tour.

⑳ ★ kids Aloha Tower Observation Deck. This 10-story building was the tallest in the islands when it was built in 1926. It welcomed thousands of visitors who arrived in Hawaii via boat. In the 1920s and '30s, "Boat Day," the arrival of a passenger ship, became a festive celebration shared by the whole community. Take in the panoramic view of Honolulu and Waikiki before you bid the island aloha. *10th floor of Aloha Tower, 1 Aloha Tower Dr.* ☎ 808/528-5700. Daily 9am–5pm.

㉑ kids Don Ho's Island Grill. Raise a glass of good cheer to your fabulous vacation as you look out over Honolulu Harbor. Order the Molokai Seafood Martini, with he'e (squid) poke, lomi salmon, and seared ahi (tuna) served in a martini glass, and start planning your next trip to Hawaii. *Aloha Tower Marketplace, 1 Aloha Tower Dr.* ☎ 8808/528-0807. www.donho.com/grill/grill.htm. $$$. ●

3 The Best Special-Interest Tours

The Best Special-Interest Tours

Honolulu & Oahu **with Kids**

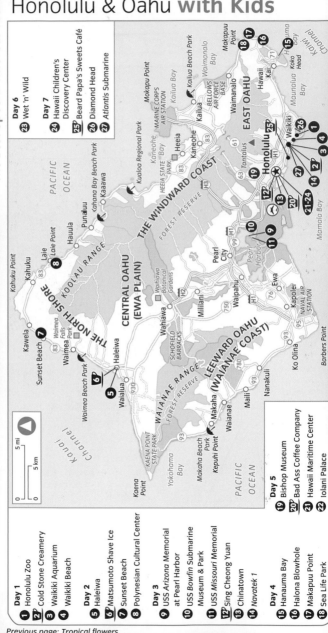

Day 1
1 Honolulu Zoo
2 Cold Stone Creamery
3 Waikiki Aquarium
4 Waikiki Beach

Day 2
5 Haleiwa
6 Matsumoto Shave Ice
7 Sunset Beach
8 Polynesian Cultural Center

Day 3
9 USS Arizona Memorial at Pearl Harbor
10 USS Bowfin Submarine Museum & Park
11 USS Missouri Memorial
12 Sing Cheong Yuan
13 Chinatown
14 Navatek 1

Day 4
15 Hanauma Bay
16 Halona Blowhole
17 Makapuu Point
18 Sea Life Park

Day 5
19 Bishop Museum
20 Bad Ass Coffee Company
21 Hawaii Maritime Center
22 Iolani Palace

Day 6
23 Wet 'n' Wild

Day 7
24 Hawaii Children's Discovery Center
25 Beard Papa's Sweets Café
26 Diamond Head
27 Atlantis Submarine

Previous page: Tropical flowers.

Families flock to Oahu not only for the island's breathtaking beauty, but also for the abundance of activities. Waikiki is famous for every type of ocean activity you can think of, plus there's the Honolulu Zoo, the Waikiki Aquarium, and fun-filled Kapiolani Park. Dotted around the rest of the Island are great family outings like Sea Life Park, the Polynesian Cultural Center, and even a water adventure park. This tour gives families a fun-filled week with something for everyone. START: **Waikiki. Trip Length: 7 days and 196 miles (315km).**

Travel Tip

See chapter 4 for kid-friendly hotel, dining, and shopping recommendations.

Day 1

1 ★★ kids **Honolulu Zoo.** If the kids aren't too tired, head for this 43-acre (17-hectare) municipal zoo. My favorite section is the 10-acre (4-hectare) African Savannah, with more than 40 African critters roaming around in the open. *Best time to go is when the gates open; the animals are more active in the morning.* ⏰ 2–3 hr. 151 Kapahulu Ave. (between Paki and Kalakaua aves.), at entrance to Kapiolani Park. ☎ 808/971-7171. www. honoluluzoo.org. $12 adults, $3 kids 6–12, free for children 5 and under, $25 family pass. Daily 9am–4:30pm.

Walk along Kapahulu Ave. toward Kalakaua Ave., then turn right on Kalakaua.

2 kids **Cold Stone Creamery.** It's not cheap, but it's close, it's air-conditioned, and it does have dreamy ice cream with about a zillion toppings to choose from (I love their brownies). *ResortQuest Waikiki Beach Hotel, 2570 Kalakaua Ave. (at Paoakalani St.).* ☎ 808/923-1656. $.

Backtrack on Kalakaua Ave.

3 ★★ kids **Waikiki Aquarium.** *See p 13, bullet* **2**.

Kids will love the hands-on exhibits at the Waikiki Aquarium.

Walk Ewa (west) along the beach until you find a spot you like.

4 ★★★ kids **Waikiki Beach.** Finish off your day with some fun in the sun. *See p 161.*

Day 2

Spend your second day on Oahu on the North Shore. Take H-1 west out of Waikiki, then take the H-2 north exit (Exit 8A) toward Mililani/ Wahiawa. After 7 miles (11km) H-2 becomes Kamehameha Hwy. (Hwy. 80). Look for the turnoff to Haleiwa town. Bus: 19, then transfer to 52.

5 ★★★ kids **Haleiwa.** Start your day exploring this famous North Shore surfing town. *See p 138, bullet* **4**.

6 ★ **kids** **Matsumoto Shave Ice.** Take time out for a cool, sweet treat at Matsumoto's. *See p 16, bullet* **11**.

Continue down Kamehameha Hwy. for about 6½ miles (10km). Bus: 52.

7 ★★★ **kids** **Sunset Beach.** Spend the rest of the morning playing on Sunset Beach. During the summer months this is a safe beach for swimming. During the winter, it's best to just sit and watch the big wave surfers. *See p 161.*

Drive another 11¼ miles (19km) down Kamehameha Hwy. to the town of Laie. Bus: 52 to Turtle Bay Resort, then 55.

8 ★★ **kids** **Polynesian Cultural Center.** Spend the rest of the afternoon and evening at this "living museum" of Polynesia. *See p 17, bullet* **13**.

Day 3
Get an early start to beat the crowds at Pearl Harbor. Drive west on H-1 past the airport to the USS *Arizona* Memorial exit, then follow the green-and-white

There's nothing like slurping up a cool cone of shave ice on a hot day.

signs; there's ample free parking. Or take the *Arizona* Memorial Shuttle Bus VIP (☎ 808/839-0911), which picks up at Waikiki hotels 6:50am–1pm ($9 per person round-trip). Bus: 20.

9 ★★★ **kids** **USS *Arizona* Memorial at Pearl Harbor.** This unforgettable memorial is Oahu's top attraction. Parents should note that strollers and diaper bags are not allowed at the memorial (you can store them at the visitor center). Also, there are no restrooms at the memorial, so be sure everyone uses

Seeing the Zoo by Moonlight

For a real treat, take the Honolulu Zoo by Twilight Tour, which offers a rare behind-the-scenes look into the lives of the zoo's nocturnal residents. Tours are Friday and Saturday from 5:30 to 7:30pm; the cost is $14 for adults and $10 for children ages 4 to 12. Other great family programs include **Snooze in the Zoo:** Discover "who is roaring and who is snoring" during the night with pizza, tours, and campfire time with s'mores, plus breakfast and a morning stroll (check website for dates). Cost is $50 for ages 4 and up. Check the website www.honoluluzoo.org for details on these special events, or call ☎ **808/971-7171.**

the ones at the visitor center. *See p 14, bullet* ④.

⑩ ★ kids USS *Bowfin* Submarine Museum & Park. *See p 47, bullet* ②.

⑪ ★ kids USS *Missouri* Memorial. *See p 47, bullet* ③.

From Arizona Memorial Dr. turn right on Kamehameha Hwy. (Hwy. 99). Take the ramp onto H-1 East toward Honolulu. Take Exit 21A and turn toward the ocean on Bishop. Stay right at the fork onto Fort St. Turn right on Beretania St. then left on Maunakea St. There's a parking garage on the corner of Maunakea and Hotel sts. Bus: 42.

⑫ ★ kids Sing Cheong Yuan. Before you start your tour of Chinatown, take a break at this small pastry shop. *See p 15, bullet* ⑧.

⑬ ★★ kids Chinatown. Plan to spend several hours in this exotic part of Honolulu. The colorful open markets, Buddhist temples, waterside walkway, and plenty of tempting restaurants should keep you occupied for a while. For complete descriptions, see my Chinatown tour on p 72.

From Sing Cheong Yuan, continue down Maunakea St., turn left on N. King St., then right on Nuuanu Ave. Make a slight left on Nimitz Hwy. (Hwy. 92). Look for the sign for Pier 6 just after Aloha Tower, and turn right. Bus: 56.

⑭ ★ kids Navatek I. Say aloha to the sun from the ocean. For details on this sunset dinner cruise, see p 15, bullet ⑨.

Day 4
From Waikiki, take H-1 East, which becomes the Kalanianaole Hwy. Look for the Koko Head

If you're lucky, your visit might coincide with the colorful spectacle of a Chinatown parade.

Regional Park on the left; the beach is on the right (ocean side). Avoid the crowds by going early, about 8am, on a weekday morning; once the parking lot's full, you're out of luck. The Hanauma Bay Shuttle Bus runs from Waikiki to Hanauma Bay every half-hour from 8:45am to 1pm. You can catch it at any city bus stop in Waikiki. It returns every hour from noon to 4pm.

⑮ ★★★ kids Hanauma Bay. Spend the morning at Oahu's best snorkeling beach (note that the beach is closed on Tues). *See p 177.*

Continue to drive east on Kalanianaole Hwy.; look for mile marker 11.

⑯ kids Halona Blowhole. *See p 143, bullet* ③.

Continue to drive east on Kalanianaole Hwy.; look for the sign for Makapuu Point.

⑰ kids Makapuu Point. Here's a chance to get out of the car and stretch your legs on a hike out to this 647-foot-high (197m) cliff and functioning lighthouse. *See p 144, bullet* ⑥.

Continue east on Kalanianaole Hwy. Bus: 58.

Family-Friendly Events

Your trip may be a little more enjoyable with the added attraction of attending a celebration, festival, or party in Honolulu, Waikiki, or other parts of the island. Check out the following events.

- **Morey World Bodyboarding Championship,** Banzai Pipeline, North Shore (☎ 808/396-2326). Early January. Participants are judged on the best wave selection and maneuvers on the wave.
- **Ala Wai Challenge,** Ala Wai Park, Waikiki (☎ 808/923-1802). Last weekend in January. This event features ancient Hawaiian games such as *ulu maika* (bowling a round stone through pegs), *oo ihe* (spear throwing), *huki kaula* (tug of war), and an outrigger canoe race. It's also a great place to hear Hawaiian music.
- **Chinese New Year,** Chinatown (☎ 808/533-3181). Late January or early February (depending on the lunar calendar). Chinatown rolls out the red carpet for this important event with a traditional lion dance, fireworks, food booths, and a host of activities.
- **Punahou School Carnival,** Punahou School, Honolulu (☎ 808/944-5753). February. This private school has everything you can imagine in a school carnival, from high-speed rides to homemade jellies. All proceeds go to scholarship funds.
- **Hawaii Challenge International Sportkite Championship,** Kapiolani Park (☎ 808/735-9059). First weekend in March. The longest-running sportkite competition in the world attracts top kite pilots from around the globe.
- **Outrigger Canoe Season,** Ala Wai Canal (☎ 808/261-6615). Weekends May to September. Canoe paddlers across the state participate in outrigger canoe races.
- **World Fire-Knife Dance Championships and Samoan Festival,** Polynesian Cultural Center, Laie (☎ 808/293-3333). Mid-May. Fire-knife dancers from around the world gather for one of the most amazing performances you'll ever see. Authentic Samoan food and cultural festivities round out the fun.
- **Ukulele Festival,** Kapiolani Park Bandstand, Waikiki (☎ 808/732-3739). Last Sunday in July. This free concert features some 600 kids (ages 4–92) strumming the ukulele. Hawaii's top musicians all pitch in.
- **Triple Crown of Surfing,** North Shore (☎ 808/638-7266). Mid-November to late December. The North Shore is on "wave watch" during this period, and when the big, monster waves roll in, the world's top professional surfers compete in events for more than $1 million in prize money.

The calm waters of Hanauma Bay make it a great place to bring novice snorkelers.

18 ★ **kids** **Sea Life Park.** This 62-acre (25-hectare) ocean theme park is one of the island's top attractions. Swim with dolphins, get up close to the sea lions, or just relax and watch the marine mammal shows. *See p 144, bullet* **4**.

To get back to Waikiki, continue on Kalanianaole Hwy. (Hwy. 72), turn left on Pali Hwy. (Hwy. 61), then take H-1 east to Waikiki. Bus: 58.

Day 5
Take Ala Wai Blvd. out of Waikiki. Turn right at Kalakaua Ave., then left on S. Beretania St. and right at Piikoi St. Make a left onto Lunalilo St., and bear left onto H-1 West. Take Exit 20B, which puts you on Haloma St. Turn right at Houghtailing St., and then left onto Bernice St. Bus: 2.

19 ★★★ **kids** **Bishop Museum.** This entrancing museum may be the highlight of your trip. It covers everything you've always wanted to know about Hawaii, from grass shacks to how a volcano works. *See p 15, bullet* **7**.

Turn right out of the parking lot onto Bernice St., left at Kapalama Ave., and right again on N. School

St. Make a right on Liliha St., a left on N. King St., and right on River St. Turn left on Nimitz Hwy. and then right at Aloha Tower Dr. Bus: A (City Express A).

20 **Bad Ass Coffee Company.** Take a break at this gourmet Hawaiian coffee. My favorite is the delicious Kona coffee, but they also offer java from Molokai, Kauai, and Maui. *Aloha Tower Marketplace, 1 Aloha Tower Dr.* ☎ *808/524-0888.* $.

Walk toward Diamond Head along the waterfront.

Kids can see dolphins, whales, sea lions, penguins, and more at Sea Life Park.

Spend a hot day splashing around at Hawaiian Waters Adventure Park.

21 ★★ **kids** **Hawaii Maritime Center.** Hawaii's rich maritime history comes alive at this museum. Call first to make sure it has reopened. *See p 22, bullet* **9**.

Walk *mauka* (inland) up Bishop St., right on S. King, and left on Richards St.

22 ★ **kids** **Iolani Palace.** If you want to really understand Hawaii, I suggest taking the Grand Tour of this royal palace, built by King David Kalakaua in 1882. ***Parents take note:*** Kids 4 and under are allowed only on the self-guided tour of the

This humpback whale skeleton hangs over the exhibits at the Hawaii Maritime Center.

basement galleries (which includes the crown jewels, ancient feather cloaks, royal china, and more). *See p 22, bullet* **10**.

To get back to Waikiki, pick up your car at Aloha Tower Marketplace and turn right on Nimitz Hwy., which becomes Ala Moana Blvd. and leads into Waikiki. TheBus: 13.

Day 6
Take H-1 west to exit 1 (Campbell Industrial Park). Make an immediate left turn to Farrington Hwy., and you will see the park on your left. Bus: B (City Express B), transfer to C (Country Express C).

23 ★ **kids** **Wet 'n' Wild.** Kids love this 29-acre (12-hectare) watertheme amusement park, formerly known as Hawaiian Waters Adventure Park. Plan to spend the whole day here. Highlights are a football field–size wave pool for bodysurfing, two 65-foot-high (20m) free-fall slides, two water-toboggan bullet slides, inner-tube slides, body-flume slides, a continuous river for floating inner tubes, and separate pools for adults, teens, and children. Restaurants, Hawaiian performances, and shops top it all off. ⏰ *All day.* 400 Farrington Hwy. (at Kalaeloa Blvd.), Kapolei. ☎ 808/674-9283. www. hawaiianwaters.com. Admission $42 adults, $17 seniors, $32 children

3–11, free for children 2 and under. Parking $5. Hours vary, but generally the park is open Mon and Thurs–Fri 10:30am–3:30pm, Sat–Sun 10:30am–4pm; closed Tues–Wed during peak (summer) season, call for hours during nonpeak season.

Day 7
Take Ala Moana Blvd. out of Waikiki. Turn left on Koula St., then right on Olomehani St. and another right on Ohe St. Bus: 42.

24 ★★ **kids** **Hawaii Children's Discovery Center.** Perfect for children ages 2 to 13, this 37,000-square-foot (3,437-sq.-m) museum of color, motion, and activities will entertain them for hours with hands-on exhibits and interactive stations. Where else can kids play volleyball with a robot, don sparkling costumes from India, or dress up as a purple octopus? Lots of summer classes and activities range from playing with clay to painting (most of them invite adults to participate, too). The Discovery Center closes at 1pm most days, so be sure to make this your first stop of the day. ⏱ 2 hr. 111 Ohe St. (at Olomehani St.), Honolulu. ☎ 808/524-5437. www.discoverycenter hawaii.org. Admission $10 children and adults, $6 seniors, free for children 1 and under. Tues–Fri 9am–1pm; Sat–Sun 10am–3pm.

Atlantis Submarine.

Retrace your route back to Ala Moana Blvd. and turn right toward Waikiki. Make a left on Piikoi St. and a right into the Ala Moana parking lot. Bus: 56.

25 **kids** **Beard Papa's Sweets Café.** The specialty here, made popular in Japan, is a baked (as opposed to fried) cream puff, made of a double layer of soft French "choux" and "pie crust" outside. The whipped cream custard filling isn't put inside until you order it—so each one is fresh. Foodland, Ala Moana Center, 1450 Ala Moana Blvd. ☎ 808/955-2806. $.

Continue toward Waikiki on Ala Moana Blvd. Turn right on Kalakaua Ave., then right on Diamond Head Rd. Just after 18th Ave. turn into Diamond Head Crater parking. Bus: 3.

26 ★ **kids** **Diamond Head.** On your last day on Oahu, get a bird's-eye view of the island from atop this 760-foot (232m) extinct volcano. See p 165.

Retrace your route back to Waikiki.

27 ★★★ **kids** **Atlantis Submarine.** Now that you've seen Oahu from the top, plunge beneath the waves and see it underwater in this high-tech submarine. See p 184.

A Week of Oahu
History & Culture

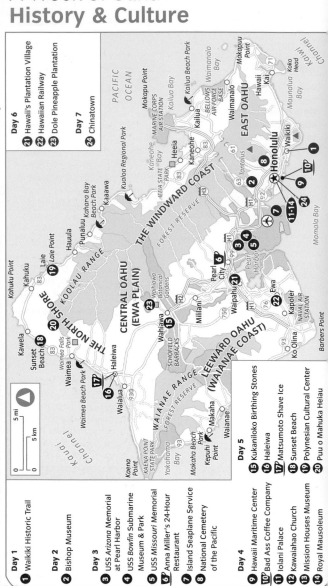

Day 1
1. Waikiki Historic Trail

Day 2
2. Bishop Museum

Day 3
3. USS Arizona Memorial at Pearl Harbor
4. USS Bowfin Submarine Museum & Park
5. USS Missouri Memorial
6. Anna Miller's 24-Hour Restaurant
7. Island Seaplane Service
8. National Cemetery of the Pacific

Day 4
9. Hawaii Maritime Center
10. Bad Ass Coffee Company
11. Iolani Palace
12. Kawaiahao Church
13. Mission Houses Museum
14. Royal Mausoleum

Day 5
15. Kukaniloko Birthing Stones
16. Haleiwa
17. Matsumoto Shave Ice
18. Sunset Beach
19. Polynesian Cultural Center
20. Puu o Mahuka Heiau

Day 6
21. Hawaii's Plantation Village
22. Hawaiian Railway
23. Dole Pineapple Plantation

Day 7
24. Chinatown

This tour covers Oahu's most sacred and historically important spots. You'll see ancient sites where wizards once healed people, visit the birthplaces of Hawaiian royalty, learn about the days of the missionaries and plantations, and reflect on the attack on Pearl Harbor. You'll visit Waikiki, downtown Honolulu, Chinatown, Central Oahu, and Pearl Harbor. **START: Waikiki. Trip Length: 7 days and 69 miles (111km).**

Day 1

① ★★ **kids** **Waikiki Historic Trail.** To get an overview of Waikiki's history, take this 4.5-mile (7.2km) walk, with stops marked by 6-foot-tall (1.8m) surfboards explaining the history of today's favorite resort area. For a full description of the trail, see my Historic Waikiki tour starting on p 50.

Day 2

Take Ala Wai Blvd. out of Waikiki. Turn right at Kalakaua Ave., then left on S. Beretania St. and right at Piikoi St. Make a left onto Lunalilo St., and bear left onto H-1 West. Take Exit 20B, which puts you on Haloma St. Turn right at Houghtailing St., and then left onto Bernice St. Bus: 2.

② ★★★ **kids** **Bishop Museum.** Take the entire day to see this entrancing museum, which could be the highlight of your trip. You'll find out about everything from grass shacks to how a volcano works. *See p 15, bullet* **⑦**.

Day 3

Get an early start to beat the crowds at Pearl Harbor. Drive west on H-1 past the airport to the USS *Arizona* Memorial exit, then follow the green-and-white signs; there's ample free parking. Or take the *Arizona* Memorial

One of many historic artifacts at the Bishop Museum.

Shuttle Bus VIP (☎ 808/839-0911), which picks up at Waikiki hotels 6:50am–1pm ($9 per person round-trip). Bus: 20.

③ ★★★ **kids** **USS *Arizona* Memorial at Pearl Harbor.** Start off your day of viewing wartime Honolulu by seeing these three important reminders of World War II. *See p 47, bullet* **④**.

④ ★ **kids** **USS *Bowfin* Submarine Museum & Park.** *See p 47, bullet* **②**.

⑤ ★ **kids** **USS *Missouri* Memorial.** *See p 47, bullet* **③**.

Turn right on Arizona Rd. and then left on Kamehameha Hwy. (Hwy. 99). Turn right on Kaonohi St. Bus: A (City Express A).

⑥ ★ **kids** **Anna Miller's 24-Hour Restaurant.** Just a couple of miles away, in Pearlridge, is this always-busy casual dining restaurant. Treat yourself to the best fresh strawberry pie on the island (with a generous helping of fluffy whipped cream). *Pearlridge Centre, 98–115 Kaonohi St. (Kamehameha Hwy.).* ☎ 808/487-2421. $.

Turn left on Kamehameha Hwy. (Hwy. 99) and merge on Hwy. 78 East. Take Exit 3 toward the Airport (Puuloa Rd., which becomes Lagoon Dr.).

7 ★★ kids **Island Seaplane Service.** See the box "See World War II History from the Air" on p 48 for details.

From Lagoon Dr. turn right on Nimitz Hwy., take H-1 East to exit 21A (Pali Hwy.). Turn right on Kuakini St., then left on Lusitana St. Right again on Concordia St. and left on Puowaina Dr., then stay on Puowaina Dr. to the end of the road. Bus: 62, transfer to 6.

8 **National Memorial Cemetery of the Pacific.** End the day seeing the final outcome of war. The National Cemetery of the Pacific (also known as "the Punchbowl") is an ash-and-lava tuff cone that exploded about 150,000 years ago—like Diamond Head, only smaller. Early Hawaiians called it *Puowaina,* or "hill of sacrifice." The old crater is a burial ground for 35,000 victims of three American wars in Asia and the Pacific: World War II, Korea, and Vietnam. Among the graves, you'll find many unmarked ones with the date December 7, 1941, carved in the headstone. ⏰ *1 hr. Punchbowl Crater, 2177 Puowaina Dr. (at the end of the road).* ☎ *808/541-1434. Free admission. Daily 8am–5:30pm (Mar–Sept to 6:30pm).*

Gardens of the Missing at the Punchbowl.

Day 4

Start off at the Hawaii Maritime Center, next to Aloha Tower.

9 ★★ kids **Hawaii Maritime Center.** Hawaii's rich maritime history comes alive at this museum. Call first to make sure it has reopened. *See p 22, bullet* **9**.

Walk next door to the Aloha Tower Marketplace.

10 **Bad Ass Coffee Company.** Whether it's hot coffee or iced you desire, your choices here include brews from beans grown in world-famous Kona or from lesser-known plantations on Maui, Molokai, and Kauai. *Aloha Tower Marketplace, 1 Aloha Tower Dr.* ☎ *808/524-0888. $.*

Walk up Bishop St. to King St. and make a right. At Richards St. turn left.

11 ★ kids **Iolani Palace.** If you want to really understand Hawaii, I suggest taking the Grand Tour of this royal palace, built by King David Kalakaua in 1882. *See p 22, bullet* **10**.

Continue to walk toward Diamond Head on S. King St. to Punchbowl St.

Mission Houses Museum.

12 ★ Kawaiahao Church. Don't miss the crowning achievement of the first missionaries in Hawaii—the first permanent stone church, complete with bell tower and colonial colonnade. *See p 23, bullet* **11**.

Continue in the Diamond Head direction on S. King St.

13 Mission Houses Museum. Step into life in 1820 among the 19th-century American Protestant missionaries. *See p 23, bullet* **12**.

Retrace your steps to your car at the Aloha Tower. Drive in the Diamond Head direction on Nimitz Hwy. and turn left on Alakea St. Turn left on Beretania St., right on Punchbowl St., then get on the Pali Hwy. north. Exit at Wylolie St. and turn left on Nuuana Ave. Bus: 4.

14 Royal Mausoleum. In the cool uplands of Nuuanu, on a 3.7-acre (1.5-hectare) patch of sacred land dedicated in 1865, is the final resting place of King Kalakaua, Queen Kapiolani, and 16 other Hawaiian royals. Only the Hawaiian flag flies over this grave, a remnant of the kingdom. ⏱ *1 hr. 2261 Nuuanu Ave. (between Wyllie and Judd sts.).* ☎ *808/536-7602. Free admission. Mon–Fri 8am–4:30pm.*

Take Nuuanu Ave. down to Nimitz Hwy., which becomes Ala Moana Blvd., into Waikiki. Bus: 4.

Day 5
Take H-1 West out of Waikiki. Take the H-2 North exit (Exit 8A) toward Mililani/Wahiawa. After 7 miles (11km), H-2 becomes Kamehameha Hwy. (Hwy. 80). Look for the sign between Wahiawa and Haleiwa, on Plantation Rd., opposite the road to Whitmore Village. No bus.

15 Kukaniloko Birthing Stones. The most sacred site in central Oahu, this is where women of ancient Hawaii gave birth to potential *alii* (royalty). *See p 137, bullet* **2**.

Many Hawaiian royals were born at this site.

Approach the Puu o Mahuka Heiau with respect; many Hawaiians consider it sacred.

Retrace your route back to Kamehameha Hwy. (Hwy. 80) and turn left. At the fork in the road, remain right, on Kamehameha Hwy. (which now becomes Hwy. 99). Follow the signs into Haleiwa.

⑯ ★★★ kids Haleiwa. Start your day exploring this famous North Shore surfing town. *See p 138, bullet* ❹.

⑰ ★ kids Matsumoto Shave Ice. Take time out for a cool, sweet treat at Matsumoto's. *See p 16, bullet* ⑪.

Continue down Kamehameha Hwy. for about 6½ miles (10km). Bus: 52.

⑱ ★★★ kids Sunset Beach. Spend the rest of the morning playing on Sunset Beach. During the summer months this is a safe beach for swimming. During the winter, it's best to just sit and watch the big wave surfers. *See p 161.*

Drive another 12 miles (19km) down Kamehameha Hwy. to the town of Laie. Bus: 52 to Turtle Bay Resort, then 55.

⑲ ★★ kids Polynesian Cultural Center. Spend the rest of the afternoon and evening at this "living museum" of Polynesia. *See p 17, bullet* ⑬.

Retrace your route back toward Haleiwa. Take Pupukea Rd. *mauka* off Kamehameha Hwy. at Foodland, and drive .7 mile (1.1km) up a switchback road. Bus: 52, then walk up Pupukea Rd.

⑳ ★ kids Puu o Mahuka Heiau. Go at sunset to feel the *mana* (sacred spirit) of this 18th-century *heiau* (temple), known as the "hill of escape." Sitting on a 5-acre (2-hectare), 300-foot (91m) bluff overlooking Waimea Bay and 25 miles (40km) of Oahu's wave-lashed North Coast, this sacrificial temple (the largest on Oahu) appears as a huge rectangle of rocks twice as big as a football field, with an altar often covered by the flower and fruit offerings left by native Hawaiians. ***Warning:*** Never walk on, climb, or even touch the rocks at a *heiau*. ⏱ *30 min. Pupukea Rd.*

Day 6
Take H-1 west to the Waikele-Waipahu exit (Exit 7); get in the left lane on exit and turn left on Paiwa St. At the fifth light, turn right onto Waipahu St.; after the second light, turn left. Bus: 58, transfer to 43.

㉑ kids Hawaii's Plantation Village. The tour of this restored 50-acre (20-hectare) village offers a glimpse back in time to when sugar planters shaped the land, economy, and culture of Hawaii. From 1852, when the first contract laborers arrived here from China, to 1947, when the plantation era ended, more than 400,000 men, women, and children from China, Japan, Portugal, Puerto Rico, Korea, and the Philippines came to work the sugar cane fields. ⏱ 1½ hr. *Waipahu Cultural Garden Park, 94–695 Waipahu St. (at Waipahu Depot Rd.), Waipahu.* ☎ *808/677-0110. www.hawaiis plantationvillage-info.com. Admission (including escorted tour) $13 adults, $10 seniors, $7 military personnel, $5 children 4–11, free for children 3 and under. Mon–Sat 10am–2pm.*

Take Farrington Hwy. to Fort Weaver Rd. (Hwy. 76) toward Ewa Beach. Turn right on Renton Rd.

㉒ kids Hawaiian Railway. All aboard! This is a train ride back into history. Between 1890 and 1947 the chief mode of transportation for Oahu's sugar mills was the Oahu Railway and Land Co.'s narrow-gauge trains. The line carried not only equipment, raw sugar, and supplies, but also passengers from one side of the island to the other. You can relive those days every Sunday with a narrated ride through Ko Olina Resort and out to Makaha. On the second Sunday of the month, you can ride on the nearly-100-year-old, custom-built, parlor-observation car (no kids 12 and under on this ride). The fare is $20. ⏱ *2 hr. 91–1001 Renton Rd., Ewa Beach.* ☎ *808/681-5461. www. hawaiianrailway.com. Admission $10 adults, $7 seniors and children 2–12. Departures Sun at 1 and 3pm.*

Retrace your route to Fort Weaver Rd. and take the H-1 East (Honolulu direction). Take exit 8B on the left and merge into H-2 North (Miilani/Wahiawa). Take Exit 8 onto Kamehameha Hwy.

㉓ kids Dole Pineapple Plantation. Concluding this day of Plantation Hawaii, this agricultural exhibit/retail area is a modern pineapple plantation with a few adventures for kids. *See p 60, bullet* **6**.

Retrace your route back on Kamehameha Hwy. to H-1, then take the H-1 to Waikiki.

Day 7
㉔ ★★ kids Chinatown. Plan to spend the entire day in this exotic part of Honolulu. Colorful open markets, Buddhist temples, a waterside walkway, and plenty of tempting restaurants will keep you occupied for hours. For complete descriptions, see my Chinatown tour beginning on p 72.

The Hawaii Plantation Village features 30 restored camp houses.

Wartime Honolulu

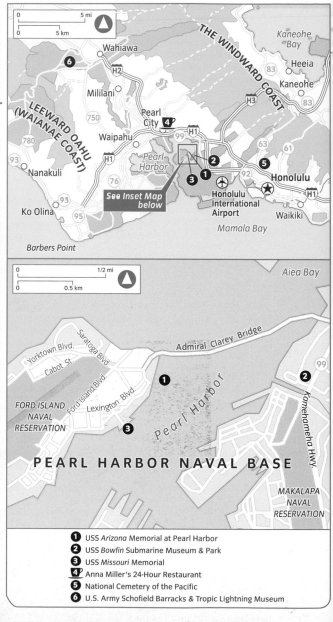

0   5 mi
0   5 km

THE WINDWARD COAST

Kāneohe Bay

Wahiawa

Heeia

Kaneohe

Mililani

Pearl City

LEEWARD OAHU (WAIANAE COAST)

Waipahu

Pearl Harbor

See Inset Map below

Nanakuli

Honolulu International Airport

Honolulu

Waikiki

Ko Olina

Barbers Point

Mamala Bay

0   1/2 mi
0   0.5 km

Aiea Bay

Yorktown Blvd.

Saratoga Blvd.

Admiral Clarey Bridge

Cabot St.

Ford Island Blvd.

FORD ISLAND NAVAL RESERVATION

Lexington Blvd.

Pearl Harbor

Kamehameha Hwy.

PEARL HARBOR NAVAL BASE

MAKALAPA NAVAL RESERVATION

1 USS *Arizona* Memorial at Pearl Harbor
2 USS *Bowfin* Submarine Museum & Park
3 USS *Missouri* Memorial
4 Anna Miller's 24-Hour Restaurant
5 National Cemetery of the Pacific
6 U.S. Army Schofield Barracks & Tropic Lightning Museum

On December 7, 1941, Hawaii's historic "day of infamy," Pearl Harbor was bombed by the Japanese, and the United States entered World War II. Honolulu has a rich history during the war years, and this 1-day tour covers the highlights. **START: Waikiki. Trip Length: 1 day and 73 miles (117km).**

Drive west on H-1 past the airport to the USS *Arizona* Memorial exit, then follow the green-and-white signs; there's ample free parking. Or take the *Arizona* Memorial Shuttle Bus VIP (☎ 808/839-0911), which picks up at Waikiki hotels 6:50am–1pm ($9 per person round-trip). Bus: 20.

1 ★★★ kids USS *Arizona* Memorial at Pearl Harbor. No trip to Honolulu would be complete without a visit to this memorial at Pearl Harbor. Get there early, preferably by the 7:30am opening—otherwise, face long lines (waits up to 3 hr.). See p 14, bullet **4**.

2 ★ kids USS *Bowfin* Submarine Museum & Park. This is a great opportunity to see what life was like on a submarine. You can go below deck of this famous vessel— nicknamed the "Pearl Harbor Avenger" for its successful attacks on the Japanese—and see how the 80-man crew lived during wartime.

The *Bowfin* Museum has an impressive collection of submarine-related artifacts. The Waterfront Memorial honors submariners lost during World War II. ⏲ *1 hr. 11 Arizona Memorial Dr. (next to the USS Arizona Memorial Visitor Center).* ☎ *808/423-1341. www.bowfin.org. Admission $10 adults, $7 active-duty military personnel and seniors, $4 children 4–12 (children 3 and under not permitted for safety reasons). Daily 7am–5pm.*

3 ★ kids USS *Missouri* Memorial. On the deck of this 58,000-ton battleship (the last one the navy built), World War II came to an end with the signing of the Japanese surrender on September 2, 1945. I recommend taking the tour, which begins at the visitor center. Guests are shuttled to Ford Island on military-style buses while listening to a 1940s-style radio program. Once on the ship, guests watch an informational film and are then free

Historical photo of USS Arizona *sinking into Pearl Harbor.*

The USS Missouri provided firepower in the battles of Iwo Jima and Okinawa.

to explore on their own or take a guided tour. Highlights of this massive battleship include the forecastle (or *fo'c's'le,* in Navy talk), where the 30,000-pound anchors are dropped on 1,080 feet (329m) of anchor chain; the 16-inch (41cm) guns, which can accurately fire a 2,700-pound (1,225kg) shell some 23 miles (37km) in 50 seconds; and the spot where the Instrument of Surrender was signed as Douglas MacArthur, Chester Nimitz, and "Bull" Halsey looked on. ⏰ *1½ hr. 11 Arizona Memorial Rd.,* ☎ *877/ MIGHTY-MO (644-4896). www.uss missouri.com. Admission $20 adults, $10 children 4–12, which includes 1 of 4 tours ranging from a guided tour to an audiovisual tour. The new Battle Station Tour (90 min.) is an additional $25 for adults and $12 for* children. *Daily 9am–5pm; guided tours 9:30am–4:30pm. Check in at the USS Bowfin Submarine Museum, next to the USS Arizona Memorial Visitor Center.*

Turn right on Arizona Rd. and then left on Kamehameha Hwy. (Hwy. 99). Turn right on Kaonohi St. Bus: A (City Express A).

4 ★ **kids** **Anna Miller's 24-Hour Restaurant.** Just a couple of miles away, in Pearlridge, is this always-busy casual dining restaurant. Treat yourself to the best fresh strawberry pie on the island (with a generous helping of fluffy whipped cream). *Pearlridge Centre, 98–115 Kaonohi St. (Kamehameha Hwy.).* ☎ *808/487-2421. $.*

See World War II History from the Air

For a unique perspective on Oahu's historical sites, I highly recommend the **Island Seaplane Service's** (☎ **808/836-6273;** www.islandseaplane.com) 1-hour tour of the island. The tour gives you aerial views of Waikiki Beach, Diamond Head Crater, Kahala's luxury estates, and the sparkling waters of Hanauma and Kaneohe bays and continues on to Chinaman's Hat, the Polynesian Cultural Center, and the rolling surf of the North Shore. The flight returns across the island, over Hawaii's historic wartime sites. Tours cost $250 per person.

Turn left on Kam Hwy. (Hwy. 99) and merge on Hwy. 78 East, which merges into H-1 East. Take Exit 21A (Pali Hwy.). Turn left on Pali Hwy., right on School St., left on Lusitana St., then right on Puowaina Dr. Stay right on Puowaina Dr. to the end of the road. Bus: 62, transfer to 6.

5 ★ National Memorial Cemetery of the Pacific.

You may know this national cemetery by its nickname, Punchbowl (ironically the Hawaiian called this area "Puowaina," or "hill of sacrifice"). Not only is the cemetery a memorial to 35,000 veterans of wars, but it also is a geological wonder—a former volcanic cone that exploded lava some 150,000 years ago.

🕑 *1 hr. Punchbowl Crater, 2177 Puowaina Dr. (at the end of the road).* ☎ *808/541-1434. Free admission. Daily 8am–5:30pm (Mar–Sept to 6:30pm).*

Retrace your route on Puowaina Dr., then go left on Lusitana St., and right on School St. Take H-1 West to H-2 North, which

The attack on Pearl Harbor outraged Americans and launched the country into World War II.

becomes Hwy. 99. Turn left on Kunia Rd., then right on Lyman Rd. (through the gate). Turn right on Flagler Rd., then left on Waianae Ave. Museum is in Bldg. 361. Bus: 6, transfer to 52, transfer to 72.

6 kids U.S. Army Schofield Barracks & Tropic Lightning Museum.

With its broad, palm-lined boulevards and Art Deco buildings, this old army cavalry post is still the largest operated by the U.S. Army outside the continental United States. You can no longer visit the barracks themselves, but the history of Schofield Barracks and the 25th Infantry Division is told in the small Tropic Lightning Museum. Displays range from a 1917 bunker exhibit to a replica of Vietnam's infamous Cu Chi tunnels. 🕑 *1 hr. Schofield Barracks, Bldg. 361, Waianae Ave.* ☎ *808/655-0438. www.25idl.army. mil/Tropic%20Lightning%20Museum/ history.htm. Free admission. Tues–Sat 10am–4pm.*

Retrace your route back to H-2, then take H-1 back to Waikiki.

A bird's-eye view of the Punchbowl.

Historic Waikiki

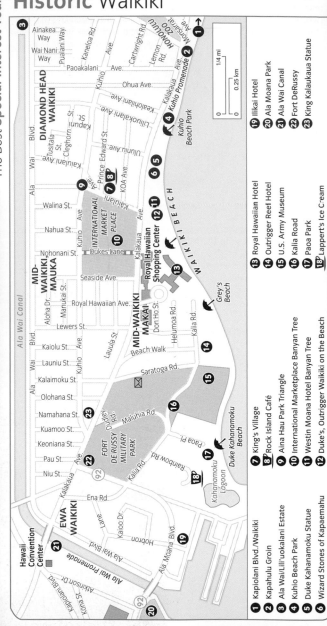

1 Kapiolani Blvd./Waikiki
2 Kapahulu Groin
3 Ala Wai/Liliʻuokalani Estate
4 Kuhio Beach Park
5 Duke Kahanamoku Statue
6 Wizard Stones of Kapaemahu
7 King's Village
8 Rock Island Café
9 Aina Hau Park Triangle
10 International Marketplace Banyan Tree
11 Westin Moana Hotel Banyan Tree
12 Duke's, Outrigger Waikiki on the Beach
13 Royal Hawaiian Hotel
14 Outrigger Reef Hotel
15 U.S. Army Museum
16 Kalia Road
17 Paoa Park
18 Lappert's Ice Cream
19 Ilikai Hotel
20 Ala Moana Park
21 Ala Wai Canal
22 Fort DeRussy
23 King Kalaukaua Statue

Spend a morning strolling through history. Each of the 21 Waikiki Historic Trail Markers, 6-foot-tall (1.8m-) surfboards, explains the history of Hawaii's favorite resort area, focusing on the time before Westerners came to its shores (I've thrown in a few extra stops along the way). You could probably speed-walk the entire route in a couple of hours, but I recommend taking all morning, stopping at each one and appreciating this culturally rich area. START: **Kapiolani Ave. (near Monsarrat Ave.). Trip Length: 4½ miles (7.2km).**

1 Kapiolani Blvd./Waikiki. In ancient times there were two *heiau* in this area that covered San Souci and Queen's Surf beaches and all of Kapiolani Park. One was *Kupalaha,* located on the shoreline at Queen's Beach and thought to be part of the *Papa'ena'ena* Heiau, where Kamehameha I made the last human sacrifice in Waikiki. The other, *Makahuna,* near Diamond Head, was dedicated to *Kanaloa,* the god of the ocean. *Kalakaua Ave. (near the Natatorium, close to Monsarrat Ave.).*

Walk Away from Diamond Head to the Groin at Kapahulu Ave.

2 Kapahulu Groin. Waikiki has always been a popular surfing site. Near here, on the slopes of Diamond Head, a *heiau* was dedicated to *he'e nalu,* or surfing, and the priests there were responsible for announcing the surfing conditions to the village below by flying a kite. *Kalakau and Kapahulu aves.*

Turn *mauka* up Kapahulu Ave. to Ala Wai Blvd.

3 Ala Wai/Liliuokalani Estate. This was the site of the estate of Queen Liliuokalani, who was overthrown by the U.S. government in 1893. She had two homes here: *Paoakalani* (royal perfume), located where the canal now stands, and *Kealohilani* (the brightness of heaven), located opposite Kuhio Beach. *Kapahulu Ave. and Ala Wai Blvd.*

Continue in the Ewa direction on Ala Wai Blvd. and turn left on Paoakalani Ave. Walk down to the beach.

4 Kuhio Beach Park. This beach park is named in honor of Prince Jonah Kalaniana'ole, Hawaii's second delegate to the U.S. Congress, 1902–22. Kalaniana'ole successfully got the passage of the Homes Commission Act, giving native Hawaiians some 200,000 acres (80,937 hectares) of land. His home, *Pualeilani* (flower from the wreath of heaven), was located on the beach here, and was given to the city when he died. *2453 Kalakaua Ave. (between Kealohilani and Liliuokalani sts.).*

Continue walking in the Ewa direction down Kalakaua Ave.

Queen Liliuokalani, Hawaii's last monarch.

Fans of Duke Kahanamoku drape his statue with leis.

⑤ Duke Kahanamoku Statue.
Olympic swimming champion, internationally known surfer, movie actor, and Hawaii's ambassador of Aloha, Duke Paoa Kahanamoku won three gold medals, two silvers, and a bronze in four Olympics. He introduced surfing to Europe, Australia, and the East Coast of the U.S., and appeared in movies from 1925 to 1933. There's no surfboard marker here, just the statue of Duke. *Kalakaua Ave. (between Liliuokalani and Uluniu sts.).*

One of the Wizard Stones.

Continue walking in the Ewa direction down Kalakaua Ave.

⑥ Wizard Stones of Kapaemahu. According to legend, four healers from Tahiti (Kapaemahu, Kahaloa, Kapuni, and Kinohi) came to Hawaii in perhaps the 15th century. Before they left, they transferred their healing powers into these stones, which were located in Kaimuki, 2 miles (3.2km) away. No one knows how the stones, which weigh approximately 8 tons (7 metric tons), got to Waikiki. *Diamond Head side of the Waikiki Police Sub-Station, 2405 Kalakaua Ave.*

At Kaiulani Ave. turn toward the mountain to Koa Ave.

⑦ King's Village. The home of King David Kalakaua (1836–91) once stood here, surrounded by towering coconut trees. The King loved dancing and revived the hula tradition, which the missionaries had just about succeeded in stamping out. He also loved to give parties and earned the nickname The Merrie Monarch. The official name for the block-long shopping center that stands here today is King's Village, but everyone calls it King's Alley. *131 Kaiulani Ave. (between Koa Ave. and Prince Edward St.).*

Inside King's Village.

8 **kids** **Rock Island Café.** Order a Cherry Coke at this nostalgic soda fountain filled with memorabilia from when "Elvis was King, Marilyn was Queen, and they both drank Coca-Cola." *King's Village, 131 Kaiulani Ave. (between Koa Ave. and Prince Edward St.).* ☎ 808-923-8033. $.

Continue *mauka* on Kaiulani Ave. to Prince Edward St.

9 **Aina Hau Park Triangle.** This tiny park was once part of the palm tree–lined grand entrance to the 10-acre (4-hectare) estate of Governor Archibald Scott Cleghorn and his wife, Hawaiian Chiefess Miriam Kapili Likelike. The Chiefess (like her sister, Liliuokalani, and her brother, Kalakaua) was a composer and wrote the song *"Ainahau"* (land of the hau tree), describing the estate of three lily ponds, 500 coconut trees, 14 varieties of hibiscus, eight kinds of mango, and a giant banyan tree. The huge, two-story Victorian home stood between what today are Cleghorn and Tusitala streets. *Kaiulani/Kuhio aves.*

Turn left on Kuhio and enter the International Marketplace.

The Westin Moana's Banyan tree.

10 **International Marketplace Banyan Tree.** At one time this area fronted the Apuakehau Stream and was the summer home of King William Kanaina Lunalilo (1835–74), who was the first elected king of Hawaii. The Hawaiians called him *ke alii lokomaikai*, or "the kind chief." His reign was only 1 year and 25 days—he died due to poor health. *Duke's Lane (between Kuhio and Kalakaua aves.).*

Walk through the International Marketplace, toward the ocean. At Kalakaua Ave. cross the street.

11 **Westin Moana Hotel Banyan Tree.** The first hotels in Waikiki were just bathhouses that offered rooms for overnight stays. The first oceanfront hotel, the Park Beach, was a home converted into a hotel with 10 rooms, one bathroom, and one telephone. Then the Moana Hotel opened its doors on March 11, 1901, with four stories (the tallest structure in Hawaii) and 75 rooms (with a bathroom and a telephone in each room). What put Waikiki on the map was Harry Owens and Webley Edwards's radio show, *Hawaii Calls*, which started in 1935. At the peak of the show's popularity, in 1952, it was broadcast to 750 stations

around the globe. *2365 Kalakaua Ave. (near Kaiulani St.).*

Next door on the Ewa side.

⑫ Duke's, Outrigger Waikiki on the Beach. The outside lanai of Duke's Canoe Club was once where the Apuakehau ("basket of dew") Stream, which flowed through the middle of Waikiki, emptied into the ocean. *Paradise of the Pacific* magazine described the river as flowing through "taro patches, rice and banana fields . . . (with) canoes gliding along the shining surface . . . (and) women and children catching shrimp in long narrow baskets, often stopping to eat a few." *3553 Kalakaua Ave. (across the street from Duke's Lane and Kaiulani St.).*

Continue down Kalakaua Ave. in the Ewa direction, turn toward the ocean at Royal Hawaiian Ave.

⑬ Royal Hawaiian Hotel. At one time, this area, known then as Helumoa, was a royal coconut grove filled with 10,000 coconut trees, first planted in the 16th century by Chief Kakuhihewa. Later Kamehameha I camped here before his conquest of Oahu. After winning battles in Nuuanu, he made Waikiki the capital of the Hawaiian islands. In 1927, the Royal Hawaii Hotel opened with 400 rooms. It cost $5 million to build.

2365 Kalakaua Ave. (Royal Hawaiian Ave.). ☎ *808/922-3111.*

Retrace your steps back to Kalakaua Ave. and turn left. Turn left (toward the ocean) at Lewers St. Turn right at Kalia Rd.

⑭ Outrigger Reef Hotel. Waikiki is known today for its incredible beauty, but in the olden days, it was known by the Hawaiians as a powerful place of healing. Very successful *kahuna la'au lapa'au* (medical physicians) lived in this area and the royal families often came here to convalesce. The beach, stretching from where the Halekkulani Hotel is today to the Outrigger Reef, was called *Kawehewehe* (removal) because if you bathed in the waters, your illness would be removed. *2169 Kalia Rd. (Lewers St.).* ☎ *808/923-3111.*

⑮ U.S. Army Museum. The grounds where the museum stands today was once the 3-acre (1.2-hectare) estate and villa of Chung Afong, Hawaii's first Chinese millionaire and member of King David Kalakaua's privy council. Afong arrived in Honolulu in 1849 and in just 6 years made a fortune in retailing, real estate, sugar, rice, and opium (he had the only government license to sell it). In 1904 the U.S. Army Corp of Engineers bought the property for

The Royal Hawaiian Hotel, also known as the "Pink Palace."

The U.S. Army Museum houses everything from ancient Hawaiian warfare items to high-tech munitions.

$28,000 to defend Honolulu Harbor. On December 7, 1976, it became a museum. *Fort DeRussy, near Saratoga and Kalia rds.* ☎ *808/955-9552. www.hiarmymuseumsoc.org. Free admission. Tues–Sat 9am–5pm.*

Continue in the Ewa direction on Kalia Rd.

16 Kalia Road. In 1897, Fort DeRussy, from Kalia Road *mauka* some 13 acres (5.3 hectares), was the largest fish pond in Waikiki. Called *Ka'ihikapu*, this pond, like the hundreds of others in Waikiki, functioned as "royal iceboxes" where *'ama'ama* (mullet) and *awa* (milkfish) were raised in brackish water. Hawaiians have lots of legends about fishponds, which they believed were protected by *mo'o* (lizards) that could grow to some 12 to 30 feet (4–9m) long. In 1908, it took the U.S. military more than 250,000 cubic yards of landfill and 1 year to cover Ka'ihikapu. *Kalia Rd. (between Saratoga Rd. and Ala Moana Blvd.) mauka to Kalakaua Ave.*

Continue in the Ewa direction on Kalia Rd.

17 Paoa Park. The 20 acres (8 hectares) where the Hilton Hawaiian Village stands today was home to Olympic champion Duke Kahanamoku's mother's family, the

Paoas. Duke's grandfather, Ho'olae Paoa, was a descendant of royal chiefs and got the land from King Kamehameha III in the Great Mahele of 1848, which allowed the king, chiefs, and commoners to claim private title to lands, and for the first time allowed foreigners to own land in Hawaii. *Kalia Rd. (bordered by Paoa Rd. and Ala Moana Ave.).*

Walk inside the Hilton Hawaiian Village to the Rainbow Bazaar.

The Hilton Hawaiian Village stands on land once owned by Duke Kamehameha's family.

18 Lappert's Ice Cream. Before you leave the Hilton Hawaiian Village, take an ice-cream break at this yummy local shop, where they have some 33 flavors. (My favorite is the Kona coffee.) *Rainbow Bazaar, Hilton Hawaiian Village, 2005 Kalia Rd. (Ala Moana Blvd.).* ☎ *808/949-4321. $.*

Make a left on Ala Moana Blvd.

19 Ilikai Hotel. Waikiki's third stream, Pi'inaio, once originated here, where the hotel's lanai is today. However, unlike the other two streams (Kuekkaunahi and Apuakehau), Pi'inaio was a muddy delta area with several smaller streams pouring in. It also was a very productive fishing area filled with reef fish, crabs, shrimp, lobster, octopus, eels, and *limu* (seaweed). However, today, Waikiki is nearly fished out. *1777 Ala Moana Blvd. (at Hobron Lane).*

Continue in the Ewa direction down Ala Moana Blvd. After you cross the bridge, look for the marker on the corner of Atkinson Dr. at the entrance to the park.

20 Ala Moana Park. In the late 1800s, Chinese farmers moved into Waikiki and converted the area now occupied by the park and shopping center into duck ponds. In 1931, the city and county of Honolulu wanted to clean up the waterfront and built a park here. In 1959, the 50 acres (20 hectares) across the street opened as one of the largest shopping centers in the U.S. *Diamond Head corner of the entrance to the park, Ala Moana Blvd. (at Atkinson Dr.).*

Turn right toward the mountains on Atkinson Dr. Bear right on Kapiolani Blvd. The Convention Center is on the corner of Kapiolani Blvd. and Kalakaua Ave. Go around the back of the Center by the Ala Wai Canal for the marker.

21 Ala Wai Canal. At the turn of the 20th century, people on Oahu were not very happy with Waikiki. The smelly duck farms, coupled with the zillions of mosquitoes from the stagnant swamp lands, did not make it a pretty picture. Work began on the Ala Wai (fresh water) Canal in 1922 and was completed in 1928. Once the canal had drained the wetlands, the taro and rice fields dried up and the duck farms and

The shady lawns and gold-sand beach of Ala Moana make it one of the island's most popular playgrounds.

fish ponds disappeared. *Ala Wai Canal Side of the Convention Center, 1801 Kalakaua Ave. (Ala Wai Canal).* ☎ 808/943-3500.

Continue in the Diamond Head direction down Kalakaua to the park on the corner of Ala Moana Blvd.

㉒ Fort DeRussy. This green recreation area was named after Brigadier General Rene E. DeRussy, Corps of Engineers, who served in the American-British War of 1812. All of Fort DeRussy and all the land from here to the foothills of Manoa Valley were planted with taro. By 1870, the demand for taro had diminished and the Chinese farmers began planting rice in the former taro fields. *Near the corner of Ala Moana Blvd. and Kalakaua Ave.*

Continue toward Diamond Head on Kalakaua Ave. to the intersection of Kuhio Ave.

㉓ King Kalakaua Statue. Next to Kamehameha I, King David Kalakaua is Hawaii's best-known king and certainly lived up to his nickname, the Merrie Monarch. He was born to royal parents in 1836, raised in the court of King Kamehameha IV,

King David Kalakaua.

and elected to the position of King in 1874, after King William Lunalilo died. During his 17-year reign he restored Hawaii's rapidly fading culture of chanting, music, and hula (which had been banned by the missionaries for years). He was also forced to sign what has been termed the "Bayonet Constitution," which restricted his royal powers, in1887. In 1890, he sailed to California for medical treatment and died in San Francisco due to a mild stroke, kidney failure, and cirrhosis. *No marker (yet); statue is located at Kuhio and Kalakaua aves. intersection.*

Waikiki: It Ain't What It Used to Be

Before Westerners showed up on Oahu, Waikiki was a 2,000-acre (809-hectare) swamp (compared to the 500 acres/202 hectares it occupies today). Waikiki (which means spouting water) was a very important area because it held the drainage basin for the 5 million gallons (18,927 cubic meters) of daily rainfall from the Koolau Mountains. When Hawaiians settled in Waikiki (which historians estimate was around A.D. 600), they slowly turned the swamp into a Hawaii version of a breadbasket: taro fields, fishponds, and gardens for fruits and vegetables. When Western boats began calling at Honolulu Harbor, they brought the pesky mosquito, which loved the swamps of Waikiki. In 1927, the just-completed Ala Wai Canal not only drained the swamps, but opened up lands that eventually became the resort area of today.

The Best Special-Interest Tours

Oahu's Best **Gardens**

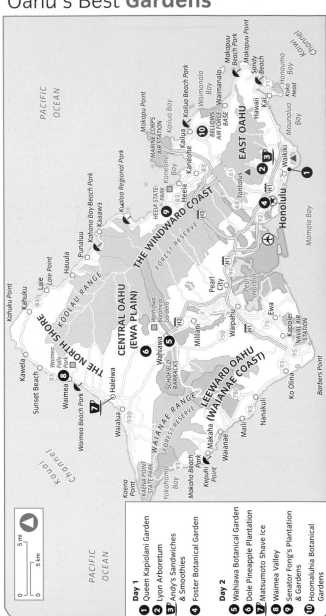

PACIFIC OCEAN

Kaiwi Channel

Mokapu Point

Mokapu Beach Park
Mokapu Point

MARINE CORPS
AIR STATION

Kailua Beach Park

Kailua Bay

Sandy Beach
Hawaii Kai

Honauma Bay
Koko Head

Waimanalo Bay

BELLOWS
AIR FORCE
BASE

Waimanalo

Kailua

Kaneohe Bay

Kaneohe

HEEIA STATE
PARK

Heeia

EAST OAHU

Waikiki

Maunalua Bay

Kualoa Regional Park

THE WINDWARD COAST

Kahana Bay Beach Park

Kaaawa

Punaluu

Hauula

Laie
Laie Point

Kahuku

Kahuku Point

Kawela

Sunset Beach

THE NORTH SHORE

Waimea

Waimea Beach Park

Haleiwa

Waialua

Kaena Point

KAENA POINT
STATE PARK

Yokohama Bay

Mokaha Beach Park

Kepuhi Point

Makaha

Waianae

Maili

Nanakuli

**LEEWARD OAHU
(WAIANAE COAST)**

WAIANAE RANGE
FOREST RESERVE

Ko Olina

Barbers Point

KAPOLEI NAVAL AIR STATION

Kapolei

Ewa

Waipahu

Pearl Harbor

Pearl City

SCHOFIELD BARRACKS

Wahiawa

Mililani

Wahiawa Botanical Gardens

**CENTRAL OAHU
(EWA PLAIN)**

KOOLAU RANGE

FOREST RESERVE

Tantalus

Honolulu

Mamala Bay

Waimea Falls Park

PACIFIC OCEAN

Kauai Channel

0   5 mi
0   5 km

Stop and smell the tuberoses. Or the plumeria. Spend a couple of days exploring the various gardens of Hawaii, from native Hawaiian plants to orchids, palms, aroids, tree ferns, heliconias, calatheas, and myriad trees. **START: Waikiki. Trip Length: 2 days and 112-miles (180km).**

Located in Waikiki next door to Kapiolani Park, on Monsarrat Ave. (between Paki and Leahi aves.). Parking entrance on Leahi Ave. Bus: 19 or 20.

Day 1

❶ Queen Kapiolani Garden. Wander into this tiny garden and smell the tropical ornamentals, hibiscus cultivars, and a small collection of native Hawaiian plants. 🕐 *30 min. Kapiolani Park, on Monsarrat Ave. (between Paki and Leahi aves.). Free admission. Open daily 24 hr.*

Take McCully St. out of Waikiki, turn right on Kapiolani Blvd., left at University Ave., and right on Oahu. Look for the slight right at Manoa Rd. Bus: B (City Express B), transfer to 5.

❷ ★ Lyon Arboretum. Six-story-tall breadfruit trees. Yellow orchids no bigger than a bus token. Ferns with fuzzy buds as big as a human head. Lyon Arboretum is 194 budding acres (79 hectares) of botanical wonders. Take the self-guided 20-minute hike through this cultivated rainforest to Inspiration Point and you'll pass more than 5,000 exotic tropical plants full of bird song. 🕐 *2–3 hr. 3860 Manoa Rd. (near the top of the road). ☎ 808/988-0456. www.hawaii.edu/lyonarboretum. Suggested donation $5 each. Mon–Fri 9am–4pm; Sat 9am–3pm.*

Retrace your route back down Manoa Rd., turn left on Oahu Ave. and then left again on E. Manoa Rd. Bus: 5.

Water lily.

❸ ★ **kids** **Andy's Sandwiches & Smoothies.** On the way down the hill, stop at this friendly neighborhood eatery. Their smoothies are terrific—try the Hi Pro (peanut butter, bananas, and apple juice with protein powder). *2904 E. Manoa Rd., opposite Manoa Marketplace. ☎ 808/988-6161. $.*

Take E. Manoa Rd. to Oahu Ave. and turn left, then left again at University and get on H-1 West to Exit 22, Vineyard Blvd. Bus: 6, transfer to City Express B.

❹ ★★ Foster Botanical Garden. The giant trees that tower over the main terrace of this leafy oasis were planted in the 1850s by William Hillebrand, a German physician and botanist, on royal land leased from Queen Emma. Today, this 14-acre (5.7-hectare) public garden, on the north side of Chinatown, is a living museum of plants, some rare and endangered, collected from the tropical regions of the world. Of

Cannonball tree at Foster Botanical Garden.

special interest are 26 "Exceptional Trees" protected by state law, a large palm collection, a primitive cycad garden, and a hybrid orchid collection. 🕐 *2–3 hr. 50 N. Vineyard Blvd. (at Nuuanu Ave.).* ☎ *808/522-7066. www.co.honolulu.hi.us/parks/hbg/fbg.htm. Admission $5 adults, $1 children 6–12. Daily 9am–4pm; guided tours Mon–Fri at 1pm (reservations recommended).*

To get back to Waikiki, drive toward Diamond Head on Vineyard Blvd., then turn right on Liliha St. Merge onto H-1 East into Waikiki. Bus: City Express B.

Day 2
Take H-1 from Waikiki to H-2, which becomes Kamehameha Hwy. (Hwy. 99). Turn right at California Ave. Bus: City Express B, transfer to 62.

⑤ Wahiawa Botanical Garden. Originally begun as an experimental arboretum by sugar planters in the 1920s, this 27-acre (11-hectare) tropical rainforest garden provides a cool, moist environment for native Hawaiian plants, palms, aroids, tree ferns, heliconias, calatheas, and epiphytic plants. Guided tours can be arranged (call in advance), but there's probably no need for it unless

you're an avid gardener. Bring mosquito repellant. 🕐 *1½–2 hr. 1396 California Ave. (at Iliwa Dr.), Wahiawa.* ☎ *808/621-7321. www.honolulu.gov/parks/hbg/wbg.htm. Free admission. Daily 9am–4pm.*

Continue on Kamehameha Hwy. to the Dole Plantation, 3 miles (5km) past Wahiawa. Bus: 62, transfer to 52.

⑥ kids Dole Pineapple Plantation. This rest stop/retail outlet/exhibit area also has an interesting self-guided tour through eight mini-gardens totaling about 1½ acres (.6 hectares). The Plantation also has a single-engine diesel locomotive that takes a 22-minute tour around 2¼ miles (3.6km) of the plantation's grounds, and the Pineapple Garden Maze, which covers more than 2 acres (.8 hectares) with a 1.7-mile (2.7km) hibiscus-lined path. 🕐 *1–2 hr. 64–1550 Kamehameha Hwy.* ☎ *808/621-8408. www.dole-plantation.com. Admission to gardens $6 adults, $4 kids (4–12); train tickets $8 adults, $6 kids; pineapple maze $6 adults, $4 kids. Daily 9am–5:30pm.*

Continue north on Kamehameha Hwy. At the traffic circle make a left into Haleiwa. Bus: 52.

⑦ ★ kids Matsumoto Shave Ice. Take a break to enjoy a cool Hawaiian treat. See p 16, bullet ⑪.

Wahiawa Botanical Garden is a lovely place for a stroll.

Continue north on Kamehameha Hwy. Bus: 52.

8 ★ kids Waimea Valley. This 1,875-acre (759-hectare) park (home to 36 botanical gardens, with about 6,000 rare species of plants and numerous Hawaiian archaeological sites) has, until recently, been under the management of the National Audubon Society. In 2008, the Office of Hawaiian Affairs took over and formed a new nonprofit corporation, Hiipaka, to run the park, with an emphasis on perpetuating and sharing the "living Hawaiian culture." The public is invited to hike the trails and spend a day in this quiet oasis. There are several free walking tours at 10, 11am, 1, and 2pm, plus cultural activities like lei-making, kappa demonstrations, hula lessons, Hawaiian games and crafts, and music and storytelling. ⏱ *2–3 hr. 59–864 Kamehameha Hwy. (Waimea Valley Rd.).* ☎ *808/638-7766. www.waimeavalley.net. Admission $13 adults, $6 seniors and children 4–12. Daily 9am–5pm.*

Continue on Kamehameha Hwy. for 30 miles (48km), then turn right on Pulama Rd. Bus: 52, which becomes 55 (stay onboard), then walk about a mile (1.6km) uphill from the stop.

9 Senator Fong's Plantation & Gardens. Senator Hiram Fong, the first Chinese American elected to the U.S. Senate, served 17 years before retiring to this 725-acre (293-hectare) tropical garden. The landscape you see today is very much like what early Polynesians saw hundreds of years ago, with forests of kukui, hala, koa, and ohia-'ai (mountain apple). Ti and pili grass still cover the slopes. It's definitely worth the hour-long guided tour. ⏱ *1 hr. 47–285 Pulama Rd., Kaneohe.* ☎ *808/239-6775. www.fonggarden.net. Admission $15 adults, $13 seniors and $9 children 5–12. Daily 10am–2pm; guided tours daily 10:30am and 1pm.*

Turn right back on Kamehameha Hwy. Continue on Kahekili Hwy., then turn left on Kulukeoe St. and right on Keneke St. Turn left to stay on Keneke St., then right on Anoi Rd. and right on Luluku Rd. Bus: 55 on Kamehameha Hwy.; it's about a mile walk to the visitor center.

10 ★ Hoomaluhia Botanical Gardens. This 400-acre (162-hectare) botanical garden at the foot of the steepled Koolau Mountains is the perfect place for a picnic. Its name means "a peaceful refuge," and that's exactly what the Army Corps of Engineers created when they installed a flood-control project here, which resulted in a 32-acre (13-hectare) freshwater lake and garden. The gardens feature geographical groupings of plantings from the major tropical regions around the world, with a special emphasis on native Hawaiian plants. ⏱ *2–3 hr. 45–680 Luluku Rd. (Visitor Center), Kaneohe.* ☎ *808/233-7323. www.co.honolulu.hi.us/parks/hbg/hmbg.htm. Free admission. Daily 9am–4pm; guided nature hikes Sat 10am and Sun 1pm.*

Continue on Luluku Rd., then turn right on Kamehameha Hwy. (Hwy. 83). Turn right on Pali Hwy., then take H-1 East back to Waikiki. Bus: 55, transfer to City Express B.

Ti leaves.

Honolulu for **Art Lovers**

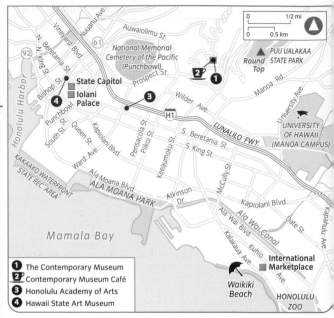

1. The Contemporary Museum
2. Contemporary Museum Café
3. Honolulu Academy of Arts
4. Hawaii State Art Museum

Even if you're not a die-hard art lover, you won't regret giving up a day for this tour. Hawaii's top three cultural galleries aren't just depositories of artwork—each is an incredible edifice in its own right. It's a part of Hawaii you won't want to miss.
START: Waikiki. Trip Length: 11 miles (18km).

Take McCully St. out of Waikiki, then turn left on Dole St. and right on Punahou St. Turn left on Nehoa St., right on Makiki St., then left on Makiki Heights Dr. Bus: 4, then about a ¾-mile (1.2km) walk up Makiki Heights Dr.

1 ★★ **kids** **The Contemporary Museum.** Honolulu's best contemporary art gallery is nestled up on the slopes of Tantalus, one of Honolulu's upscale residential communities, and is renowned for its 3 acres (1.2 hectares) of Asian gardens (with reflecting pools, sun-drenched terraces, and views of Diamond Head).

Even if you don't venture inside any of the Museum's buildings, exploring the grounds alone is worth the trip. ⏱ 1½–2 hr. 2411 Makiki Heights Dr. (near Mott-Smith Dr.). ☎ 808/526-0232. www.tcmhi.org. Tickets $8 adults, $6 seniors and students, free for children 12 and under, free for all the third Thurs of each month. Tues–Sat 10am–4pm; Sun noon–4pm.

2 ★ **Contemporary Museum Café.** After you've wandered the grounds and the exhibits, treat yourself to the sinfully delicious flourless chocolate cake and a just-brewed

Shangri La in Hawaii

In the late 1930s, heiress Doris Duke developed her dream property and dubbed it "Shangri La." It reflects Duke's love of both Hawaii and the Middle East by featuring an extensive collection of Islamic art and architecture blended with Hawaii's sweeping ocean views, exotic gardens, and water features. Tours originate at the Honolulu Academy of Arts, 900 S. Beretania St. (at Ward Ave.), and cost $25. Reservations are required (book way in advance; this tour is popular). For more information, visit www.shangrilahawaii.org or call ☎ **808/532-DUKE** (3853).

latte at this intimate cafe. *Contemporary Museum, 2411 Makiki Heights Dr. (near Mott-Smith Dr.).* ☎ *808/ 523-3362. www.tcmhi.org. $$.*

Turn left at Mott-Smith Dr. then right on Piikoi St., left on Pensacola St., and right on Beretania St. Bus: Walk 1 mile (1.6km) to the stop at Pensacola St. and Wilder Ave. to catch bus 18.

❸ ★★★ **kids** **Honolulu Academy of Arts.** The state's only general fine arts museum features one of the top Asian art collections in the country. Also on exhibit are American and European masters and prehistoric works of Mayan, Greek, and Hawaiian art. The museum's award-winning architecture is a paragon of graciousness, featuring magnificent courtyards, lily ponds, and sensitively designed galleries. 🕐 *2–3 hr. 900 S. Beretania St. (at Ward Ave.).* ☎ *808/ 532-8700, or 808/532-8701 for recording. www.honoluluacademy.org. $10 adults; $5 students, seniors, and military personnel; free for children 11 and under; free the third Sun of the month (11am–5pm) and first Wed of the month. Tues–Sat 10am–4:30pm; Sun 1–5pm. Guided tours (included in admission price) Tues–Sat 10:15am, 11:30am, and 1:30pm; Sun 1:15pm.*

Drive Ewa on Beretania St. and turn left on Richards St. Park at a meter on the street. Bus: Walk about a half-mile down Beretania St. to Punchbowl St., get on bus 13.

❹ ★★ **kids** **Hawaii State Art Museum.** This historic building was once the Royal Hawaiian Hotel, built in 1872 during the reign of King Kamehameha V. All of the 360 works on display were created by artists who live in Hawaii. 🕐 *2–3 hr. 250 S Hotel St. (at Richards St.).* ☎ *808/586-0900. www.state.hi.us/sfca. Free admission. Tues–Sat 10am–4pm and first Fri of every month 5–9pm.*

From Richards St. turn left on King St., then take a slight right at Kapiolani Blvd., right on Piikoi, and left on Ala Moana Blvd. into Waikiki. Bus: Walk 1 block toward the ocean to King St., then walk toward Diamond Head 2 blocks to Punchbowl St. to catch City Express B.

Antoine Bourdelle's La Grande Penelope at the Honolulu Academy of Arts.

Romantic Honolulu & Oahu

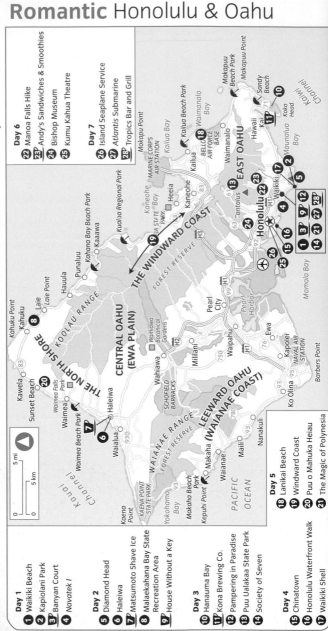

Day 1
① Waikiki Beach
② Kapiolani Park
③ Banyan Court
④ Navatek I

Day 2
⑤ Diamond Head
⑥ Haleiwa
⑦ Matsumoto Shave Ice
⑧ Malaekahana Bay State Recreation Area
⑨ House Without a Key

Day 3
⑩ Hanauma Bay
⑪ Kona Brewing Co.
⑫ Pampering in Paradise
⑬ Puu Ualakaa State Park
⑭ Society of Seven

Day 4
⑮ Chinatown
⑯ Honolulu Waterfront Walk
⑰ Waikiki Shell

Day 5
⑱ Lanikai Beach
⑲ Windward Coast
⑳ Puu o Mahuka Heiau
㉑ The Magic of Polynesia

Day 6
㉒ Manoa Falls Hike
㉓ Andy's Sandwiches & Smoothies
㉔ Bishop Museum
㉕ Kumu Kahua Theatre

Day 7
㉖ Island Seaplane Service
㉗ Atlantis Submarine
㉘ Tropics Bar and Grill

What could be more romantic than a vacation in Waikiki, where the gentle breezes caress your skin, the sensuous aroma of tropical flowers wafts through the air, and the relaxing sound of the rolling surf beckons lovers from around the globe? Below is a suggested tour for discovering not only the exotic isle of Oahu, but also each other. START: Waikiki. Trip Length: 7 days and 271 miles (436km).

Day 1

1 ★★★ Waikiki Beach. Your vacation starts when the warm sand covers your toes and the salt air kisses your face. Take a stroll hand-in-hand down this famous beach. *See p 161.*

Walk down Kalakaua Ave.

2 ★★ Kapiolani Park. If you aren't too tired from your trip, take a stroll around this tropical park. Stop to smell the flowers and kiss your sweetie. See my tour of the park beginning on p 86.

Walk back to Waikiki on Kalakaua Ave. Just across the street from Kaiulani St.

3 Banyan Court. After all that walking, sit oceanside at this outdoor bar and order an exotic drink such as a mai tai. *Moana Surfrider, 2365 Kalakaua Ave. (Kaiulani St.).* ☎ *808/921 4600. $$.*

From Waikiki take Ala Moana Blvd. to Aloha Tower Marketplace, Pier 6. Bus: 19 or 20.

4 ★ Navatek I. Spend your first evening in Paradise watching the sun set in the Pacific offshore on a dinner cruise. *See p 15, bullet 9.*

Day 2

Drive to the intersection of Diamond Head Rd. and 18th Ave. Follow the road through the tunnel (which is closed 6pm–6am) and park in the lot. Bus: 58 (from the Ala Moana Shopping Center).

5 ★ Diamond Head. You'll probably be up early on your first day in Hawaii before you get used to the time difference. So get up and greet the sun by hiking up to Waikiki's most famous landmark. You'll get a bird's-eye view of the island from atop this 760-foot (232m) extinct volcano. *See p 165.*

Take H-1 west out of Waikiki, then take the H-2 north exit (Exit 8A)

A couple enjoying some time on the beach.

toward Mililani/Wahiawa. After 7 miles (11km) H-2 becomes Kamehameha Hwy. (Hwy. 80). Look for the turnoff to Haleiwa town. Bus: 19, then transfer to 52.

6 ★★★ **kids** **Haleiwa.** Spend the rest of your morning exploring this famous North Shore surfing town. *See p 138, bullet* **4**.

7 ★ **kids** **Matsumoto Shave Ice.** For a tropical taste of the islands, stop at this nearly 50-year-old shop where Hawaii's rendition of a snow cone is served *See p 16, bullet* **11**.

Continue down Kamehameha Hwy. Bus: 52.

8 ★★★ **Malaekahana Bay State Recreation Area.** Take a picnic lunch to this secluded beach park. (I suggest getting a burger or sandwich from Kua Aina, 66–160 Kamehameha Hwy. in Haleiwa, ☎ 808/637-6067.) If you go during the week, you may have a stretch of beach all to yourself. Plan to spend the entire afternoon here relaxing on the beach, swimming, or snorkeling. *See p 167*.

Retrace your route back to Honolulu: Take Kamehameha Hwy. (Hwy. 83) to Hwy. 99 to H-2 to H-1 to Waikiki. Bus: 52, transfer to City Express B.

9 ★★★ **House Without a Key.** Watch the sunset from the beach at this exquisitely beautiful resort in Waikiki. See p 14, bullet **3**

Day 3
From Waikiki, take H-1 East, which becomes the Kalanianaole Hwy. Look for the Koko Head Regional Park on the left; the beach is on the right (ocean side). Avoid the

Float among the abundant brightly colored fish in Hanauma Bay.

crowds by going early, about 8am, on a weekday morning; once the parking lot's full, you're out of luck. The Hanauma Bay Shuttle Bus runs from Waikiki to Hanauma Bay every half-hour from 8:45am to 1pm. You can catch it at any city bus stop in Waikiki. It returns every hour from noon to 4pm.

10 **Hanauma Bay.** Rent a mask, snorkel, and fins and head out to Oahu's premiere snorkeling area to discover the incredible beauty of Hawaii's underwater world. *Note:* The beach is closed on Tuesdays. *See p 177*.

Return to Kalanianaole Hwy. (Hwy. 72) heading back to Waikiki.

11 **Kona Brewing Co.** Stop by this local brewing company to sample some of their locally made beer, like the Fire Rock Pale Ale or the Lilikoi Wheat Ale (or the nonalcoholic Gingerade, made from organic ginger). *Koko Marina Center, 7192 Kalanianaole Hwy. (Lunalilo Home Rd.).* ☎ *808/394-5662. $$.*

Trace your route back to Waikiki.

The Lei

There's nothing like a lei. The stunning tropical beauty of the delicate garland, the deliciously sweet fragrance of the blossoms, the way the flowers curl softly around your neck. There's no doubt about it: Getting lei'd in Hawaii is a sensuous experience. Leis are much more than just a decorative necklace of flowers; they're also one of the nicest ways to say hello, good-bye, congratulations, I salute you, my sympathies are with you, or I love you. The custom of giving leis can be traced back to Hawaii's very roots; according to chants, the first lei was given by Hiiaka, the sister of the volcano goddess Pele, who presented Pele with a lei of lehua blossoms on a beach in Puna. Leis are the perfect symbol for the islands: They're given in the moment and their fragrance and beauty are enjoyed in the moment, but even after they fade, their spirit of aloha lives on.

⓬ Pampering in Paradise.
Spend the afternoon at a spa getting pampered. For my top spa picks, see the box "Pampering in Paradise" on p 107.

From Waikiki, take Ala Wai Blvd. to McCully St., turn right, and drive *mauka* beyond the H-1 on-ramps to Wilder St. Turn left and go to Makiki St. Turn right and continue onward and upward about 3 miles (4.8km).

⓭ ★ Puu Ualakaa State Park.
One of the island's most romantic sunset views is from this 1,048-foot

Oahu's spas offer unique Hawaiian treatments.

(319m) hill named for sweet potatoes. Get there before sunset to see the panoramic view of the entire coastline. *See p 21, bullet ❻.*

Retrace your route to back to Waikiki.

⓮ ★ Society of Seven. Spend the evening with your honey at this popular nightclub featuring a blend of skits, Broadway hits, popular music, and costumed musical acts. *See p 30.*

Day 4
⓯ ★★★ Chinatown. Explore this exotic neighborhood with the help of the tour starting on p 72. Be sure to shop for a lei for your sweetie.

Walk down Bethel St. toward the ocean to the Aloha Tower.

⓰ ★ Honolulu Waterfront Walk. Continue your day of exploring Honolulu with the tour on p 82. But start out by going up to the top of the Aloha Tower and seeing Honolulu from this bird's-eye view. Finish your tour of the Waterfront by having dinner at Chai's Island Bistro (see p 131).

Chinatown is one of the best places to shop for leis.

Take Ala Wai Blvd. into Waikiki. TheBus: 19 or 20.

17 ★★ Waikiki Shell. Find out if there's anything playing at Waikiki's best outdoor venue, this open amphitheater in Kapiolani Park. *See p 89.*

Day 5

Take the H-1 to the Pali Hwy. (Hwy. 61) to Kailua, where it then becomes Kailua Rd. as it proceeds through town. At Kalaheo Ave., turn right and follow the coast about 2 miles (3.2km) to Kailua Beach Park; just past it, turn left at the T-intersection and drive uphill on Aalapapa Dr., a one-way

Lanikai Beach.

street that loops back as Mokulua Dr. Park on Mokulua, and walk down any of the eight public-access lanes to the shore. Bus: 20, transfer to 57, transfer to 70.

18 ★★ Lanikai Beach. Escape to the windward side and spend the morning (when the sun is the best) at this tiny, off–the-beaten-track beach. *See p 157.*

From Lanikai take Kawailoa Rd., which becomes Kalaheo Ave., which becomes Kaneohe Bay Dr. Turn left on Kamehameha Hwy. (Hwy. 83). Bus: 57, transfer to 55, transfer to 52.

19 ★★ Windward Coast. After a morning at the beach, take a drive along the windy windward coast. Have fun trying to pronounce the tongue-twisting names of the towns. See the tour starting on p 142.

From Kahana continue on Kame-hameha Hwy. (Hwy. 83) to Pupukea Rd., just after Pupukea Beach Park. Turn toward the mountain on Pupukea Rd. to Puu o Mahuka Heiau.

20 ★ Puu o Mahuka Heiau. It will take you about 30 to 45 minutes to drive here from Kahana Bay; time your drive so you can be at this historic heiau as the sun sets. *See p 44, bullet 20.*

Take Kamehameha Hwy. (Hwy. 83) to Hwy. 99, to H-2, to H-1, to Waikiki. Bus: 52, transfer to City Express B.

㉑ ★ The Magic of Polynesia. Back in Waikiki, watching Hawaii's top magic show with illusionist John Hirokana will enthrall you. *See p 133.*

Day 6
Take McCully St. out of Waikiki toward the mountains. Turn right onto Kapiolani Blvd., then left onto University Ave. and drive through the University of Hawaii campus. Turn right onto Manoa Rd. The trail head, marked by a footbridge, is at the end of Manoa Rd., past Lyon Arboretum. Park in the Paradise Park neighborhood. Bus: TheBus 5.

㉒ Manoa Falls Hike. Take your sweetheart on this easy, .75-mile (1.2km; one-way) hike in a warm, tropical rainforest just minutes from Waikiki. In less than an hour you'll be at the idyllic Manoa Falls. *See p 167.*

Retrace your route back down Manoa Rd., turn left on Oahu Ave., then left again on E. Manoa Rd.

㉓ ★ kids Andy's Sandwiches & Smoothies. After hiking in the rainforest, stop by this neighborhood eatery and grab a smoothie and a healthy snack (try the mango muffins). *2904 E. Manoa Rd., opposite Manoa Marketplace.* ☎ 808/988-6161. *$.*

Drive down E. Manoa Rd., turn left on Oahu Ave., take a slight left on University Ave., then get on H-1 West. Take exit 20A (Likelike Hwy.), then turn right on Bernice St. Bus: 5, transfer to City Express B.

Steal a kiss and a great photo op at Manoa Falls.

㉔ ★★★ Bishop Museum. Spend the rest of the day wandering through this treasure-trove of Hawaiian culture, flora, and fauna. *See p 15, bullet ➐.*

From Bernice turn right on Houghtailing St., then left at N. King St. Turn right on Nuuanu Ave., then left on Merchant St. Bus: 1.

㉕ ★★ Kumu Kahua Theatre. Check out a local play at this intimate theater, which features local playwrights. *See p 134.*

Continue on Merchant St., then turn right on Bishop St. Go left at Ala Moana Blvd. back to Waikiki. Bus: B (City Express B).

Day 7
㉖ ★★ Island Seaplane Service. On your last day on Oahu, take to the air and see this magnificent island from a seaplane. *See p 30.*

Retrace your route down Lagoon Dr., then turn right on Nimitz Hwy., which becomes Ala Moana Blvd. into Waikiki. Bus: 31, transfer to 19.

㉗ ★★★ *Atlantis* Submarine.
After seeing the island from the air, plunge beneath the waves (without getting wet) and see the island from the Neptunian perspective. *See p 184.*

Walk back to the Hilton Hawaiian Village Resort.

⓲ Tropics Bar and Grill. Plop down in this beachfront outdoor cafe and order a mai tai to toast your Hawaiian vacation and start planning your next trip to Paradise. *Hilton Hawaiian Village, beachfront Alii Tower, 2005 Kalia Rd.* ☎ *808/949-4321. $$.* ●

Getting Married in Paradise

Honolulu and Waikiki are a great place for a wedding. Not only does the entire island exude romance and natural beauty, but after the ceremony, you're only a few steps away from the perfect honeymoon.

The easiest way to plan your wedding is to let someone else handle it at the resort or hotel where you'll be staying. Most Waikiki resorts and hotels have wedding coordinators who can plan everything from a simple (relatively) low-cost wedding to an extravaganza that people will talk about for years.

You will need a marriage license: Contact the Marriage License Office, Room 101 (First floor) of the Health Department Building, 1250 Punchbowl St. (corner of Beretania and Punchbowl sts.; ☎ 808/586-4545; www.state.hi.us/doh/records/vr_marri.html). Open Monday through Friday from 8am to 4pm. Once in Hawaii, the prospective bride and groom must go together to the marriage-licensing agent to get a license. A license costs $60 and is good for 30 days. The only requirements for a marriage license are that both parties are 15 years of age or older (applicants 15–17 years old must have proof of age, written consent of both parents, and the written approval of the judge of the family court) and are not more closely related than first cousins.

Almost half of the 20,000 couples who get married in Hawaii every year come from somewhere else.

Historic **Chinatown**

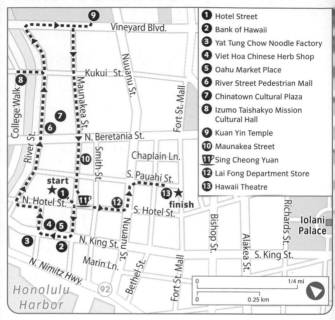

1 Hotel Street
2 Bank of Hawaii
3 Yat Tung Chow Noodle Factory
4 Viet Hoa Chinese Herb Shop
5 Oahu Market Place
6 River Street Pedestrian Mall
7 Chinatown Cultural Plaza
8 Izumo Taishakyo Mission Cultural Hall
9 Kuan Yin Temple
10 Maunakea Street
11 Sing Cheong Yuan
12 Lai Fong Department Store
13 Hawaii Theatre

Honolulu's historic Chinatown is a mix of Asian cultures all packed into a small area where tangy spices rule the cuisine, open-air markets have kept out the mini-malls, and acupuncture and herbal remedies have paved the way to good health. The jumble of streets bustles with residents and visitors from all over the world; a cacophony of sounds, from the high-pitched bleating of vendors in the market to the lyrical dialects of the retired men "talking story" over a game of mah-jongg. No trip to Honolulu is complete without a visit to this exotic, historic district. Plan at least 2 hours, more if you love to browse. **START: North Hotel and Maunakea sts. Parking is scarce, so I recommend taking bus 2 or 20. If you insist on driving, take Ala Moana Blvd. and turn right on Smith St.; make a left on Beretania St. and a left again at Maunakea St. The city parking garage is on the Ewa (west) side of Maunakea St., between North Hotel and North King sts.**

1 ★ **kids** **Hotel Street.** During World War II, Hotel Street was synonymous with good times. Pool halls and beer parlors lined the blocks,

Previous page: Waikiki Beach and Diamond Head.

and prostitutes were plentiful. Nowadays, the more nefarious establishments have been replaced with small shops, from art galleries to specialty boutiques. Wandering up and down this street, head to the intersection with Smith Street. On the Diamond

You can easily spend half a day exploring the colorful streets of Chinatown.

Head (east) side of Smith, you'll notice stones in the sidewalk; they were taken from the sandalwood ships, which came to Hawaii empty of cargo except for these stones, which were used as ballast on the trip over. *Hotel St., between Maunakea and Bethel sts.*

When you've finished exploring Hotel St., head back to Maunakea St. and turn toward the ocean.

2 kids **Bank of Hawaii.** This unusual-looking bank is not the conservative edifice you might expect—it's guarded by two fire-breathing-dragon statues. *101 N. King St. (Maunakea St.).* ☎ *808/532-2480.*

Turn right onto King St.

3 ★ kids **Yat Tung Chow Noodle Factory.** The delicious, delicate noodles that star in numerous Asian dishes are made here. There aren't any tours of the factory, but you can look through the window, past the white cloud of flour that hangs in the air, and watch as dough is fed into rollers at one end of the noodle machines, and perfectly cut noodles emerge at the other end. *150 N. King St. (Maunakea St.).* ☎ *808/531-7982. Mon–Sat 6am–3pm.*

4 kids **Viet Hoa Chinese Herb Shop.** Here, Chinese herbalists act as both doctors and dispensers of herbs. There's a wall of tiny drawers all labeled in Chinese characters; the herbalist pulls out bits and pieces ranging from dried flowers to mashed antelope antler. The patient then takes the concoction home to brew into a strong tea. *162 N. King St. (Maunakea St.).* ☎ *808/523-5499. Mon–Sat 8:30am–5pm; Sun 8:30am–2pm.*

Cross to the south side of King St., where, just west of Kekaulike St., you come to the most-visited part of Chinatown, the open-air market.

5 ★★ kids **Oahu Market Place.** Those interested in Asian cooking will find all the necessary ingredients here, including pigs' heads, poultry (some still squawking), fresh octopuses, pungent fish sauce, and 1,000-year-old eggs. The friendly vendors are happy to explain their wares and give instructions on how to prepare these exotic treats. The market has been at this spot since 1904. ⏲ *1 hr. N. King and Kekaulike sts. Daily 6am–6pm.*

Follow King down to River St. and turn right toward the mountains. A range of inexpensive restaurants lines River St. from King to Beretania sts. You can get the best Vietnamese and Filipino food

Shop for delicacies such as dragon fruit at Chinatown markets.

Bargaining: A Way of Life in Chinatown

In Chinatown, nearly every purchase—from chicken's feet to an 18-carat gold necklace—is made by bargaining. It's the way of life for most Asian countries—and part of the fun and charm of shopping in Chinatown. The main rule of thumb when negotiating a price is respect. The customer must have respect for the merchant and understand that he's in business to make money. This respect is coupled with the understanding that the customer does not want to be taken advantage of and would like the best deal possible.

Keep in mind two rules when bargaining: cash and volume. Don't even begin haggling if you're not planning to pay cash. The second you pull out a credit card (if the merchant or vendor will even accept it), all deals are off. And remember, the more you buy, the better the deal the merchant will extend to you.

Significant savings can be realized for high-ticket items like jewelry. The price of gold in Chinatown is based on the posted price of the tael (a unit of weight, slightly more than an ounce), which is listed for 14-, 18-, and 24-carat gold, plus the value of the labor. There's no negotiating on the tael price, but the cost of the labor is where the negotiations begin.

in town in these blocks, but go early—lines for lunch start at 11:15am.

6 kids **River Street Pedestrian Mall.** The statue of Chinese revolutionary leader Sun Yat-sen marks the beginning of this wide mall, which borders the Nuuanu Stream. It's lined with shade trees, park benches, and tables where seniors gather to play mah-jongg and checkers. There are plenty of takeout restaurants nearby if you'd like to eat lunch outdoors. *N. Beretania St. to Vineyard Blvd.*

7 ★ kids **Chinatown Cultural Plaza.** This modern complex is filled with shops featuring everything from tailors to calligraphers (most somewhat more expensive than their streetside counterparts), as well as numerous restaurants, Asian magazine vendors, and even a small

post office for those who want to mail cards home with the "Chinatown" postmark. The best feature of the plaza is the **Moongate Stage** in the center, the site of many cultural presentations, especially around the Chinese New Year. ⏱ *30 min. 100 N. Beretania St. (Vineyard Blvd.).* ☎ *808/521-4934.*

Continue up the River Street Mall and cross the Nuuanu Stream via the bridge at Kukui St.

8 kids **Izumo Taishakyo Mission Cultural Hall.** This small wooden Shinto shrine, built in 1923, houses a male deity (look for the X-shaped crosses on the top). Members of the faith ring the bell out front as an act of purification when they come to pray. Inside the temple is a 100-pound sack of rice, symbolizing good health. ⏱ *15 min. 215 N. Kukui St.* ☎ *808/538-7778.*

You'll find leis of all descriptions in the shops on Maunakea Street.

Walk a block toward the mountains to Vineyard Blvd.; cross back over Nuuanu Stream, past the entrance of Foster Botanical Gardens.

⑨ kids Kuan Yin Temple. This Buddhist temple, painted in a brilliant red with a green ceramic-tiled roof, is dedicated to Kuan Yin Bodhisattva, the goddess of mercy, whose statue towers in the prayer hall. The temple is still a house of worship, not an exhibit, so enter with respect and leave your shoes outside. You may see people burning paper "money" for prosperity and good luck, or leaving flowers and fruits at the altar (gifts to the goddess). 🕐 *15 min. 170 N. Vineyard Blvd. (Nuuanu St.).* ☎ *808/533-6361.*

Continue down Vineyard and then turn right (toward the ocean) on:

⑩ ★★ kids Maunakea Street. Numerous lei shops line this colorful street, which is the best place in all of Hawaii to get a deal on leis. The size, color, and design of the leis made here are exceptional. *Between Beretania and King sts.*

⑪ ★ kids Sing Cheong Yuan. Grab an Asian pastry (my picks: moon cakes and almond cookies) at this tempting shop, which also has a wide selection of dried and sugared candies (ginger, pineapple, and lotus root) that you can eat as you stroll or give

The Izumo Shinto shrine.

as an exotic gift to friends back home. *1027 Maunakea St. (near King St.).* ☎ *808/531-6688. Daily 6am–4:30pm. $.*

Turn left on King St. and walk in the Diamond Head (east) direction to Nuuanu Ave., then turn left on Nuuanu Ave to:

⑫ ★ Lai Fong Department Store. Before you enter this classic Chinatown store, owned by the same family for more than 80 years, check out the sidewalks on Nuuanu Avenue—they're made of granite blocks used as ballast on ships that brought tea from China to Hawaii in the 1800s. This store sells everything from precious antiques to god awful knickknacks to rare Hawaiian postcards from the early 1900s. But it has built its reputation on its fabulous selection of Chinese silks, brocades, and custom dresses. *118 Nuuanu Ave. (Hotel St.).* ☎ *808/537-3497. Mon–Sat 9am–7:30pm.*

At Pauahi St., turn toward Diamond Head and walk up to Bethel St.

⑬ ★★★ kids Hawaii Theatre. This restored 1920 Art Deco theater is a work of art in itself. It hosts a variety of programs, from the Hawaii International Film Festival to Hawaiian concerts. *1130 Bethel St. (at Pauahi St.).* ☎ *808/528-0506.*

Walking the Beach of **Waikiki**

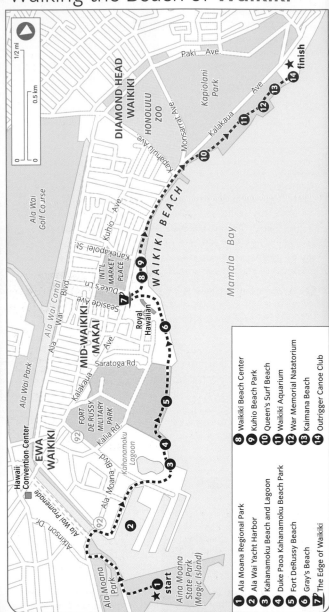

1 Ala Moana Regional Park
2 Ala Wai Yacht Harbor
3 Kahanamoku Beach and Lagoon
4 Duke Paoa Kahanamoku Beach Park
5 Fort DeRussy Beach
6 Gray's Beach
7 The Edge of Waikiki
8 Waikiki Beach Center
9 Kuhio Beach Park
10 Queen's Surf Beach
11 Waikiki Aquarium
12 War Memorial Natatorium
13 Kaimana Beach
14 Outrigger Canoe Club

start

finish

Just the name Waikiki conjures images of Paradise. Only the *alii* (royalty) lived on Waikiki Beach in the 1800s. After the overthrow of the Hawaiian Monarchy, in 1893, accommodations for visitors to Hawaii were built with the first large hotel in Waikiki, the Moana (on the same spot where the Sheraton Moana Surfrider is today), which opened in 1901. During the 20th century, Waikiki went from a wetland, with ducks and water, to 3 miles (4.8km) of hotels, condominiums, restaurants, and shops. The very word "Waikiki" translates into spouting water, referring to the numerous springs and streams which flowed (and generally flooded) this now-famous destination area. In January 1922, the Waikiki Reclamation project dredged the Ala Wai Canal to drain the area and also buried the springs, ponds, and marshes. The area you see today is surprisingly nearly all man-made, even the famous beach is made from sand shipped in from the island of Molokai. Although most people think of Waikiki Beach as just one long beach, it actually is a series of small beaches. Plan at least 2 to 3 hours to walk this incredible beach area (and more if you plan on swimming along the way). **START: Take Ala Moana Blvd. out of Waikiki in the Ewa (or west) direction. Turn into the Ala Moana Region Park at Atkinson Dr. and park your car here. Even easier—take bus 19 or 20 and you don't have to worry about parking.**

1 **Ala Moana Regional Park.** Walk toward the ocean along the peninsula facing Waikiki. Hard to believe that this 76-acre (31-hectare) park was once a garbage dump. Today, the park is filled with picnickers, joggers, sunbathers, lawn bowlers, tennis players, and model-airplane flyers, and that's just on land. A popular swimming site, the ocean also is attractive to fishermen and surfers (several surf sites offshore include Big Rights, Big Lefts, Bay Haleiwa, Concessions, and Bomboras), and on a calm day, even scuba divers jump into the water. If you're lucky you may see Hawaiian outrigger canoe paddlers practicing in the Ala Wai Canal.

Next, trace your steps back to Ala Moana Blvd., turn right toward Waikiki, and cross over the bridge. Turn right (toward the ocean) at Holomoana St. and head for the ocean to the harbor.

2 **Ala Wai Yacht Harbor.** The largest of all the small boat harbors

Ala Wai Yacht Harbor.

in Hawaii, this harbor accommodates slightly more than 700 boats and is the host of one of the longest running ocean yacht races, the Transpac sailing race (which begins in Los Angeles and ends at the harbor), an event that takes place every 2 years. There are a couple of yacht clubs in the harbor: the Waikiki Yacht Club and the Hawaii Yacht Club, which are both private clubs.

Unless you belong to a yacht club that has reciprocal relations with these clubs, you will not be able to enter.

At the ocean end of the harbor, continue down the beach on the sand, just before the Hilton Hawaiian Village.

③ Kahanamoku Beach and Lagoon. In 1955, Henry J. Kaiser built Hawaii's first resort in Hawaii, the Hilton Hawaiian Village. To improve this beautiful area, he also dredged a swimming area along the beach and a lagoon inland, to which he imported sand. The area is named after Duke Paoa Kahanamoku (1890–1968), who spent most of his childhood swimming in this area and who later became a gold medalist in swimming in the 1912, 1920, and 1924 Olympic games. He is credited with spreading the sport of surfing to the California coast and to Australia. Offshore is one of Waikiki's surf sites, Kaisers. If the waves are right, you can see the surfers at the west

Kahanamoku Beach and Lagoon.

end of the channel leading to the Ala Wai Harbor.

Continue down the beach toward Diamond Head, on the other side of the Hilton Hawaii Village. At the end of Paoa Place, opposite the catamaran pier, is:

Hawaii's Early History

Paddling outrigger sailing canoes, the first ancestors of today's Hawaiians followed the stars, waves, and birds across the sea to Hawaii, which they called "the land of raging fire." Those first settlers were part of the great Polynesian migration that settled the vast triangle of islands stretching between New Zealand, Easter Island, and Hawaii. No one is sure when they arrived in Hawaii from Tahiti and the Marquesas Islands, some 2,500 miles (4,023km) to the south, but recent archaeological digs at the Maluuluolele Park on Maui date back to A.D. 700–900.

All we have today are some archaeological finds, some scientific data, and ancient chants to tell the story of Hawaii's past. The chants, especially the *Kumulipo*, which is the chant of creation and the litany of genealogy of the *alii* (high-ranking chiefs) who ruled the islands, talk about comings and goings between Hawaii and the islands of the south, presumed to be Tahiti. In fact, the channel between Maui, Kahoolawe, and Lanai is called *Kealaikahiki*, or "the pathway to Tahiti."

④ Duke Paoa Kahanamoku Beach Park. This tiny (.5-acre/.2-hectare) park is also named after Hawaii's top water man (see ③). There are restrooms and showers here and it is a great spot for snorkeling, windsurfing, swimming, and, of course, surfing (when the southerly winds are blowing). It's known to local surfers as Number Fours, or just Fours.

Continue down the beach toward Diamond Head.

⑤ Fort DeRussy Beach. One of the best-kept secrets in Waikiki, this long stretch of sand beach (some say the largest in Waikiki) is generally less crowded than other parts of Waikiki. The beach fronts the military reservation of Fort DeRussy Park (named after Brigadier General Rene Edward DeRussy, a member of the Engineer Corps in the War of 1812 and the Civil War). In the park on the east end is the Hale Koa Hotel (for military personnel only), and on the Diamond Head end is the U.S. Army Museum. On the ocean side of the park are food and beach equipment rentals, concessions, picnic tables,

restrooms, and showers. Offshore lies another popular surf site, Number Threes, or just Threes

Continue down the beach toward Diamond Head. Look for the sandy area between Halekulani Hotel and the Sheraton Waikiki shaded by a single hau tree.

⑥ Gray's Beach. Ancient Hawaiians called this area "Kawehewehe" (the removal), and revered the beach and the waters offshore as a sacred healing spot. The Halekulani (house befitting heaven) Hotel site was once a boardinghouse owned in 1912 by La Vancha Maria Chapin Gray, who called her accommodations "Gray's-by-the-Sea." The popular swimming area facing her boardinghouse became known as Gray's. By the 1920s the boardinghouse had been sold and expanded into a hotel named Halekulani. One of the guests at the hotel, Earl Derr Biggers, wrote a murder mystery, *The House Without a Key*, based on Honolulu residents who never locked their doors (at that time). The hero of the book was a Chinese detective named Charlie Chan (based on an actual detective in the Honolulu Police Department, Chang Apana). The House Without a Key is a restaurant in the Halekulani today. The beach area is a safe swimming spot for families. Offshore are a couple of surf sites: Populars and Paradise.

Continue down the beach toward Diamond Head. At the Sheraton Waikiki, head toward the swimming pool area.

⑦ The Edge of Waikiki. If it is after 10am, stop for liquid libation, overlooking the new Infinity pool. Be sure to check out the "Vint-Edge" list of cocktails (from the 1940s to 1950). If you are hungry, Chef Ryan Loo has created "Hawaiian-inspired cuisine" ranging from sandwiches to

Gray's Beach.

Military memorablilia at the U.S. Army Museum at Fort DeRussy.

soups to salads. *Sheraton Waikiki, 2255 Kalakaua Ave.* ☎ *808/922-4422. Daily 10am–9pm. $.*

Continue down the beach toward Diamond Head. Just after the Sheraton Moana Surf Rider and before the Kapahulu Groin, look inland for:

8 **Waikiki Beach Center.** In addition to the Police substation here, you'll find the Stones of Kapaemahu, the Duke Kahanamoku statue, and the Prince Kuhio statue. The Stones represent four famous holy men, legendary for their powers of healing and wisdom (Kapaemahu, Kahaloa,

Kuhio Beach Park.

Kapuni, and Kinohi). Plus the center has restrooms, showers, picnic tables, and ocean equipment rentals.

Continue down the beach toward Diamond Head. On the ocean side of the Sheraton Moana Surf Rider and before the Kapahulu Groin is:

9 **Kuhio Beach Park.** In 1951 this large pedestrian groin was built into the ocean, an extension of the storm drain that runs under Kapahulu Avenue and allows visitors to walk out to a great scenic point to view Waikiki. The beach is named after Jonah Kuhio Kalaniana'ole, son of Kekauliki Kinoiki II and High Chief David Kahalepouli Pi'ikoi, born on March 26, 1871, on Kauai. His mother died soon after his birth and he was adopted by Kapi'olani (his mother's sister) and her husband, David Kalakaua. When Kalakaua became King in 1874, Kuhio became prince. He never served as Hawaiian royalty—the monarchy was overthrown in 1896. However, he was elected as Hawaii's delegate to congress in 1902, where he served until his death in 1922. Kuhio Beach Park fronts the site of Kuhio's home, Pualeilani (which means *flower from a wreath of heaven*), where in 1918 he removed the fence around his home and opened the beach to the people of Hawaii. To the west end of the park are two famous surf sites: Queen's and Canoes.

10 Queen's Surf Beach. King David Kalakaua dedicated this park to his wife, Queen Kapiolani. This beach is the former site of an oceanfront mansion that was later converted to a restaurant and nightclub called Queen's Surf, which was torn down in 1971. Surfing is the most popular activity here, but the area is also great for swimming and fishing. You'll find food stands, picnic tables, restrooms, showers, and ocean equipment concessions here. Surf sites offshore include the Walls, good for bodysurfers and bodyboarders only, no board surfing. Farther out to sea (beyond the line of buoys) is a famous surfboarding area known as Cunha's, which means "where the big waves roll in."

11 Waikiki Aquarium. See p 13, bullet **2**.

12 War Memorial Natatorium. At the end of World War I, Hawaii (which was just a territory at the time, not yet a state) constructed a memorial to recognize the veterans from Hawaii who had lost their lives in the war. In the 1920s competitive swimming was very popular in the islands. Swim meets were usually held in Honolulu Harbor at the time because there were not any suitable swimming pools. The Natatorium, an Olympic-size swimming pool, was added to the veterans memorial and dedicated by Olympic swimming medalist Duke Kahanamoku in 1927. Over the years it fell into disrepair and was finally closed in 1979. Much political discussion remains today over repair and the question of whether to restore the pool or tear it down. Still, good snorkeling, fishing, and swimming can be found offshore.

13 Kaimana Beach. Named after Kaimana Hila (Diamond Head), this popular beach also is called San Souci Beach, after an old beachfront rental called Sans Souci. (*Sans souci* is French for "without a care.") I think this is the best family beach in Waikiki: The wide reef offshore protects the shallow, sandy bottom, making it perfect for small children. You may see a parade of open ocean swimmers and kayakers who enter the water here to get to deep waters offshore. Also offshore is a great surfing site called Old Man's.

14 Outrigger Canoe Club. The tiny beach fronting this private club, founded in 1908 to "preserve and promote the sports of surfing and canoe paddling," marks the end of the Waikiki Beach area. There are no public amenities here, but the waters offshore are good for snorkeling, swimming, and, when the waves are right, surfing.

Kaimana Beach is a wonderful spot for families.

Historic Honolulu

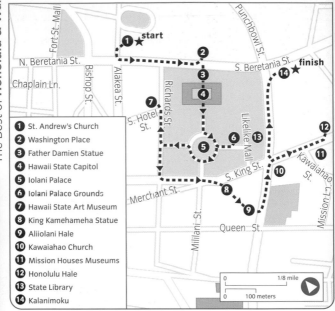

1 St. Andrew's Church
2 Washington Place
3 Father Damien Statue
4 Hawaii State Capitol
5 Iolani Palace
6 Iolani Palace Grounds
7 Hawaii State Art Museum
8 King Kamehameha Statue
9 Aliiolani Hale
10 Kawaiahao Church
11 Mission Houses Museums
12 Honolulu Hale
13 State Library
14 Kalanimoku

The 1800s were a turbulent time in Hawaii. By the end of the
1790s, Kamehameha the Great had united all the islands. Foreigners then began arriving by ship—first explorers, then merchants, and in
1820, missionaries. By 1872, the monarchy had run through the Kamehameha line and in 1873 David Kalakaua was elected to the throne.
Known as "the Merrie Monarch," Kalakaua redefined the monarchy by
going on a world tour, building Iolani Palace, having a European-style
coronation, and throwing extravagant parties. By the end of the 1800s,
however, the foreign sugar growers and merchants had become
extremely powerful in Hawaii. With the assistance of the U.S. Marines,
they orchestrated the overthrow of Queen Liliuokalani, Hawaii's last
reigning monarch, in 1893. The United States declared Hawaii a territory
in 1898. You can witness the remnants of these turbulent years in just a
few short blocks. Allow 2 to 3 hours for this tour. **START: St. Andrew's
Church, Beretania and Alakea sts. Take Ala Moana Blvd. in the Ewa direction to Nimitz Highway. Turn right on the next street on your right
(Alakea St.). After you cross Beretania St., there's a parking garage across
from St. Andrews Church. Bus: 1, 2, 3, 4, 11, 12, or 50.**

1 **St. Andrew's Church.** The
Hawaiian monarchs were greatly

influenced by the royals in Europe.
When King Kamehameha IV saw the

Stained-glass window at St. Andrew's.

grandeur of the Church of England, he decided to build his own cathedral. He and Queen Emma founded the Anglican Church of Hawaii in 1858. The king, however, didn't live to see the church completed; he died on St. Andrew's Day, 4 years before King Kamehameha V oversaw the laying of the cornerstone in 1867. This French-Gothic structure was shipped in pieces from England and reassembled here. Don't miss the floor-to-eaves hand-blown stained-glass window that faces the setting sun. In the glass is a mural of Reverend Thomas Staley (Hawaii's first bishop), King Kamehameha IV, and Queen Emma. *224 Queen Sq. (between Beretania and Alakea sts.).* ☎ *808/524-2822.*

Next, walk down Beretania St. in the Diamond Head direction.

② Washington Place. Once the residence of the Governor of Hawaii (sorry, no tours; just peek through the iron fence), this house occupies a distinguished place in Hawaii's history. The Greek revival–style home was built in 1842 by a U.S. sea captain named John Dominis. The sea captain's son, also named John, married a beautiful Hawaiian princess, Lydia Kapaakea, who later became Hawaii's last queen, Liliuokalani. When the queen was overthrown by U.S. businessmen in 1893, she moved out of Iolani Palace and into her husband's inherited home, Washington Place, where she lived until her death in 1917. On the left side of the building, near the sidewalk, is a plaque inscribed with the words to one of the most popular songs written by Queen Liliuokalani, "Aloha Oe" ("Farewell to Thee"). *Beretania St. (between Queen Emma and Punchbowl sts.).* ☎ *808/586-0240.*

Cross the street and walk to the front of the Hawaii State Capitol.

③ ★ Father Damien Statue. The people of Hawaii have never forgotten the sacrifice this Belgian priest made to help the sufferers of leprosy when he volunteered to work with them in exile on the Kalaupapa Peninsula on the island of Molokai. After 16 years of service, Father Damien died of leprosy, at the age of 49. *Beretania St. (between Queen Emma and Punchbowl sts.).*

Washington Place.

The Hawaii State Capitol.

Behind Father Damien's statue.

④ ★ kids Hawaii State Capitol.
Here's where Hawaii's state legislators work from mid-January to the end of April every year. The building's unusual design has palm tree–shaped pillars, two cone-shaped chambers (representing volcanoes) for the legislative bodies, and, in the inner courtyard, a 600,000-tile mosaic of the sea created by a local artist. A reflecting pool (representing the sea) surrounds the entire structure. You are welcome to go into the rotunda and see the woven hangings and murals at the entrance, or take the elevator up to the fifth floor for a spectacular view. *415 Beretania St.* ☎ *808/586-0034.*

Walk down Richards St. toward the ocean.

⑤ ★ kids Iolani Palace. If you want to really understand Hawaii, I suggest taking the "Grand Tour" of this royal palace. *See p 22, bullet ⑩.*

⑥ ★ kids Iolani Palace Grounds. You can wander around the grounds at no charge. The ticket window to the palace and the gift shop are in the former barracks of the Royal Household Guards. The domed pavilion on the grounds was originally built as a Coronation Stand by King Kalakaua. Later he used it as a Royal Bandstand for concerts (King Kalakaua, along with Herni Berger, the first Royal Hawaiian Bandmaster,

wrote "Hawaii Pono'i," the state anthem). Today the Royal Bandstand is still used for concerts by the Royal Hawaiian Band. *At S. King and Richards sts.* ☎ *808/522-0832.*

Turn in the Ewa direction, cross Richards St., and walk to the corner of Richards and Hotel sts.

⑦ ★ kids Hawaii State Art Museum. *See p 63, bullet ④.*

Walk makai down Richards St. and turn left (toward Diamond Head) on S. King St.

⑧ ★ kids King Kamehameha Statue. The striking black-and-gold bronze statue is a replica of the man who united the Hawaiian Islands. The best day to see the statue is on June 11 (King Kamehameha Day), when it is covered with leis in honor of Hawaii's favorite son. *Juncture of King, Merchant, and Mililani sts.*

⑨ Aliiolani Hale. The name translates to "House of Heavenly Kings." This distinctive building, with a clock tower, now houses the State Judiciary Building. King Kamehameha V originally wanted to build a palace here and commissioned the Australian architect Thomas Rowe in 1872. However, it ended up as the first major government building for the Hawaiian monarchy.

The construction of Iolani Palace nearly bankrupted the Hawaiian kingdom.

Statue of King Kamehameha, draped with leis.

Kamehameha V didn't live to see it completed, and King David Kalakaua dedicated the building in 1874. Ironically, less than 20 years later, on January 17, 1893, Stanford Dole, backed by other prominent sugar planters, stood on the steps to this building and proclaimed the overthrow of the Hawaiian monarchy and the establishment of a provisional government. *417 S. King St. (between Mililani and Punchbowl sts.).* ☎ *808/539-4999. Mon–Fri 9am–4pm for self-guided tours.*

Walk toward Diamond Head on King St.; at the corner of King and Punchbowl, stop in at:

⑩ ★ **Kawaiahao Church.** Don't miss this crowning achievement of the first missionaries in Hawaii—the first permanent stone church, complete with bell tower and colonial colonnade. *See p 23, bullet* ⑪.

Cross the street, and you'll see the:

⑪ ★ **Mission Houses Museum.** Step into 1820 and see what life was like among the 19th-century American Protestant missionaries. *See p 23, bullet* ⑫.

Cross King St. and walk in the Ewa direction to the corner of Punchbowl and King sts.

⑫ **Honolulu Hale.** The Honolulu City Hall, built in 1927, was designed by Honolulu's most famous architect, C. W. Dickey. His Spanish

mission–style building has an open-air courtyard, which is used for art exhibits and concerts. *530 S. King St. (Punchbowl St.).* ☎ *808/523 4385. Mon–Fri 8am–5pm.*

Cross Punchbowl St. and walk *mauka* (inland).

⑬ **State Library.** Anything you want to know about Hawaii and the Pacific can be found here, at the main branch of the state's library system. Located in a restored historic building, it has an open garden courtyard in the middle, great for stopping for a rest on your walk. *478 S. King St. (Punchbowl St.).* ☎ *808/586-3617. Mon and Wed 10am–5pm; Thurs 9am–8pm; Tues and Fri–Sat 9am–5pm.*

Head *mauka* up Punchbowl to the corner of Punchbowl and Beretania sts.

⑭ **Kalanimoku.** A beautiful name, "Ship of Heaven," has been given to this dour state office building. Here you can get information on hiking and camping in state parks (from the Department of Land and Natural Resources). *1151 Punchbowl St. (Beretania St.).* ☎ *808/587-0320. Mon–Fri 8am–5pm.*

Retrace your steps in the Ewa direction down Beretania to Alakea back to the parking garage.

Kawaiahao Church was built from 14,000 coral blocks.

Kapiolani Park

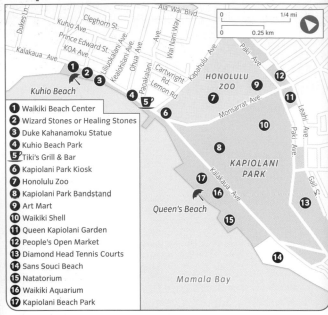

1 Waikiki Beach Center
2 Wizard Stones or Healing Stones
3 Duke Kahanamoku Statue
4 Kuhio Beach Park
5 Tiki's Grill & Bar
6 Kapiolani Park Kiosk
7 Honolulu Zoo
8 Kapiolani Park Bandstand
9 Art Mart
10 Waikiki Shell
11 Queen Kapiolani Garden
12 People's Open Market
13 Diamond Head Tennis Courts
14 Sans Souci Beach
15 Natatorium
16 Waikiki Aquarium
17 Kapiolani Beach Park

On June 11, 1877 (King Kamehameha Day), King David Kalakaua donated some 140 acres (57 hectares) of land to the people of Hawaii for Hawaii's first park. He asked that the park be named after his beloved wife, Queen Kapiolani, and he celebrated the opening of this vast grassy area with a free concert and "high stakes" horse races (the king loved gambling). The horse races, and the gambling that accompanied it, were eventually outlawed, but the park lives on. Just a coconut's throw from the high-rise concrete jungle of Waikiki lies this grassy oasis dotted with spreading banyans, huge monkeypod trees, blooming royal poincianas, and swaying ironwoods. From Waikiki, walk toward Diamond Head on Kalakaua Avenue. If you're coming by car, the cheapest parking is metered street parking on Kalakaua Avenue adjacent to the park. **START: Waikiki Beach Center, Kalakaua Ave., Diamond Head side of the Westin Moana Hotel, across the street from the Hyatt Regency. Bus: 19 or 20.**

1 Waikiki Beach Center. On the ocean side of Kalakaua Avenue, next to the Westin Moana Hotel, is a complex of restrooms, showers, surfboard lockers, rental concessions, and the Waikiki police substation. *2435 Kalakaua Ave., Diamond Head side of the Westin Moana Hotel.*

A tranquil pond in Kapiolani Park.

❷ Wizard Stones or Healing Stones.

These four basalt boulders, which weigh several tons apiece and sit on a lava rock platform, are held sacred by the Hawaiian people. The story goes that sometime before the 15th century, four powerful healers from Moaulanuiakea (in the Society Islands), named Kapaemahu, Kahaloa, Kapuni, and Kinohi, lived in Waikiki. After years of healing the people and the *alii* of Oahu, they wished to return home. They asked the people to erect four monuments made of bell stone, a basalt rock that was found in a Kaimuki quarry and that produced a bell-like ringing when struck. The healers spent a ceremonious month transferring their spiritual healing power, or *mana*, to the stones. The great mystery is how the boulders were transported from Kaimuki to the marshland near Kuhio Beach in Waikiki. *Diamond Head side of the police substation, Kalakaua Ave.*

❸ Duke Kahanamoku Statue.

Here, cast in bronze, is Hawaii's most famous athlete, also known as the father of modern surfing. Duke (1890–1968) won Olympic swimming medals in 1912, 1920, and 1924. He was enshrined in both the Swimming Hall of Fame and the Surfing Hall of Fame. He also traveled around the world promoting surfing. *Just west of the stones, Kalakaua Ave.*

❹ Kuhio Beach Park.

The two small swimming holes here are great, but heed the warning sign: Watch out for holes. There actually are deep holes in the sandy bottom, and you may suddenly find yourself in very deep water. The best pool for swimming is the one on the Diamond Head end, but the water circulation is questionable—there sometimes appears to be a layer of suntan lotion floating on the surface. If the waves are up, watch the boogie boarders surf by the seawall. They ride toward the wall and at the last minute veer away with a swoosh. *2453 Kalakaua Ave. (between Liliuokalani and Paoakalani aves.).*

Cross Kalakaua Ave. and walk toward Paoakalani St.

Kuhio Beach Park.

5 Tiki's Grill & Bar. Stop for lunch at this casual eatery on the second floor of the ResortQuest Waikiki Beach Hotel overlooking Waikiki Beach. The menu is American with Pacific Rim influences; seafood dishes are especially good. *2570 Kalakaua Ave. (at Paoakalani St.).* ☎ *808/923-TIKI (8454). Daily 10:30am–midnight. $$.*

Walk *mauka* down Kalakaua Ave. to Kapahulu Ave., then walk toward Diamond Head to the entrance of Kapiolani Park.

6 Kapiolani Park Kiosk. This small display stand contains brochures and actual photos of the park's history. It also carries information on upcoming events at the various sites within the park (the aquarium, the zoo, Waikiki Shell, and Kapiolani Bandstand). An informative map will help to orient you to the park grounds. *Corner of Kalakaua and Kapahulu aves.*

Continue up Kapahulu Ave.

7 Honolulu Zoo. The best time to see the city's 42-acre (17-hectare) zoo is as soon as the gates open at 9am—the animals seem to be more active and it's a lot cooler than walking around at midday in the hot sun. *See p 33, bullet 1.*

If you're traveling with kids, plan to spend at least half a day at the Honolulu Zoo.

Trace your steps back to Kapahulu and Kalakaua aves. and head *mauka* down Monsarrat Ave.

8 Kapiolani Park Bandstand. Once upon a time, from 1937 to 2002, the Kodak Hula Show presented the art of hula to visitors, with some 3,000 people filling bleachers around a grassy stage area every day. The Kodak Hula Show is gone now, but the Bandstand is still used for concerts and special events. *Inside Kapiolani Park.*

Back on Monsarrat Ave., on the fence facing the zoo.

The Waikiki Shell.

9 Art Mart. The Artists of Oahu Exhibit is the new official name of this display, where local artisans hang their artwork on a fence for the public to view and buy. Not only do you get to meet the artists, but you also have an opportunity to purchase their work at a considerable discount from the prices you'll see in galleries. *Monsarrat Ave. Sat–Sun and Wed 10am–4pm.*

Cross Monsarrat Ave.

10 Waikiki Shell. This open-air amphitheater hosts numerous musical shows, from the Honolulu Symphony to traditional Hawaiian music. *2805 Monsarrat Ave.* ☎ *808/527-5400.*

Continue walking down to the end of the block to the corner of Monsarrat and Paki aves.

11 Queen Kapiolani Garden. You'll see a range of hibiscus plants and dozens of varieties of roses, including the somewhat rare Hawaiian rose. The tranquil gardens are always open and are a great place to wander and relax. *Corner of Monsarrat and Paki aves.*

Across the street.

12 People's Open Market. The farmer's market with its open stalls is an excellent spot to buy fresh produce and flowers. *Monsarrat and Paki aves. Wed 10–11am.*

Continue in the Diamond Head direction down Paki Ave.

13 Diamond Head Tennis Courts. Located on the *mauka* side of Paki Avenue, the nine free city and county tennis courts are open for play daily during daylight hours. Tennis etiquette suggests that if someone is waiting for a court, limit your play to 45 minutes. *3908 Paki Ave.* ☎ *808/971-7150.*

Turn onto Kalakaua Ave. and begin walking back toward Waikiki.

14 Sans Souci Beach. This is one of the best swimming beaches in Waikiki. The shallow reef, which is close to shore, keeps the waters calm. Farther out there's good snorkeling in the coral reef by the Kapua Channel. Facilities include outdoor showers and a lifeguard. *Next to the New Otani Kaimana Beach Hotel, 2863 Kalakaua Ave.*

Keep walking toward Waikiki.

15 Natatorium. This huge concrete structure next to the beach is both a memorial to the soldiers of World War I and a 100-meter saltwater swimming pool. Opened in 1927, when Honolulu had hopes of hosting the Olympics, the ornate swimming pool fell into disuse and disrepair after World War II, and was finally closed in 1979. *2815 Kalakaua Ave.*

Next door.

16 Waikiki Aquarium. Try not to miss this stop—the tropical aquarium is worth a peek if only to see the only living chambered nautilus born in captivity. *See p 13, bullet* **2**.

17 Kapiolani Beach Park. Relax on the stretch of grassy lawn alongside the sandy beach, one of the best-kept secrets of Waikiki. This beach park is much less crowded than the beaches of Waikiki, plus it has adjacent grassy lawns, barbecue areas, picnic tables, restrooms, and showers. The swimming is good here year-round, there's a surfing spot known as "Public's" offshore, and there's always a game going at the volleyball courts. The middle section of the beach park, in front of the pavilion, is known as Queen's Beach or Queen's Surf and is popular with the gay community. *2745 Kalakaua Ave.*

Dining Best Bets

Best **Bistro**
★ Chai's Island Bistro Honolulu
$$$ *Aloha Tower Marketplace,
1 Aloha Tower Dr. (p 131)*

Best **Breakfast**
★★ Hula Grill Waikiki $$ *2335 Kalakaua Ave. (p 97)*

Best **Buffet**
★ Prince Court $$$$ *100 Holomoana St. (p 100)*

Best **Burger**
★ Kua Aina $ *1116 Auahi St. (p 98)*

Best **Casual Chinese**
★★ Little Village Noodle House $
1113 Smith St. (p 99)

Best **Dim Sum**
★ Legend Seafood Restaurant $
100 N. Beretania St. (p 98)

Best for **Families**
★★ Kaka'ako Kitchen $ *1200 Ala Moana Blvd. (p 97)*

Best **French/Vietnamese**
★★ Duc's Bistro $$ *1188 Maunakea St. (p 96)*

Best **Hawaii Regional Cuisine**
★★★ Alan Wong's Restaurant
$$$$ *1857 S. King St. (p 94)*

Best for **under $10**
★★ Nico's At Pier 38 $ *1133 N.
Nimitz Hwy. (p 99)*

Best **Steakhouse**
★ d.k. Steakhouse $$$$ *2552 Kalakaua Ave. (p 96)*

Best **Late-Night Meals**
★ Eggs 'n Things $ *343 Saratoga
Rd. (p 96)*

Most **Romantic**
★★★ La Mer $$$$ *2199 Kalia Rd.
(p 98)*

Best **Splurge**
★★★ Chef Mavro Restaurant
$$$$$ *1969 S. King St. (p 95)*

Best **Sunday Brunch**
★★★ Orchids $$$$$ *2199 Kalia Rd.
(p 100)*

Best **Sushi**
★★ Sansei Seafood Restaurant &
Sushi Bar $$$ *2552 Kalakaua Ave.
(p 101)*

Best **Sunset Views**
★ Duke's Waikiki $$ *2335 Kalakaua
Ave. (p 96)*

Best **View of Waikiki**
★ Hau Tree Lanai $$$ *2863 Kalakaua Ave. (p 97)*

You'll find beautiful food and beautiful people at the Diamond Head Grill.

Waikiki's Best **Dining**

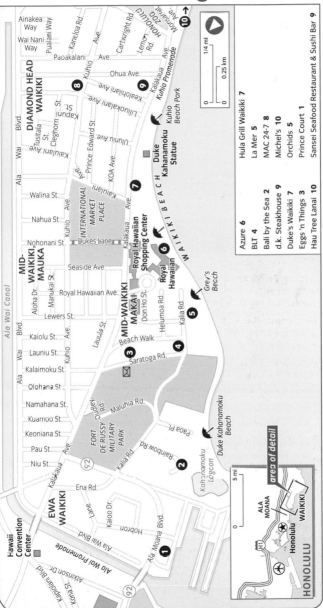

Honolulu's Best **Dining**

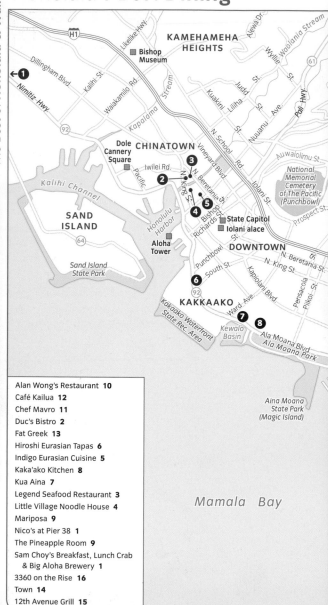

KAMEHAMEHA HEIGHTS

Bishop Museum

Dole Cannery Square

CHINATOWN

Iwilei Rd.

Kalihi Channel

SAND ISLAND

Honolulu Harbor

Aloha Tower

Sand Island State Park

National Memorial Cemetery of The Pacific (Punchbowl)

State Capitol
Iolani alace

DOWNTOWN

KAKKAAKO

Kakaako Waterfront State Rec. Area

Kewalo Basin

Ala Moana Park

Aina Moana State Park (Magic Island)

Mamala Bay

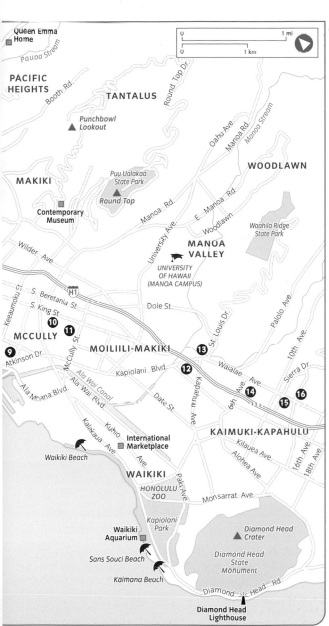

Honolulu & Waikiki Restaurants **A to Z**

★★★ Alan Wong's Restaurant

MCCULLY *HAWAII REGIONAL CUISINE* James Beard Award winner Chef Alan Wong, worshiped by foodies across the state, serves brilliantly creative and irresistibly cutting-edge cuisine in a casual, sometimes noisy room that is always packed, so book in advance. I love the ginger-crusted onaga. *1857 S. King St. (between Kalakaua Ave. and McCully St.).* ☎ *808/949-2526. Entrees $30–$50; 5-course sampling menu $75 ($105 with wine); chef's 7-course tasting menu $95 ($135 with wine). AE, DC, MC, V. Dinner daily. TheBus: 13. Map p 92.*

★★★ Azure Restaurant WAIKIKI

SEAFOOD For a night of romance, this lantern-lit, oceanside restaurant at the Royal Hawaiian Hotel prepares fresh fish with a mixture of French and Hawaiian influences. Dine in plush banquettes with comfy pillows or rent a beachfront cabana and have your own intimate dining area. Hawaii's fresh fish (most just bought that morning from the Honolulu Fish Market) is the star of the menu. Tasting menus and prix-fixe menus are available. Service is top-notch. *Royal*

Kona Kampachi at Bali by the Sea.

Hawaiian Hotel, 2259 Kalakaua Ave. ☎ *808/823-7311. www.royalhawaiian.com. Reservations recommended. Entrees $32–$60; 3-course prix-fixe dinner $59. AE, DC, MC, V. Dinner daily. TheBus: 13. Map p 91.*

★★ Bali by the Sea WAIKIKI

CONTINENTAL/PACIFIC RIM Get a window seat at sunset for oceanfront dining on herb-infused rack of lamb or Kona lobster. Choose from a host of mouthwatering desserts. Best time to dine: Fridays to see the 7:30pm fireworks. *Hilton Hawaiian Village, 2005 Kalia Rd. (Ala Moana*

Room Service from 50 Different Restaurants

Don't let the room service menu in your hotel room limit you; **Room Service in Paradise** (☎ **808/941-DINE** [3463]; www.941-dine.com) delivers almost a dozen different cuisines (from American/Pacific Rim to Italian to sandwiches and burgers) from oodles of restaurants to your hotel room. You can check out menus online or pick up one of its magazines in various Waikiki locations. There's an $8.25 to $9.25 delivery charge in Waikiki (more in outlying areas).

Blvd.). ☎ 808/941-2254. Entrees $30–$65. AE, DC, DISC, MC, V. Dinner Tues–Sat. Bus: 19 or 20. Map p 91.

★★★ **BLT Steak** WAIKIKI *STEAK-HOUSE* BLT Steak does not stand for bacon-lettuce-tomato, but for Bistro Laurent Tourondel, the French-trained chef who began his franchise of well-known steakhouses in New York City. This big (4,000-sq.-ft./372-sq-m) restaurant sits on the ground floor of the newly opened (2010) Trump International Hotel. The service is impeccable and so is the food. If you are a carnivore, this steakhouse is for you. The steaks come from Wagyu beef in the Midwest, broiled at 1,700°F and finished with herb butter and an option of nine sauces (ranging from red wine to a dreamy Roquefort). In true steakhouse tradition, everything is a la carte—appetizers, meats, sides, and dessert. **Budget Travelers Note:** They serve a very large portion prix-fixe meal with appetizer, entree, side dish, and dessert for $60. *Trump International Hotel, 223 Saratoga Rd.* ☎ 808/683-7440. www.bltsteak.com. *Reservations recommended. Entrees $29–$42; prix-fixe dinner $60 for 3 courses. AE, DC, MC, V. Dinner daily. Bus: 13. Map p 91.*

★★**Café Kailua** HONOLULU *COFFEE SHOP* Hidden in a strip mall next to the freeway is this treasure, a European-style bistro/country cafe where breakfast is always served. Owner/chef Chrissie "Kaila" Castillo serves up all her favorites—do not miss the incredibly fluffy pancakes or the yummy frittata—in a relaxed casual atmosphere (notice the trickling fountain). **Warning:** This place is packed at breakfast and lunch. I suggest going late for breakfast (after 9:30am) and lunch (after 1:30pm) so you won't have to wait for a table. Even if you do run into a long line, grab a latte, read a newspaper, and relax—the food is well worth the wait. *Market City Shopping Center, 2919 Kapiolani Rd (at Harding St.).* ☎ 808/732-3330. *Breakfast and lunch entrees $9–$13. Cash only. Breakfast and lunch daily. Bus: 4 (get off at University Ave. and S. King St.) and walk to Kapiolani. Map p 92.*

★★★ **Chef Mavro Restaurant** MCCULLY *PROVENÇAL/HAWAII REGIONAL* If you have only 1 night on Oahu, splurge at this intimate dining experience in a nontouristy neighborhood. James Beard Award winner Chef George Mavro's inspired menu (roast pork with apple quinoa or poached fresh fish with sago-coconut nage, Thai herbs, limu, and lime froth) features perfect wine pairings. *1969 S. King St. (McCully St.).* ☎ 808/944-4714. *Prix fixe $69–$165 ($117–$250*

d.k. Steakhouse, one of Chef D. K. Kodama's popular restaurants (also check out Sansei Seafood).

Duc's Bistro.

w/wine pairings). AE, DC, DISC, MC, V. Dinner Tues–Sun. Bus: 13, transfer to 1. Map p 92.

★ **d.k. Steakhouse** WAIKIKI *STEAK* Attention meat lovers: This is the ultimate steakhouse for the 21st century at very reasonable prices (especially for Waikiki). Book an outside table on the lanai to see the sunset on Waikiki Beach. *Waikiki Beach Marriott Resort, 2552 Kalakaua Ave. (Ohua Ave.).* ☎ 808/931-6280. Main courses $18–$80. AE, DISC, MC, V. Dinner daily. Bus: 19 or 20. Map p 91.

★★ **Duc's Bistro** CHINATOWN *FRENCH/VIETNAMESE* Dine on Honolulu's best French/Vietnamese cuisine—from seafood spring rolls to steak au poivre—in a quietly elegant restaurant that features live music nightly. *1188 Maunakea St. (Beretania St.).* ☎ 808/531-6325. Entrees $12–$20. AE, DC, DISC, MC, V. Lunch Mon–Fri, dinner Mon–Sat. Bus: 19 or 20. Map p 92.

★ **kids Duke's Waikiki** WAIKIKI *STEAK/SEAFOOD* This open-air dining room (outfitted in surfing memorabilia) overlooking Waikiki Beach is the best spot to watch the sunset. Hawaiian musicians serenade diners lingering over a menu ranging from burgers to fresh fish. *Outrigger Waikiki on the Beach, 2335 Kalakaua Ave. (next door to Royal Hawaiian*

Shopping Center).* ☎ 808/922-2268. Entrees $20–$32. AE, DC, DISC, MC, V. Breakfast, lunch & dinner daily. Bus: 19 or 20. Map p 91.

★ **kids Eggs 'n Things** WAIKIKI *BREAKFAST* This popular breakfast-only eatery is famous for its huge plates of food, now at a new location. *343 Saratoga Rd.* ☎ 808/949-0820. Breakfast entrees $7–$12; lunch/dinner entrees $9.25–$13. DISC, MC, V. Daily 6am–2pm and 5–10pm. Bus: 19 or 20. Map p 91.

★★ **The Fat Greek** KAIMUKI *GREEK* This tiny hole-in-the-wall with just counter service has wonderful Greek dishes at money-saving prices. The food is terrific. Try the Papa Special, New Zealand rack of lamb marinated in the "special" house sauce with rosemary and garlic plus potato wedges and a Greek salad for just $20; or shawarma, lamb and beef in a pita with tzatkiki sauce and salad for $10; or the daily specials from moussaka to kabobs to souvlakia. The atmosphere at this charming dive involves a blaring television in the enclosed dining area. *1140 12th Ave.* ☎ 808/735-7581. Reservations recommended for groups. Main courses $12–$28. AE, DISC, MC, V. Lunch & dinner daily. Bus: 13, get off at Kapahulu and Campbell aves., walk to Date St and Kapahulu Ave., and transfer to

Duke's Waikiki.

Dining in Waikiki 24-7

If you get the late-night munchies, your best bet in Waikiki is **MAC 24-7** at the **Hilton Waikiki Prince Kuhlo Hotel,** 2500 Kuhio Ave. (at Liliuokalani Ave.; ☎ 808/921-5564). The menu features hotel coffee shop "comfort" food, reasonably priced for Waikiki (most entrees in the $13–$18 range).

Get breakfast all day (and all night on weekends) at Eggs 'n Things.

bus 3, then get off at Koko Head and Waialae aves. Map p 92.

★ **kids Hau Tree Lanai** WAIKIKI *PACIFIC RIM* Located under a giant hau tree right on the beach (just a few yards from the waves), this informal eatery has the best view of Waikiki Beach. Breakfast is my favorite—especially the taro pancakes. *New Otani Kaimana Beach Hotel, 2863 Kalakaua Ave. (across from Kapiolani Park).* ☎ *808/921-7066. Entrees: breakfast $12–$16, lunch $13–$17, dinner $30–$39. AE, DC, DISC, MC, V. Breakfast, lunch & dinner daily. Bus: 19 or 20. Map p 91.*

★ **Hiroshi Eurasian Tapas** RESTAURANT ROW *EURO-ASIAN FUSION* This is my pick for the best tapas (small plates) on the island. Go with as many people as possible so you can sample lots—some favorite items include truffled crab cake and kampachi carpaccio. *Restaurant*

Row, 500 Ala Moana Blvd. (between Punchbowl and South sts.). ☎ *808/533-HIRO (4476). Tapas $8.50–$17; larger plates $22–$37. AE, DISC, MC, V. Dinner daily. Bus: 19 or 20. Map p 92.*

★★ **kids Hula Grill Waikiki** WAIKIKI *HAWAIIAN REGIONAL* This is the best place for breakfast in Waikiki: Not only does this bistro have a terrific ocean view (clear to Diamond Head), but the food is also fabulous (crab cake eggs Benedict, Maui pineapple-and-coconut pancakes) and prices are reasonable. *Outrigger Waikiki on the Beach, 2335 Kalakaua Ave. (next to Royal Hawaiian Shopping Center).* ☎ *808/923-HULA (4852). Breakfast items $6–$14; dinner main courses $17–$33. AE, DC, MC, V. Breakfast & dinner daily. Bus: 19 or 20. Map p 91.*

★★ **Indigo Eurasian Cuisine** CHINATOWN *EURASIAN* Dine in an elegant indoor setting or in a tropical garden, with an East-West menu ranging from pot stickers to plum-glazed baby back ribs. *1121 Nuuanu Ave. (Pauahi St.).* ☎ *808/521-2900. Lunch buffet $16; dinner main dishes $22–$35. DC, DISC, MC, V. Lunch Tues–Fri, dinner Tues–Sat. Bus: 19 or 20. Map p 92.*

★★ **kids Kaka'ako Kitchen** HONOLULU *GOURMET PLATE LUNCHES* Bring the family for local home-style cooking at budget prices. (It's owned by chef Russell Siu of 3660 on the **Risee;** see

Don't be deterred by the Styrofoam plates: Kaka'ako Kitchen serves fabulous Hawaiian home-style food.

p 101.) The catch: It's served on Styrofoam plates in a warehouse ambience. *Ward Centre, 1200 Ala Moana Blvd. (Kamakee St.).* ☎ *808/596-7488. Entrees: breakfast $5–$9, lunch & dinner $7–$13. AE, MC, V. Breakfast & lunch daily, dinner Mon–Sat. Bus: 19 or 20. Map p 92.*

★ **kids Kua Aina** HONOLULU *AMERICAN* This branch of the ultimate sandwich shop (the original is on the North Shore) is very popular—I recommend calling ahead for

Kua Aina is a great place to get a sandwich on the go.

takeout and going to the beach. The excellent sandwich selection includes burgers and a legendary mahimahi with Ortega chile and cheese. *Ward Village, 1116 Auahi St. (Kamakee St.).* ☎ *808/591-9133. Sandwiches and burgers $4.50–$9. MC, V. Lunch & dinner daily. Bus: 19 or 20. Map p 92.*

★★★ **La Mer** WAIKIKI *NEOCLASSIC FRENCH* This second-floor oceanfront bastion of haute cuisine is the place to go for a romantic evening. Michelin award–winning chef Yves Garnier prepares classical French dishes with fresh island ingredients (hamachi with pistachio, shrimp on black risotto, and scallops with ratatouille served with a saffron sauce). *Halekulani Hotel, 2199 Kalia Rd. (Lewers St.).* ☎ *808/923-2311. Prix-fixe menus $90 for 2 courses, $120 for 3 courses, $135 for 4 courses; $150 for "Ultimate" dinner. AE, DC, MC, V. Dinner daily. Bus: 19 or 20. Map p 91.*

★ **kids Legend Seafood Restaurant** CHINATOWN *DIM SUM/ SEAFOOD* This is my favorite dim sum eatery. It's not fancy, but who cares with the creative dim sum coming out of the kitchen (ranging from deep-fried taro puffs to prawn dumplings). The clientele are mainly Chinese-speaking diners, so you know it's authentic. *Chinese Cultural Plaza, 100 N. Beretania St. (Maunakea St.).* ☎ *808/532-1868. Dim sum under $7. AE, DC, MC, V. Breakfast Sat–Sun, lunch & dinner daily. Bus: 19 or 20. Map p 92.*

★★ kids **Little Village Noodle House** CHINATOWN *CHINESE* My pick for the best Chinese food served "simple and healthy" (its motto) is this tiny neighborhood restaurant with helpful waitstaff and even parking in the back (unheard of in Chinatown). Try the honey-walnut shrimp or the garlic eggplant. The menu includes Northern, Canton, and Hong Kong–style dishes. *1113 Smith St. (between King and Pauahi sts.).* ☎ *808/545-3008. Entrees under $15. AE, DISC, MC, V. Lunch & dinner daily. Bus: 19 or 20. Map p 92.*

★★ kids **Mariposa** ALA MOANA *AMERICAN/PACIFIC RIM* High ceilings inside and outside tables with views of Ala Moana Park pair beautifully with a menu of Pacific and American specialties (from a king crab, shrimp, and mussel risotto, to pan-roasted Hawaiian snapper). At

Steamed clams at Mariposa.

lunch, order the signature starter: the popover with *poha* (gooseberry) butter. *Neiman Marcus, Ala Moana Center, 1450 Ala Moana Blvd. (Piikoi St.).* ☎ *808/951-3420. Entrees: lunch $14–$24 (prix-fixe lunches $25–$35), dinner $27–$36 (prix-fixe dinner $55–$65). AE, DC, MC, V. Lunch & dinner daily. Bus: 19 or 20. Map p 92.*

★★ **Michel's** WAIKIKI *FRENCH/ HAWAII REGIONAL* One side of this 45-year-old classic French restaurant opens to the ocean view (get there for sunset), but the food is the real draw. Tuxedo-clad waiters serve classic French cuisine with an island infusion (lobster bisque, steak Diane, and a Caesar salad made at your table) in an elegantly casual atmosphere. *Colony Surf Hotel, 2895 Kalakaua Ave. (across from Kapiolani Park).* ☎ *808/923-6552. Entrees $36–$50. AE, DC, DISC, MC, V. Dinner daily. Bus: 19 or 20. Map p 91.*

★★ kids **Nico's At Pier 38** IWILEI *FRESH FISH* I never miss a chance to eat at this tiny takeout place, which serves up gourmet French cuisine produced island-style in Styrofoam takeout containers at frugal prices. My favorite is the furikake–pan-seared ahi with the addicting ginger garlic cilantro dip, served with greens or macaroni salad for $8.75. *Pier 38, 1133 N. Nimitz Hwy. (Alakawa St.).*

☎ 808/540-1377. Entrees: breakfast $2.75–$7, lunch $6.50–$10. Breakfast & lunch Mon–Sat. Bus: 19 or 20. Map p 92.

★★★ **kids** Orchids WAIKIKI *INTERNATIONAL/SEAFOOD* This is the best Sunday brunch in Hawaii, with an outstanding array of dishes from popovers to sushi to an omelet station. The setting is extraordinary (right on Waikiki Beach), and the food is excellent. *Halekulani Hotel, 2199 Kalia Rd. (Lewers St.).* ☎ 808/923-2311. *Dinner entrees $26–$51; Sun brunch $55 adults, $29 children 5–12. AE, DC, MC, V. Breakfast, lunch & dinner Mon–Sat, brunch & dinner Sun. Bus: 19 or 20. Map p 91.*

★★ **kids** The Pineapple Room ALA MOANA *HAWAII REGIONAL* Culinary icon Chef Alan Wong's bistro features gustatory masterpieces that will probably leave you wanting to come back to try breakfast, lunch, and dinner, just to see what else he will present. Expect anything from *moi* (served whole and steamed Chinese-style) to apple curry–glazed pork chops with pumpkin and mascarpone purée and mango chutney. *Macy's, 1450 Ala Moana Blvd. (Piikoi St.).* ☎ 808/945-6573. *Entrees: lunch $11–$18, dinner $26–$38. AE, DC, MC, V. Breakfast Sat–Sun, lunch daily,*

dinner Mon–Sat. Bus: 19 or 20. Map p 92.

★ **kids** Prince Court WAIKIKI *CONTEMPORARY ISLAND CUISINE* Floor-to-ceiling windows, sunny views of the harbor, and top-notch buffets are Prince Court's attractions. The best are the Friday and Saturday seafood buffets featuring sushi, Vietnamese pho, crab, oysters, shrimp, scallops, and even prime rib. *Hawaii Prince Hotel Waikiki, 100 Holomoana St. (Ala Moana Blvd.).* ☎ 808/944-4494. *Dinner prix fixe and buffet $37–$57 (no a la carte for dinner), breakfast buffet $21, weekend brunch $37, luncheon buffet $25, seafood dinner buffet $45. AE, DC, MC, V. Breakfast, lunch (or brunch) & dinner daily. Bus: 19 or 20. Map p 91.*

kids Sam Choy's Breakfast, Lunch, Crab & Big Aloha Brewery IWILEI *ISLAND CUISINE/SEAFOOD* Chef/restaurateur Sam Choy's crab house features gigantic meals (fried poke, Cajun seared ahi) and several varieties of Big Aloha beer, brewed on-site. The unusual decor includes a sampan boat smack in the middle of the 11,000-sq.-ft. (1,022-sq.-m) restaurant. *580 Nimitz Hwy. (between Pacific and Kukahi sts.).* ☎ 808/545-7979. *Entrees: breakfast $8–$15, lunch $12–$36, dinner $20–$47. AE,*

The sushi bar at Sansei's.

Ahi Katsu at 3660 On the Rise.

DC, DISC, MC, V. Breakfast, lunch & dinner daily. Bus: 19 or 20. Map p 92.

★★ **Sansei Seafood Restaurant & Sushi Bar** WAIKIKI SUSHI/ ASIAN–PACIFIC RIM   Perpetual award winner D. K. Kodama's Waikiki restaurant is known not only for its extensive menu, but also for Kodama's outrageous sushi creations (he's my favorite sushi chef). Examples include seared foi gras nigiri sushi (duck liver lightly seared over sushi rice, with caramelized onion and ripe mango) or the wonderful mango crab salad hand roll (mango, blue crab, greens, and peanuts with a sweet Thai-chili vinaigrette). *Waikiki Beach Marriott Resort, 2552 Kalakaua Ave. (Paoakalani Ave.).* ☎ *808/931-6286. Sushi $8–$20; entrees $16–$43. AE, DISC, MC, V. Dinner daily. Bus: 19 or 20. Map p 91.*

★★★ **3660 On the Rise** KAIMUKI EURO-ISLAND   In his elegant 200-seat restaurant, chef Russell Siu adds Asian and local touches to the basics: rack of lamb with macadamia nuts, filets of catfish in *ponzu* (a Japanese sauce), and seared ahi salad with grilled shiitake mushrooms. Save room for the warm chocolate cake. *3660 Waialae Ave. (Koko Head Ave.).* ☎ *808/737-1177. Entrees $19–$59, prix fixe $40. AE, DC, DISC, MC, V. Dinner Tues–Sun. No bus service. Map p 92.*

★ **Town** KAIMUKI CONTEMPORARY ITALIAN   The latest hip restaurant along Waialae's miracle mile of "in" spots is a surprisingly delicious place to eat. Dine on ahi tartar on risotto cakes or outstanding gnocchi in a metro high-tech atmosphere (highly polished concrete floors, stainless steel tables, and incredibly uncomfortable chairs). Lunches consist of sandwiches, salads, and pastas, and the recently added breakfast menu includes frittata of the day, eggs, and wonderful baked goods. *3435 Waialae Ave. (at 9th St.).* ☎ *808/735-5900. Entrees: breakfast $5–$9.50, lunch $10–$15, dinner $19–$26. AE, MC, V. Breakfast, lunch & dinner Mon–Sat. No bus service. Map p 92.*

★ **kids 12th Avenue Grill** KAIMUKI RETRO-AMERICAN   All 14 tables in this tiny, upscale neighborhood diner are packed every night with people hungry for good ol' American food, but a little more sophisticated than what Mom used to make. Try gourmet macaroni and smoked Parmesan cheese, smoked trout, or grilled pork chop with apple chutney. *1145-C 12th Ave. (at Wailalea Ave.).* ☎ *808/732-9469. Entrees: small plates $6–$12, large plates $18–$32. MC, V. Dinner Mon–Sat. No bus service. Map p 92.*

Poi, that humble Hawaiian staple, is often served at luaus; I recommend the one at the Royal Hawaiian (p 110).

Lodging Best Bets

Most **Romantic**
★★ Royal Hawaiian $$$$ *2259 Kalakaua Ave. (p 110)*

Most **Historic**
★★ Moana Surfrider, a Westin Resort $$$$ *2365 Kalakaua Ave. (p 107)*

Most **Luxurious**
★★★ Halekulani $$$$ *2199 Kalia Rd. (p 105)*

Best **Moderately Priced**
★ Ilima Hotel $$ *445 Nohonani St. (p 106)*

Best **Budget Hotel**
★ Royal Grove Hotel $ *151 Uluniu Ave. (p 109)*

Best **for Kids**
★★★ Embassy Suites Hotel—Waikiki Beach Walk $$$$ *201 Beach Walk (p 104)*

Best **Value**
★ The Breakers $$ *250 Beach Walk (p 104)*

Hippest Hotel
★★ Waikiki Parc $$$ *2233 Helumoa Rd. (p 110)*

Best **View of Waikiki Beach**
★★ Hilton Hawaiian Village Beach Resort & Spa $$$ *2005 Kalia Rd. (p 106)*

Best **View of Ala Wai Harbor**
★★ Hawaii Prince Hotel Waikiki $$$$ *100 Holomoana St. (p 105)*

Best **View of Fort DeRussy Park**
★ Outrigger Luana Waikiki $$$ *2045 Kalakaua Ave. (p 108)*

Most **Serene**
★ Royal Garden at Waikiki $$ *440 Olohana St. (p 109)*

Best **Hi-Tech Gadgets**
★★ Hotel Renew $$$ *129 Paoakalani Ave. (p 106)*

Best **Hidden Gem**
★ New Otani Kaimana Beach Hotel $$$ *2863 Kalakaua Ave. (p 108)*

Best **Boutique Hotel**
★ DoubleTree Alana Hotel Waikiki $$ *1956 Ala Moana Blvd. (p 104)*

Best **Family Condo**
★★ Outrigger Waikiki Shore Condominium $$$ *2161 Kalia Rd. (p 109)*

Vera Wang suite at the Halekulani.

Waikiki's Best **Lodging**

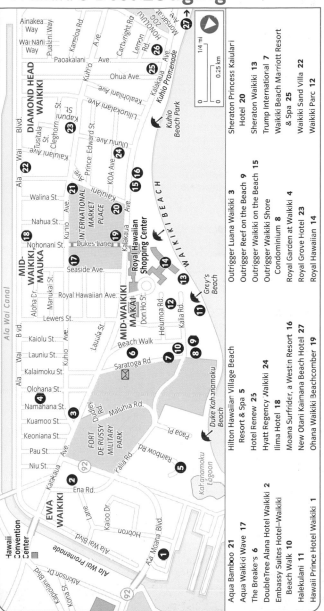

Aqua Bamboo **21**

Aqua Waikiki Wave **17**

The Breake's **6**

DoubleTree Alana Hotel Waikiki **2**

Embassy Suites Hotel–Waikiki Beach Walk **10**

Halekulani **11**

Hawaii Prince Hotel Waikiki **1**

Hilton Hawaiian Village Beach Resort & Spa **5**

Hotel Renew **25**

Hyatt Regency Waikiki **24**

Ilima Hotel **18**

Moana Surfrider, a Westin Resort **16**

New Otani Kaimana Beach Hotel **27**

Ohana Waikiki Beachcomber **19**

Outrigger Luana Waikiki **3**

Outrigger Reef on the Beach **9**

Outrigger Waikiki on the Beach **15**

Outrigger Waikiki Shore Condominium **8**

Royal Garden at Waikiki **4**

Royal Grove Hotel **23**

Royal Hawaiian **14**

Sheraton Princess Kaiulari Hotel **20**

Sheraton Waikiki **13**

Trump International **7**

Waikiki Beach Marriott Resort & Spa **25**

Waikiki Sand Villa **22**

Waikiki Parc **12**

Waikiki Hotels **A to Z**

★ **Aqua Bamboo** MID-WAIKIKI MAUKA   I love the intimacy of this boutique hotel, decorated with an Asian flair (with kitchenettes or kitchens). Other pluses: only a block from Waikiki beach, complimentary continental breakfast, spa on property, and personal service. Minus: not enough parking for all rooms. *2425 Kuhio Ave. (at Kaiulani Ave.).* ☎ *800/367-5004 or 808/922-7777. www.aquaresorts.com. 90 units. Doubles $85–$159; studio doubles $111–$179; 1-bedroom from $170; all units w/breakfast. AE, DISC, MC, V. Bus: 19 or 20. Map p 103.*

★ **Aqua Waikiki Wave** MID-WAIKIKI MAUKA   Recently renovated rooms with hip decor, flatscreen TVs, and free Wi-Fi have put this formerly dreary hotel on the map. Located in a not-very-hip neighborhood next door to International Marketplace, about a 10-minute walk to the beach. *2299 Kuhio Ave. (at Duke's Lane), Honolulu, HI 96817.* ☎ *866/406-2782 or 808/922-1262. www.aquaresorts.com. 247 units. Doubles $94–$115; suites from $135; all units w/breakfast. AE, DISC, MC, V. Bus: 19 or 20. Map p 103.*

★ **kids The Breakers** MID-WAIKIKI MAKAI   One of Waikiki's best deals: This two-story 1950s budget hotel is a terrific buy for a family (kitchenette in all rooms) and just a 2-minute walk to the beach, numerous restaurants, and shopping. Expect comfortable budget accommodations with tropical accents. *250 Beach Walk (between Kalakaua Ave. and Kalia Rd.).* ☎ *800/426-0494 or 808/923-3181. www.breakers-hawaii.com. 64 units. Doubles $120–$130 (extra person $20 per day); garden suites $185 ($205 for 3, $225 for 4, and $245 for 5). AE, DC, MC, V. Bus: 19 or 20. Map p 103.*

★ **DoubleTree Alana Hotel Waikiki** EWA   This boutique hotel (operated by the Hilton Hawaiian Village) is a welcome oasis of small, but comfortable rooms, and offers amenities of a more luxurious hotel at more affordable prices. Great location, too: Waikiki Beach is a 10-minute walk away, and the convention center is about a 7-minute walk. *1956 Ala Moana Blvd. (near Kalakaua Ave.).* ☎ *800/222-TREE (8733) or 808/941-7275. www.doubletree.com. 317 units. Doubles $134; suites from $189. AE, DC, DISC, MC, V. Bus: 19 or 20. Map p 103.*

★★★ **kids Embassy Suites Hotel—Waikiki Beach Walk** MID-WAIKIKI MAKAI   Opened in

DoubleTree Alana Hotel.

Hawaiiana Hotel.

2007, this ultraluxurious one- and two-bedroom hotel chain, famous for its complimentary "cooked to order" breakfast and evening cocktail reception, has a great location just 1 block from the beach. The newly opened Waikiki Beach Walk provides plenty of shops and restaurants on property as well. Prices may seem high, but it pencils out to a deal for families. *201 Beach Walk (at Kalia Rd).* ☎ *800/EMBASSY (362-2779) or 808/921-2345. www.waikiki beach.embassysuites.com. 421 suites. Doubles $239–$319 1-bedroom; 2-bedroom $439–$600. AE, DC, DISC, MC, V. Bus: 19 or 20. Map p 103.*

★★★ **kids Halekulani** MID-WAIKIKI MAKAI This is my favorite hotel in all Hawaii—the ultimate heavenly Hawaii luxury accommodations, spread over 5 acres (2 hectares) of prime Waikiki beachfront.

Some 90% of the large rooms (620 sq. ft./58 sq. m) face the ocean, and all have furnished lanais and top-drawer amenities. This is the best Waikiki has to offer. *2199 Kalia Rd. (at Lewers St.).* ☎ *800/367-2343 or 808/923-2311. www.halekulani.com. 455 units. Doubles $460–$680; suites from $875. AE, DC, MC, V. Bus: 19 or 20. Map p 103.*

★★ **Hawaii Prince Hotel Waikiki** EWA For a vacation with a view and the feel of a palace, stay in these striking twin 33-story high-tech towers, where service is priority. All bedrooms face the Ala Wai Yacht Harbor, with floor-to-ceiling sliding-glass windows (sorry, no lanais). The higher the floor, the higher the price. Ala Moana Center is a 10-minute walk away and Waikiki's beaches are just a 5-minute walk. *100 Holomoana St. (just across Ala Wai Canal Bridge).* ☎ *800/321-OAHU*

Waikiki Neighborhoods

The neighborhoods in Waikiki can be divided up into four districts: **Ewa** (the western end of Waikiki from Ala Wai Canal to Fort DeRussy Park), **Mid-Waikiki Makai** (from the ocean up to Kalakaua Ave. and from Fort DeRussy Park to Kaiulani St.), **Mid-Waikiki Mauka** (mountain side of Kalakaua Ave. to Ala Wai Blvd. and from Kalaimoku St. to Kaiulani St.), and **Diamond Head** (from the ocean to Ala Wai Blvd. and from Kaiulani to Diamond Head).

(6248) or 808/956-1111. www.prince resortshawaii.com. 521 units. Doubles $199–$249; suites from $379. AE, DC, DISC, MC, V. Bus: 19 or 20. Map p 103.

★★ kids **Hilton Hawaiian Village Beach Resort & Spa** EWA Sprawling over 20 acres (8 hectares), this is Waikiki's biggest resort—with tropical gardens dotted with exotic wildlife (flamingos, peacocks, and even penguins), award-winning restaurants (the Golden Dragon, and Bali by the Sea, p 94), 100 different shops, a secluded lagoon, two minigolf courses, and a gorgeous stretch of Waikiki Beach. A wide choice of accommodations, from simple hotel rooms to ultra-deluxe, are housed in five towers. 2005 Kalia Rd. (at Ala Moana Blvd.). ☎ 800/HILTONS (445-8667) or 808/949-4321. www.hiltonhawaiian village.com. 2,860 units. Doubles $199–$610; suites from $305. AE, DISC, MC, V. Bus: 19 or 20. Map p 103.

★★ **Hotel Renew** DIAMOND HEAD This boutique is a gem among aging Waikiki hotels, an oasis of tranquillity and excellent taste in a sea of schlock. True to its name, Hotel Renew recently underwent several million dollars' worth of renovations—every single surface was redone. The result is a quiet, Zen-like decor, just a block from the

beach, with complimentary gourmet breakfast, lots of high-tech gadgets, and a free fitness center and yoga classes. 129 Paoakalani Ave. (at Lemon Rd.). ☎ 866/406-2782 or 808/687-7700. www.aquaresorts. com. 70 units. Doubles $128–$155. AE, DC, MC, V. Bus: 19 or 20. Map p 103.

★ kids **Hyatt Regency Waikiki** DIAMOND HEAD This is one of Waikiki's largest hotels, with two 40-story towers covering nearly an entire city block, located across the street from Waikiki Beach. The location is great, there's a good children's program, and guest rooms are large and luxuriously furnished, but personally I find it too big and too impersonal, with service to match. 2424 Kalakaua Ave. (between Kaiulani St. and Uluniu Ave.). ☎ 800/233-1234 or 808/923-1234. www.waikiki.hyatt.com. 1,230 units. Doubles $220–$539; Regency Club doubles $469–$569. AE, DC, DISC, MC, V. Bus: 19 or 20. Map p 103.

★ kids **Ilima Hotel** MID-WAIKIKI MAUKA Local residents frequent this 17-story, condo-style hotel that offers value for your money: huge rooms (with full kitchen), walking distances to restaurants and shops, and low prices. The only two caveats: It's a 15-minute hike to the beach, and there aren't any ocean views. 445

Lobby of the Moana Surfrider.

Pampering in Paradise

Hawaii's spas have raised the art of relaxation and healing to a new level, as traditional Greco-Roman–style spas have evolved into airy, open facilities that embrace the tropics. Today's spas offer a wide diversity of treatments, many including traditional Hawaiian massages and ingredients. There are even side-by-side massages for couples, and duo massages—two massage therapists working on you at once.

Of course, all this pampering doesn't come cheap. Massages are generally $175 to $275 for 50 minutes and $275 to $350 for 80 minutes; body treatments are in the $175 to $275 range; and alternative healthcare treatments can be as high as $200 to $300. But you may think it's worth the expense to banish your tension and stress.

My picks for Waikiki's best spas:

- **Most Relaxing: SpaHalekulani** From the time you step into the elegantly appointed, intimate spa and experience the foot massage to the last whiff of fragrant maile, their signature scent, you will be transported to nirvana. Spa connoisseurs should try something unique, like the Polynesian Nonu, a Samoan-inspired massage using stones. Halekulani Hotel; ☎ **808/923-2311;** www.halekulani.com.
- **Best Facial: Abhasa Waikiki Spa** This contemporary spa, spread out over 7,000 square feet (650 sq. m), concentrates on natural, organic treatments in a soothing atmosphere, where the smell of eucalyptus wafts through the air. Their specialty is an anti-aging facial using caviar that promises to give you a refreshed, revitalized face immediately. Royal Hawaiian Hotel; ☎ **808/922-8200;** www.abhasa.com.
- **Best Spa Menu: Mandara Spa** A great selection of 300 treatments from around the globe, ranging from a Balinese facial to a Javanese Lulur rub to a Shirodhara Ayurvedic Massage, plus each of the 25 luxury treatment rooms has its own exotic private garden. Hilton Hawaiian Village Beach Resort & Spa; ☎ **808/947-9750;** www.mandaraspa.com.

Nohonani St. (near Ala Wai Blvd.). ☎ 800/801-9366 or 808/923-1877. www.HotelWaikiki.com. 99 units. Doubles $188–$268; 1-bedroom (rate for 4) $230–$280; 2-bedroom (rate for 4, sleeps up to 6) $300–$350; 3-bedroom (rate for 6, sleeps up to 8) $560–$600. AE, DC, DISC, MC, V. Bus: 19 or 20. Map p 103.

★★ kids **Moana Surfrider, a Westin Resort** MID-WAIKIKI MAKAI Old Hawaii reigns here; I recommend staying in the historic Banyan Wing, where rooms are modern replicas of Waikiki's first hotel (built in 1901). Outside is a prime stretch of beach and an oceanfront courtyard centered

Enjoying a massage as ocean breezes caress your skin is pure bliss.

around a 100-year-old banyan tree, where there's live music in the evenings. *2365 Kalakaua Ave. (across from Kaiulani St.). ☎ 800/325-3535 or 808/922-3111. www.moana-surf rider.com. 793 units. Doubles $235–$310; suites from $1,050. AE, DC, MC, V. Bus: 19 or 20. Map p 103.*

★ **kids New Otani Kaimana Beach Hotel** DIAMOND HEAD   This is one of Waikiki's best-kept secrets: a boutique hotel nestled on the beach at the foot of Diamond Head, with Kapiolani Park just across the street. Skip the inexpensive, teeny-tiny, barely-room-for-two rooms and go for the parkview studios with kitchens.

Outrigger Reef on the Beach.

2863 Kalakaua Ave. (near Waikiki Aquarium, across from Kapiolani Park). ☎ 800/356-8264 or 808/923-1555. www.kaimana.com. 124 units. Doubles $175–$450; studios from $215; junior suites from $325; regular suites from $515. AE, DC, DISC, MC, V. Bus:19 or 20. Map p 103.

kids Ohana Waikiki Beach-comber MID-WAIKIKI MAUKA   One of the main pluses here is the location—a block from the beach, across the street from the upscale Royal Hawaiian Shopping Center, and walking distance to restaurants. Rooms are stylish and contemporary. *2300 Kalakaua Ave. (at Duke's Lane). ☎ 800/622-4646 or 808/922-4646. www.waikikibeach comber.com. 495 units. Doubles $319–$389; 1-bedroom $509; 2-bedroom $749–$1,700. AE, DC, MC, V. Bus: 19 or 20. Map p 103.*

★ **kids Outrigger Luana Waikiki** EWA   Families take note: This midsize hotel offers studios with kitchenettes and 1-bedrooms with full kitchens. You also get terrific views of Fort DeRussey park and the ocean in the distance. *2045 Kalakaua Ave. (at Kuhio Ave.). ☎ 800/OUTRIGGER (688-7444) or 808/955-6000. www.outrigger.com. 205 units. Doubles $229–$269 1-bedroom $409–$519. AE, DC, DISC, MC, V. Bus: 19 or 20. Map p 103.*

The Royal Garden room at the Royal Hawaiian Hotel.

★ kids **Outrigger Reef on the Beach** MID-WAIKIKI MAKAI This three-tower megahotel's prime beachfront location and loads of facilities (including a 5,000-sq.-ft./465-sq.-m spa) make it one of the chain's most attractive properties. A recent multimillion-dollar renovation upgraded furniture and spruced up the bathrooms. Even the standard rooms are large and comfortable. *2169 Kalia Rd. (at Beach Walk).* ☎ *800/OUTRIGGER (688-7444) or 808/923-3111. www.outrigger.com. 883 units. Doubles $369–$679. AE, DC, DISC, MC, V. Bus: 19 or 20. Map p 103.*

★★ kids **Outrigger Waikiki on the Beach** MID-WAIKIKI MAKAI I'd pick this Outrigger to stay in: Not only does it have an excellent location on Waikiki Beach, but also with some $20 million invested into guest room renovations and upgrades (oversize Jacuzzi bathtubs with ocean views in some rooms), coupled with the great dining (Duke's and Hula Grill; see p 97), it offers more for the money. *2335 Kalakaua Ave. (between the Royal Hawaiian Shopping Center and the Moana Surfrider).* ☎ *800/OUTRIGGER (688-7444) or 808/923-0711. www.outrigger.com. 525 units.*

Doubles $179–$509. AE, DC, DISC, MC, V. Bus: 19 or 20. Map p 103.

★★ kids **Outrigger Waikiki Shore Condominium** MID-WAIKIKI MAKAI One of the few condominiums on Waikiki Beach offers guests a terrific location (right on Waikiki Beach, close to shopping and restaurants), a spectacular panoramic view, daily maid service, and fully equipped kitchens. *2161 Kalia Rd. (at Saratoga Rd.).* ☎ *800/OUT-RIGGER (688-7444). www.outrigger. com. 168 units. Doubles $305 studio; 1-bedroom $335–$445; 2-bedroom $525–$725. AE, DC, DISC, MC, V. Bus: 19 or 20. Map p 103.*

★ **Royal Garden at Waikiki** EWA For people looking for a quieter stay, this elegant boutique hotel, tucked away on a side street, offers rooms with pantry kitchenettes. The beach is a few blocks away, but at these prices, it's worth the hike. *440 Olohana St. (between Kuhio Ave. and Ala Wai Blvd.).* ☎ *800/367-5666 or 808/943-0202. www.royalgardens.com. 210 units. Doubles $185–$300. AE, DC, DISC, MC, V. Bus: 19 or 20. Map p 103.*

★ kids **Royal Grove Hotel** DIAMOND HEAD This is a great bargain for frugal travelers and families; the budget accommodations are no-frill (along the lines of a Motel 6), but the family-owned hotel has genuine aloha for all the guests and Waikiki Beach is a 3-minute walk away. *151 Uluniu Ave. (between Prince Edward and Kuhio aves.).* ☎ *808/923-7691. www.royal grovehotel.com. 85 units. Doubles $55–$70, 1-bedroom $90–$100. AE, DC, DISC, MC, V. Bus: 19 or 20. Map p 103.*

★★ kids **Royal Hawaiian** MID-WAIKIKI MAKAI The symbol of Waikiki, this flamingo-pink oasis, nestled in tropical gardens, offers rooms in both the 1927 historic wing (my favorites, with carved wooden doors, four-poster canopy beds, flowered wallpaper, and period furniture) and modern oceanfront towers. The beach outside is the best in Waikiki for sunbathing. *2259 Kalakaua Ave. (at Royal Hawaiian Ave.).* ☎ *800/325-3535 or 808/923-7311. www.sheraton.com. 527 units. Doubles $350–$500. AE, MC, V. Bus: 19 or 20. Map p 103.*

★ kids **Sheraton Princess Kaiulani Hotel** MID-WAIKIKI MAUKA Across the street from the beach, this moderately priced (for Waikiki),

At the Sheraton Waikiki 1,200 units have ocean views.

29-story, three-tower hotel features double-insulated doors with sound-proofing (Waikiki can be noisy at night) in their modestly decorated rooms. *120 Kaiulani Ave. (at Kalakaua Ave.).* ☎ *800/325-3535 or 808/922-5811. www.princess-kaiulani. com. 1,150 units. Doubles $260–$450. AE, DC, MC, V. Bus: 19 or 20. Map p 103.*

★ kids **Sheraton Waikiki** MID-WAIKIKI MAKAI It's hard to get a bad room here—the hotel sits right on Waikiki Beach: a whopping 1,200 units have ocean views, and 650 overlook Diamond Head. However, this is a megahotel, with two 30 story towers and an immense lobby. It's a frequent favorite of conventions and can be crowded, noisy, and overwhelming (not to mention the long wait at the bank of nearly a dozen elevators). *2255 Kalakaua Ave. (at Royal Hawaiian Ave.).* ☎ *800/325-3535 or 808/922-4422. www.sheraton.com. 1,852 units. Doubles $199–$245. AE, DC, DISC, MC, V. Bus: 19 or 20. Map p 103.*

kids **Waikiki Beach Marriott Resort & Spa** DIAMOND HEAD Pluses: It's across the street from the beach, has renovated rooms, and boasts great restaurants (Sansei Seafood Restaurant & Sushi Bar and d.k. Steakhouse; see p 91). The minus: Rack rates are way too high—check their website for 40% off. *2552 Kalakaua Ave. (at Ohua Ave.).* ☎ *800/367-5370 or 808/922-6611. www.marriottwaikiki.com. 1,310 units. Doubles $370–$470. AE, DC, DISC, MC, V. Bus: 19 or 20. Map p 103.*

★★ **Waikiki Parc** MID-WAIKIKI MAKAI Recently redesigned and renovated, especially for the 20s and 30s crowd, this "hidden" luxury hotel (operated by the Halekulani) offers lots of bonuses: It's just 100

Waikiki Parc.

yards (91m) from the beach, has modern high-tech rooms, hosts frequent wine-party receptions, and offers first-class service. *2233 Helumoa Rd. (at Lewers St.).* ☎ *800/422-0450 or 808/921-7272. www. waikikiparchotel.com. 297 units. Doubles $285–$415. AE, DC, MC, V. Bus: 19 or 20. Map p 103.*

kids **Waikiki Sand Villa** MID-WAIKIKI MAUKA   Budget travelers, take note: This very affordable 10-story hotel is located on the quieter side of Waikiki, with medium-size rooms and studio apartments with kitchenettes (fridge, stove, and microwave). It's a 10-minute walk to the beach. *2375 Ala Wai Blvd. (at Kanekapolei Ave.).* ☎ *800/247-1903 or 808/922-4744. www.waikiki sandvillahotel.com. 214 units. Doubles $73–$110; studios w/kitchenette $130; suites from $230; all units w/ breakfast. AE, DC, DISC, MC, V. Bus: 19 or 20. Map p 103.*

Shopping Best Bets

Best **Alohawear**
★★ Bailey's Antiques & Aloha Shirts, *517 Kapahulu Ave. (p 116)*

Best **Alohawear for Kids**
★ Hilo Hattie, *700 N. Nimitz Hwy.; and Ala Moana Center, 1450 Ala Moana Blvd. (p 117 and 125)*

Best **Antiques**
★ Antique Alley, *1347 Kapiolani Blvd. (p 117)*

Best **Place to Browse**
★★★ Native Books Na Mea Hawaii, *1050 Ala Moana Blvd. (p 122)*

Best **Cookies**
Yama's Fish Market, *2332 Young St. (p 121)*

Best **European Bakery**
★ Cake Works, *2820 S. King St. (p 118)*

Best **Exotic Foods**
★ Asian Grocery, *1319 S. Beretania St. (p 119)*

Best **Fashion Deals**
★ Avanti Fashion, *2160 Kalakaua Ave. (p 116)*

Best **Gifts**
★★★ Nohea Gallery, *1050 Ala Moana Blvd. (p 122)*

Best **Health Food Store**
Down to Earth, *2525 S. King St. (p 123)*

Best **Hawaii Artist**
★ Pegge Hopper Gallery, *1164 Nuuanu Ave. (p 117)*

Best **Hawaiian Books**
★ Rainbow Books and Records, *1010 University Ave. (p 119)*

Best **Hawaiian CDs**
★★ Shop Pacifica, *1525 Bernice St. (p 123)*

Best **Hawaiian Memorabilia**
★ Hula Supply Center, *2346 S. King St. (p 122)*

Aloha shirts at Bailey's Antiques.

Best **Place for a Lei**
★ Cindy's Lei Shoppe, *1034 Mau-nakea St. (p 121)*

Best **Made-in-Hawaii Products**
★★ It's Chili in Hawaii, *2080 S. King St. (p 119)*

Best **Pastries**
★ Cafe Laufer, *3565 Waialae Ave. (p 118)*

Best **Shopping Center**
★★ Ala Moana Center, *1450 Ala Moana Blvd. (p 123)*

Best **Shopping-as-Entertainment**
★★ Honolulu Fish Auction, *Pier 38, 1131 N. Nimitz Hwy. (p 121)*

Best **Sinfully Delicious Bakery**
★★ Honolulu Chocolate Co., *1200 Ala Moana Blvd. (p 119)*

Best **Sushi Takeout**
★ Sushi Company, *1111 McCully St. (p 121)*

Best **T-Shirt**
★ Local Motion, *Ala Moana Shop-ping Center, 1450 Ala Moana Blvd., and in the Waikiki Sheraton, 2255 Kalakaua Ave. (p 125)*

Best **Wine & Liquor**
Fujioka's Wine Merchants, *2919 Kapiolani Blvd. (p 119)*

Waikiki's Best **Shopping**

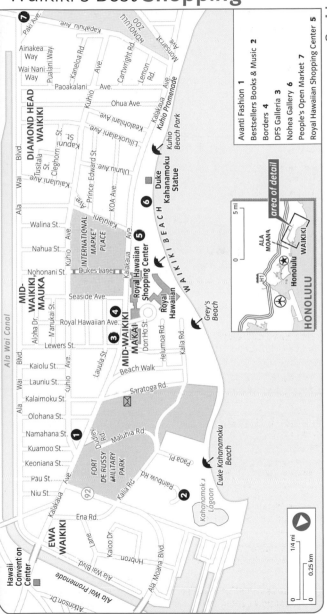

Shopping Best Bets

Avanti Fashion **1**
Bestsellers Books & Music **2**
Borders **4**
DFS Galleria **3**
Nohea Gallery **6**
People's Open Market **7**
Royal Hawaiian Shopping Center **5**

area of detail

HONOLULU

HONOLULU

ALA
MOANA

WAIKIKI

5 mi

0

0   5 km

Honolulu's Best **Shopping**

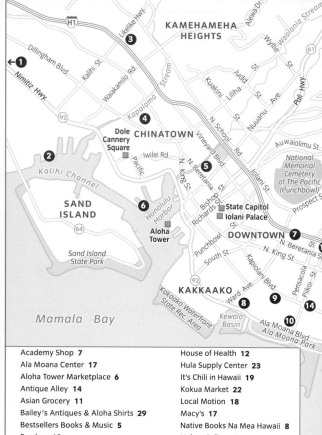

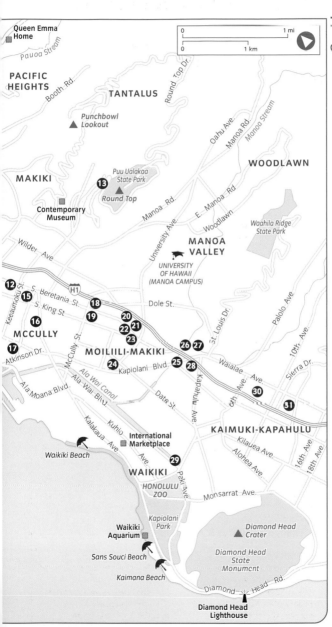

Chinatown's Best **Shopping**

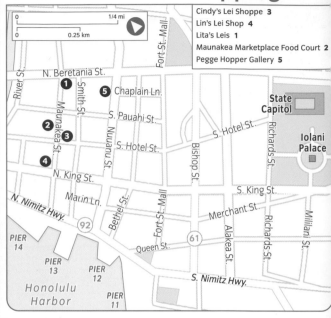

Cindy's Lei Shoppe **3**
Lin's Lei Shop **4**
Lita's Leis **1**
Maunakea Marketplace Food Court **2**
Pegge Hopper Gallery **5**

Honolulu & Waikiki
Shopping A to Z

Alohawear

★ **Avanti Fashion** WAIKIKI   This leading retro aloha shirt label turns out stunning hip and nostalgic silk shirts and dresses in authentic 1930s to 1950s fabric patterns. *2160 Kalakaua Ave. (at Kuhio St.).* ☎ *808/924-3232. www.avantishirts. com. AE, DC, DISC, MC, V. Bus: 19 or 20. Map p 113.*

★★ **Bailey's Antiques & Aloha Shirts** KAPAHULU   Honolulu's largest selection (thousands) of vintage, secondhand, and nearly new aloha shirts and other collectibles fill this eclectic emporium, as well as old ball gowns, feather boas, fur

stoles, leather jackets, 1930s dresses, and scads of other garments. *517 Kapahulu Ave. (at Castle*

Antique Alley.

Pegge Hopper is known for her paintings of Hawaiian women.

St.). ☎ 808/734-7628. www.aloha shirts.com. DISC, MC, V. Bus: 13 or 14. Map p 114.

★ **kids** **Hilo Hattie** IWILEI, ALA MOANA, WAIKIKI Hawaii's largest manufacturer of Hawaiian fashions has become "hip" in the last few years with inexpensive silk aloha shirts as well as brand-name aloha shirts like Tommy Bahama and the store's own Hilo Hattie label. *700 N. Nimitz Hwy. (at Pacific St.).* ☎ 808/ 535-6500. Also at Ala Moana Center, 1450 Ala Moana Blvd. (at Piikoi). ☎ 808/973-3266. Bus: 19 or 20. www.hilohattie.com. AE, DISC, MC, V. Map p 114 and 125.

Macy's ALA MOANA If it's alo-hawear, Macy's has it. The extensive aloha shirt and muumuu departments here feature just about every label you can think of, with a selection—in all price ranges—that changes with the times. *Ala Moana Center, 1450 Ala Moana Blvd. (at Atkinson Dr.).* ☎ 808/941-2345. www.macys.com. AE, DISC, MC, V. Bus: 19 or 20. Map p 114.

Reyn's ALA MOANA Reyn's used to be a prosaic line but has stepped up its selection of women's and men's alohawear with contemporary fabric prints and stylings that

appeal to a trendier clientele. *Ala Moana Center, 1450 Ala Moana Blvd. (at Piikoi).* ☎ 808/949-5929. www.reyns.com. AE, DC, DISC, MC, V. Bus: 19 or 20. Map p 114.

Antiques & Collectibles

★ **Antique Alley** KAKAAKO This narrow shop is chockablock with collections ranging from old Hawaiian artifacts and surfing and hula nostalgia to estate jewelry, antique silver, Hawaiian bottles, collectible toys, pottery, cameras, Depression glass, linens, plantation photos, and a wide selection of nostalgic items from Hawaii and across America. *Located behind America's Mattress, 1347 Kapiolani Blvd. (at Piikoi).* ☎ 808/941-8551. AE, MC, V. Bus: 2. Map p 114.

T. Fujii Japanese Antiques MOILIILI This is a long-standing icon in Hawaii's antiques world and an impeccable source for ukiyo-e prints, scrolls, obis, Imari porcelain, tansus, tea-ceremony bowls, and screens, as well as contemporary ceramics from Mashiko and Kasama, with prices from $25 to $18,000. *1016-B Kapahulu Ave. (King St. and H1).* ☎ 808/732-7860. www.tfujii antiques.com. MC, V. Bus: 14. Map p 114.

Art

Gallery at Ward Centre ALA MOANA This cooperative gallery of Oahu artists features fine works in all media, including paper, clay, scratchboard, oils, watercolors, collages, woodblocks, lithographs, glass, jewelry, and more. *Ward Centre, 1200 Ala Moana Blvd. (at Auahi St.).* ☎ 808/597-8034. www.gwc-fineart.com. AE, DC, DISC, MC, V. Bus: 19 or 20. Map p 114.

★ **Pegge Hopper Gallery** CHINATOWN One of Hawaii's most popular artists, Hopper displays her widely collected paintings in her attractive gallery, which has become quite the gathering place for exhibits ranging from Tibetan sand painting by saffron-robed monks to the most avant-garde printmaking in the islands. *1164 Nuuanu Ave. (between Beretania and Pauahi sts.).* ☎ *808/524-1160. www.peggehopper.com. AE, DC, MC, V. Bus: B, 19, or 20. Map p 116.*

Bakeries

★ kids **Cafe Laufer** WAIALAE This small, cheerful cafe features frilly decor and sublime pastries— from apple scones and Linzer tortes to fruit flan, decadent chocolate mousse, and carrot cake—to accompany the latte and espresso. *3565 Waialae Ave. (at 11th Ave.).* ☎ *808/735-7717. www.cafelaufer. com. AE, DISC, MC, V. Map p 114.*

★ kids **Cake Works** MOILIILI Local residents love this top-notch European bakery, which sells everything from lavishly tiered wedding cakes to killer carrot cakes, chocolate decadence cakes, and all manner of baked sweets that line the counters calling your name. *2820 S.*

Finger sandwiches at Cafe Laufer.

A sugar cookie from Cake Works

King St., across from the Hawaiian Humane Society (at Waialae Ave.). ☎ *808/946-4333. MC, V. Bus: 4. Map p 114.*

Foodland KAKAAKO This grocery story flies in dough from Los Angeles's famous La Brea bakery and bakes it fresh at this location, so you can pick up fresh-from-the-oven organic wheat, rosemary olive oil, roasted garlic, potato-dill, and other spectacular breads. *1460 S. Beretania St. (between Kalakaua Ave. and Makiki St.).* ☎ *808/949-4365. www. foodland.com. AE, DISC, MC, V. Bus: 2. Map p 114.*

Sconees WAIALAE Formerly Bea's Pies, this unique bakery has fantastic scones, yummy pumpkin-custard pies, and tempting Danishes. *1117 12th Ave. (at Harding).* ☎ *808/734-4024. No credit cards. Map p 114.*

Bookstores
Bestsellers Books & Music DOWNTOWN/WAIKIKI Hawaii's largest independent bookstore has a complete selection of nonfiction and fiction titles with an emphasis on Hawaiian books and music. *1001 Bishop St. (at Hotel St.).* ☎ *808/528-2378. Bus: 4. Also in the Hilton*

Hawaiian Village, 2005 Kalia Rd. (at Ala Moana Blvd.). ☎ 808/953-2378. Bus: 19 or 20. www.bestsellers.com. AE, MC, V. Maps p 113 and 114.

Borders WAIKIKI/ALA MOANA Borders is a beehive of literary activity, with weekly signings, prominent local and mainland musicians at least monthly, and special events almost daily that make this store a major Honolulu attraction. *Royal Hawaiian Shopping Center, 2201 Kalakaua Ave.* ☎ 808/922-4154. Bus: 19 or 20. Also in the Ward Centre, 1200 Ala Moana Blvd. (at Auahi St.). ☎ 808/591-8995. Bus: 19 or 20. www.bordersstores.com. AE, DC, DISC, MC, V. Maps p 113 and 114.

Rainbow Books and Records MOILIILI   A little weird but totally lovable, especially among students and eccentrics (and insatiable readers), this tiny bookstore is notable for its selection of popular fiction, records, and Hawaii-themed books, secondhand and reduced. *1010 University Ave. (at King St.).* ☎ 808/ 955-7994. AE, DISC, MC, V. Bus: 4. Map p 114.

Edibles

★ **Asian Grocery** KAKAAKO This store supplies many of Honolulu's Thai, Vietnamese, Chinese, Indonesian, and Filipino restaurants with authentic spices, rice, noodles, produce, sauces, herbs, and other adventurous ingredients. Heaven for foodies. *1319 S. Beretania St. (between Piikoi and Keeaumoku sts.).* ☎ 808/593-8440. www.asian food.com. MC, V. Bus: 2. Map p 114.

Don Quijote KAKAAKO   You can find everything at this huge emporium, ranging from takeout sushi, Korean *kal bi*, pizza, Chinese food, flowers, and Mrs. Fields cookies to Kau navel oranges, macadamia nuts, Kona coffee, Chinese taro, and other Hawaii products. *801 Kaheka*

You'll find all kinds of Hawaiian goodies at Don Quijote.

St. (at Kahunu St.). ☎ 808/973-4800. AE, DISC, MC, V. Bus: 2. Map p 114.

Fujioka's Wine Merchants MOILIILI   Oenophiles flock here for a mouthwatering selection of wines, single-malt Scotches, and affordable, farm-raised caviar—food and libations for all occasions. *Market City Shopping Center, 2919 Kapiolani Blvd. (at S. King St.), lower level.* ☎ 808/739-9463. AE, DC, DISC, MC, V. Bus: 14. Map p 114.

★★ **Honolulu Chocolate Co.** ALA MOANA   Life's greatest pleasures are dispensed here with abandon: expensive gourmet chocolates made in Honolulu, Italian and Hawaiian biscotti, boulder-size turtles (caramel and pecans covered with chocolate), truffles, and my favorites—the dark-chocolate-dipped macadamia nut clusters (heavenly). *Ward Centre, 1200 Ala Moana Blvd. (at Auahi St.).* ☎ 808/591-2997. www.honoluluchocolate.com. AE, DC, MC, V. Bus: 19 or 20. Map p 114.

★★ **It's Chili in Hawaii** MCCULLY This is *the* oasis for chile-heads, a house of heat with endorphins

Rocky Road bites from Honolulu Chocolate Co.

aplenty and good food to accompany the hot sauces from around the world, including a fabulous selection of made-in-Hawaii products. Every Saturday free samples of green-chile stew are dished up to go with the generous hot-sauce tastings. *2080 S. King St., Ste. 105 (between McCully and Wiliwili sts.).* ☎ *808/945-7070. MC, V. Bus: 6. Map p 114.*

Maunakea Marketplace Food Court CHINATOWN Hungry patrons line up for everything from pizza and plate lunches to quick, authentic, and inexpensive Vietnamese, Thai, Italian, Chinese, Japanese, and Filipino dishes. The best seafood fried rice comes from the woks of **Malee Thai/Vietnamese Cuisine**—it's perfectly flavored, with morsels of fish, squid, and shrimp. **Tandoori Chicken Cafe** serves a fount of Indian culinary pleasures, from curries and jasmine-chicken rice balls to spiced rounds of curried potatoes and a wonderful lentil dal. **Masa's** serves bento and Japanese dishes, such as miso eggplant, that are famous. You'll find the best dessert around at **Pho Lau,** which

serves haupia (coconut pudding), tapioca, and taro in individual baskets made of pandanus. Join in the spirit of discovery at the produce stalls (pungent odors, fish heads, and chicken feet on counters—not for the squeamish). Vendors sell everything from fresh ahi and whole snapper to yams and taro, seaweed, and fresh fruits and vegetables. *1120 Maunakea St. (between N. Hotel and Pauahi sts.), Chinatown.* ☎ *808/524-3409. No credit cards. Bus: 2. Map p 116.*

★ People's Open Market
WAIKIKI Truck farmers from all over the island bring their produce to Oahu's neighborhoods in regularly scheduled, city-sponsored open markets, held Monday through Saturday at various locations. *Paki/Monsarrat aves.* ☎ *808/527-5167. www.honolulu.gov/parks/programs/pom/index1.htm. Map p 113.*

R. Field Wine Co.
KAKAAKO Richard Field—oenophile, gourmet, and cigar aficionado—moved his wine shop and thriving gourmet store into this grocery store. You'll find all manner of epicurean delights, including wines and single-malt Scotches. *Foodland Super Market, 1460 S. Beretania St. (between Kalakaua Ave. and Makiki*

Hawaiian hot sauces at It's Chili in Hawaii.

St.). ☎ 808/596-9463. AE, DISC, MC,
V. Bus: 2. Map p 114.

★ Sushi Company

MCCULLY   Forget about going to a
sushi bar when you can get takeout
at this small, incredible sushi store.
You'll get fast-food sushi of non-fast-
food quality, all at great prices. *1111
McCully St. (between King and Beretania sts.).* ☎ *808/947-5411. No
credit cards. Bus: 6. Map p 114.*

*Sushi Company has great takeout at bar-
gain prices.*

Fashion

House of Flys WAIKIKI   This
store, owned by local surfers and
sports enthusiasts, draws in the
20-something crowd with events
such as DJ nights or a skateboard-a-
thon in the nearby parking lot.
Come here for hip sports clothing.
*2330 Kalakaua Ave. (between Duke
Lane and Kaiulani Ave.), upper floor
of the International Marketplace.*
☎ *808/923-3597. AE, DC, DISC, MC,
V. Bus: 19 or 20.*

Kicks KAKAAKO   Attention
sneaker aficionados, collectors, and
those looking for shoes as a fashion
statement: This is your store. You'll
find limited editions and classic foot-
wear by Nike and Adidas, plus
trendy clothing lines. *1530 Makaloa
St. (between Kooaumoku and
Amana sts.).* ☎ *808/941-9191.
www.kickshawaii.com. AE, DISC, MC,
V. Bus: 13.*

Fish Markets

★★ KIDS Honolulu Fish Auc-

tion IWILEI   If you want to experience the high drama of fish buying,
head to this auction at the United
Fishing Agency, where fishermen
bring their fresh catch in at 5:30am
(sharp) Monday through Saturday,
and buyers bid on a variety of fish,
from fat tunas to weird-looking
hapupu. *Pier 38, 1131 N. Nimitz
Hwy.* ☎ *808/536-2148. No credit
cards. Bus: 42. Map p 114.*

★ Tamashiro Market

IWILEI   Good service and the most
extensive selection of fresh fish in
Honolulu have made this the grand-
daddy of fish markets. You'll find
everything from live lobsters and
crabs to fresh slabs of ahi to whole
onaga and *ehu. 802 N. King St.
(between Palama St. and Austin
Lane), Kalihi.* ☎ *808/841-8047. MC,
V. Bus: 42. Map p 114.*

Yama's Fish Market MOILI-
ILI   Known for its inexpensive fresh
fish, tasty poke, lomi salmon, and
many varieties of prepared seafood,
Yama's also has a variety of prepared foods and bakery items (their
chocolate chip/mac nut cookies are
peerless). *2332 Young St. (Hoawa
Lane).* ☎ *808/941-9994. www.
yamasfishmarket.com. DC, DISC, MC,
V. Bus: 6. Map p 114.*

Flowers & Leis

★ KIDS Cindy's Lei Shoppe CHI

NATOWN   I love this lei shop
because it always has unusual leis
such as feather dendrobiums, fire-
cracker combinations, and everyday
favorites like ginger, tuberose,
orchid, and pikake. Its "curb service" allows you to phone in your
order and pick up your lei curb-
side—a great convenience on this

busy street. *1034 Maunakea St. (at Hotel St.).* ☎ *808/536-6538. MC, V. Bus: 2. Map p 116.*

Lin's Lei Shop CHINATOWN   Features creatively fashioned, unusual leis. *1017-A Maunakea St. (at King St.).* ☎ *808/537-4112. AE, DISC, MC, V. Bus: 19 or 20. Map p 116.*

Lita's Leis CHINATOWN   This small lei shop features fresh puakenikeni, gardenias that last, and a supply of fresh and reasonable leis. *59 N. Beretania St. (between Maunakea and Smith sts.).* ☎ *808/521-9065. AE, DISC, MC, V. Bus: 19 or 20. Map p 116.*

★ Rainforest Plantes et Fleurs KAPAHULU   For special-occasion designer bouquets or leis, this is the place. Custom-designed leis and special arrangements come complete with cards in Hawaiian, with English translations. *1016 Kapahulu Ave. (between H-1 and Kehei Place).* ☎ *808/591-9999. AE, DC, DISC, MC, V. Map p 114.*

Rudy's Flowers MOILIILI   The best prices on roses, Micronesian ginger leis, and a variety of cut

Rudy's Flowers.

blooms. *2357 S. Beretania St. (at Isenberg St.).* ☎ *808/944-8844. www.rudysflowers.com. AE, DISC, MC, V. Bus: 6. Map p 114.*

Hawaiiana Gifts
★ kids Hula Supply Center MOILIILI   Hawaiiana meets kitsch. This shop's marvelous selection of souvenirs and memorabilia of Hawaii includes Day-Glo cellophane skirts, bamboo nose flutes, T-shirts, hula drums, shell leis, feathered rattle gourds, lauhala accessories, fiber mats, and a wide assortment of pareu fabrics. *1008 C Isenberg St.* ☎ *808/941-5379. www.hulasupply center.com. MC, V. Bus: 6. Map p 114.*

★★★ kids Native Books Na Mea Hawaii ALA MOANA   This is a browser's paradise, featuring a variety of Hawaiian items from musical instruments to calabashes, jewelry, leis, and books to contemporary Hawaiian clothing, Hawaiian food products, and other high-quality gift items. *Ward Warehouse, 1050 Ala Moana Blvd. (at Ward Ave.).* ☎ *808/596-8885. www.nativebookshawaii.com. AE, DISC, MC, V. Bus: 19 or 20. Map p 114.*

★★★ kids Nohea Gallery ALA MOANA/WAIKIKI   A fine showcase for contemporary Hawaii art, Nohea celebrates the islands with thoughtful, attractive selections like pit-fired raku, finely turned wood vessels, jewelry, handblown glass, paintings, prints, fabrics (including Hawaiian-quilt cushions), and furniture. *Ward Warehouse, 1050 Ala Moana Blvd. (at Ward Ave.).* ☎ *808/596-0074. www.noheagallery.com. Bus: 19 or 20. AE, DC, DISC, MC, V. Also at Moana Surfider, 2365 Kalakaua Ave. (at Kaiulani Ave.).* ☎ *808/923-6644. Maps p 113 and 114.*

Health Food Stores

Down to Earth MOILIILI Located near the University of Hawaii, this locally owned store sells organic vegetables and vegetarian bulk foods. All with good prices, they've got a strong selection of supplements and herbs and a vegetarian juice-and-sandwich bar. *2525 S. King St.* ☎ *808/947-7678. AE, DISC, MC, V. Bus: 4. Map p 114.*

House of Health HONOLULU This tiny store features competitive prices and a wide selection of health food supplements. There's no produce, but there are frozen vegetarian foods, bulk grains, and healthful snacks. *1541 S. Beretania St. (at Kalalaua St.).* ☎ *808/955-6118. AE, DISC, MC, V. City Express B. Map p 114.*

Kokua Market HONOLULU This health food cooperative is one of Honolulu's best sources for organic vegetables It also has an excellent variety of cheeses, pastas, bulk grains, sandwiches, salads, prepared foods, organic wines, and an expanded vitamin section. *2643 S. King St. (at University Ave.).* ☎ *808/941-1922. AE, DISC, MC, V. Bus: 4. Map p 114.*

Museum Stores

★ kids **Academy Shop** KAKAAKO The place to go for art books, jewelry, basketry, ethnic fabrics, native crafts from all over the world, posters, books, and fiber vessels and accessories. *Honolulu Academy of Arts, 900 S. Beretania St. (at Ward Ave.).* ☎ *808/532-8703. www.honoluluacademy.org. AE, DISC, MC, V. Bus: 2, 13, or City Express B. Map p 114.*

★ **Contemporary Museum Gift Shop** MAKIKI HEIGHTS I love the glammy selection of jewelry and novelties, such as the twisted-wire wall hangings, at this browser-friendly shop. Pick up avant-garde

Academy Shop, at the Honolulu Academy of Arts.

jewelry, cards and stationery, books, home accessories, and gift items made by artists from Hawaii and across the country. *2411 Makiki Heights Rd. (between Round Top Dr. and Mott-Smith Dr.).* ☎ *808/523-3447. www.tcmhi.org. AE, DC, DISC, MC, V. Map p 114.*

★★ kids **Shop Pacifica** KALIHI Plan to spend time browsing through the local crafts (including terrific Niihau shell leis), lauhala and Cook Island woven products, Hawaiian music tapes and CDs, pareu, and a vast selection of Hawaii-themed books that anchor this gift shop. *Bishop Museum, 1525 Bernice St. (between Kalihi St. and Kapalama Ave.).* ☎ *808/848-4158. www.bishopmuseum.org. AE, DC, DISC, MC, V. Bus: 2. Map p 114.*

Shopping Centers

★★ kids **Ala Moana Center** ALA MOANA Nearly 400 shops and restaurants sprawl over several blocks, making this Hawaii's largest shopping center catering to every imaginable need, from upscale (**Neiman Marcus, Tiffany,** and **Chanel**) to mainland chains (**Gap, Banana Republic, DKNY,** and **Old Navy**), to department stores **(Macy's,**

You'll find everything from upscale boutiques to mainland chains at Ala Moana Shopping Center.

Sears), to practical touches, such as banks, a foreign-exchange service **(Travelex),** a U.S. Post Office, several optical companies (including 1-hr. service by **LensCrafters**), and a handful of smaller locally owned stores (**Islands' Best** and **Splash! Hawaii**). The **food court** is abuzz with dozens of stalls purveying Cajun food, pizza, plate lunches, vegetarian fare, green tea, panini, and countless other treats. *1450 Ala Moana Blvd. (between Kaheka and*

Piikoi sts.). ☎ *808/955-9517. www. alamoanacenter.com. AE, DC, DISC, MC, V. Bus: 8, 19, or 20. Map p 114.*

Aloha Tower Marketplace HONOLULU HARBOR Dining and shopping prospects abound here: **Hawaiian Pacific Crafts, Hawaiian Ukulele Company, Sunglass King, Don Ho's Island Grill, Chai's Island Bistro,** and **Gordon Biersch Brewery Restaurant.** *1 Aloha Tower Dr. (at Bishop St.).* ☎ *808/528-5700. www.alohatower. com. AE, DC, DISC, MC, V. Bus: 19 or 20. Map p 114.*

DFS Galleria WAIKIKI "Boat days" is the theme at this Waikiki emporium, a three-floor extravaganza of shops ranging from the superluxe (like **Givenchy** and **Coach**) to the very touristy, with great Hawaii food products **(Big Island Candies),** aloha shirt and T-shirt shops, surf and skate equipment, a terrific Hawaiian music department, and a labyrinth of fashionable stores thrown in to complete the retail experience. *330 Royal Hawaiian Ave. (at Kalakaua Ave.).* ☎ *808/931-2655. www.dfs galleria.com. AE, DC, MC, V. Bus: 19 or 20. Map p 113.*

Bad Ass Coffee Cafe at the Aloha Tower Marketplace.

★ **Royal Hawaiian Shopping Center** WAIKIKI After 2 years and $84 million in remodeling and renovations, a larger, upscale shopping center opened in 2007 with new shops, restaurants, a nightclub and theater, entry porte-cochere, and even a garden grove of 70 coconut trees with an entertainment area. The result is a 293,000-square-foot (27,220-sq.-m) open-air mall with 110 stores, restaurants, and entertainment options on four levels. Shops range from **Hilo Hattie** to **Cartier, Hermès,** and **Salvatore Ferragamo.** *2201 Kalakaua Ave. (at Royal Hawaiian Ave.).* ☎ *808/922-0588. www.shopwaikiki. com. AE, DC, DISC, MC, V. Bus: 19 or 20. Map p 113.*

★ **kids** **Ward Centre** ALA MOANA Great restaurants **(Kakaako Kitchen, Kua Aina)** and shops **(Crazy Shirts Factory Outlet, Paper Roses, Honolulu Chocolate Co., The Gallery,** and **Borders)** make this a popular place, bustling with browsers. *200 Ala Moana Blvd. (at Kamakee St.).* ☎ *808/591-8411. www.victoriaward. com. AE, DC, DISC, MC, V. Bus: 19 or 20. Map p 114.*

kids **Ward Entertainment Center** ALA MOANA This is the place for eating, drinking, and entertainment. You'll find a 16-movie megaplex; eateries such as **Dave & Buster's, Buca di Beppo,** and **Cold Stone Creamery;** retail therapy including **Nordstrom Rack, Office Depot,** and **Pier 1 Imports;** and the ubiquitous **Starbucks Coffee.** *At the corner of Auahi and Kamakee sts.* ☎ *808/591-8411. www.victoriaward.com. AE, DC, DISC, MC, V. Bus: 19 or 20. Map p 114.*

★ **kids** **Ward Warehouse** ALA MOANA Older than its sister properties (see above), Ward Warehouse remains a popular stop for dining

(Old Spaghetti Factory, Honolulu Cookie Company) and shopping **(Native Books & Beautiful Things, Nohea Gallery).** *1050 Ala Moana Blvd. (at Ward Ave.).* ☎ *808/591-8411. www.victoria ward.com. AE, DC, DISC, MC, V. Bus: 19 or 20. Map p 114.*

T-Shirts

Hawaiian Island Creations ALA MOANA This supercool surf shop offers sunglasses, sun lotions, surf wear, surfboards, skateboards, and accessories galore. *Ala Moana Center, 1450 Ala Moana Blvd. (between Piikoi and Kaheka sts.).* ☎ *808/973-6780. www.hicsurf.com. AE, DISC, MC, V. Bus: 19 or 20. Map p 114.*

★ **kids** **Local Motion** ALA MOANA The icon of surfers and skateboarders, both professionals and wannabes, has everything from surfboards, T-shirts, alohawear, and casual wear, to countless accessories for life in the sun. *Ala Moana Shopping Center, 1450 Ala Moana Blvd. (between Kaheka and Piikoi sts.).* ☎ *808/979-7873. www. localmotionhawaii.com. AE, DISC, MC, V. Bus: 19 or 20. Map p 114.*

Hawaiian Island Creations.

Nightlife & Performing Arts
Best Bets

Best Place to **Celebrate St. Patrick's Day**
★ Murphy's Bar & Grill, *2 Merchant St. (p 129)*

Best for **Hawaiian Music**
★★★ House Without a Key, *Halekulani Hotel, 2199 Kalia Rd. (p 132)*

Best **Club for Jazz**
★★ Indigo's, *1121 Nuuanu Ave. (p 129)*

Best **Club for Concerts**
★ Pipeline, *805 Pohukaina St. (p 130)*

Most **Romantic Place for Sunset**
★★ Banyan Veranda, *Moana Surfrider, 2365 Kalakaua Ave. (p 131)*

Best Place to **People-Watch at Sunset**
★★ Duke's Canoe Club, *Outrigger Waikiki on the Beach Hotel, 2335 Kalakaua Ave. (p 131)*

Best **Luau**
Royal Hawaiian Hotel, *2259 Kalakaua Ave. (p 132)*

Best **Performing Arts Center**
★★ Neal Blaisdell Center, *777 Ward Ave. (p 133)*

Best for **Outdoor Concerts**
★★ Waikiki Shell, *2805 Monsarrat Ave. (p 134)*

Best for **Film Buffs**
★★ The Movie Museum, *3566 Harding Ave. (p 131)*

Best **Magic Show**
★ "The Magic of Polynesia," Ohana Waikiki Beachcomber, *2300 Kalakaua Ave. (p 133)*

Best **Musical Show**
★ Society of Seven, Outrigger Waikiki on The Beach, *2335 Kalakaua Ave. (p 133)*

Most **Historic Theater**
★★★ Hawaii Theatre, *1130 Bethel St. (p 134)*

Best Place to See **Locally Written and Produced Plays**
★★ Kumu Kahua Theatre, *46 Merchant St. (p 134)*

Watch the sun set and listen to Hawaiian music at Duke's Canoe Club.

Waikiki's Best **Nightlife**

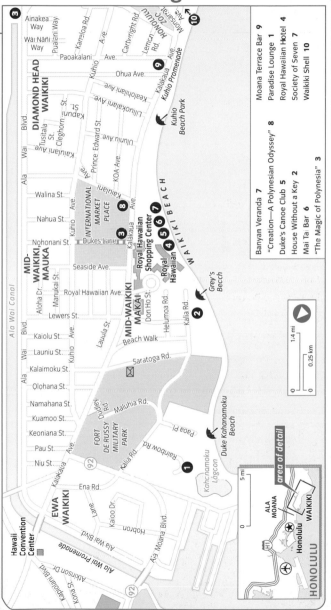

Banyan Veranda **7**
"Creation—A Polynesian Odyssey" **8**
Duke's Canoe Club **5**
House Without a Key **2**
Mai Ta Bar **6**
"The Magic of Polynesia" **3**

Moana Terrace Bar **9**
Paradise Lounge **1**
Royal Hawaiian Hotel **4**
Society of Seven **7**
Waikiki Shell **10**

Honolulu's Best **Nightlife**

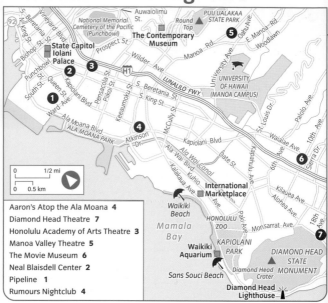

Aaron's Atop the Ala Moana **4**
Diamond Head Theatre **7**
Honolulu Academy of Arts Theatre **3**
Manoa Valley Theatre **5**
The Movie Museum **6**
Neal Blaisdell Center **2**
Pipeline **1**
Rumours Nightclub **4**

Chinatown & Downtown Honolulu's Best **Nightlife**

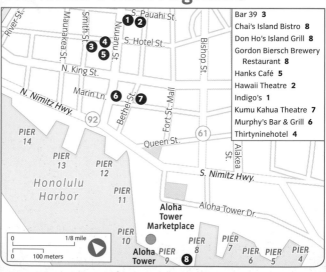

Bar 39 **3**
Chai's Island Bistro **8**
Don Ho's Island Grill **8**
Gordon Biersch Brewery
  Restaurant **8**
Hanks Café **5**
Hawaii Theatre **2**
Indigo's **1**
Kumu Kahua Theatre **7**
Murphy's Bar & Grill **6**
Thirtyninehotel **4**

Nightlife & Performing Arts
A to Z

Bars & Cocktail Lounges

Aaron's Atop the Ala Moana
ALA MOANA   For the more mature set: Take in the best view in town (from the 36th floor of the hotel), watch the Honolulu city lights wrap around the room, and cha-cha-cha to the vertigo! There's live music and dancing nightly, a lengthy dinner menu, and an appetizer menu nightly from 5pm. *In the Ala Moana Hotel, 410 Atkinson Dr. (next to the Ala Moana Shopping Center).* ☎ 808/955-4466. Bus: 19 or 20. Map p 128.

★ Gordon Biersch Brewery Restaurant ALOHA TOWER   A new stage area allows diners to swing to jazz, blues, and island riffs. *1 Aloha Tower Dr., on the waterfront between piers 8 and 11, Honolulu Harbor (at Bishop St.).* ☎ 808/599-4877. www.gordonbiersch.com. Map p 128.

Hanks Café DOWNTOWN   This tiny, kitschy, friendly pub has live music nightly, open-mic nights, and special events that attract great talent and a supportive crowd. On some nights the music spills out into the streets, and it's so packed you have to press your nose against the window to see what you're missing.

1038 Nuuanu Ave. (between Hotel and King sts.). ☎ 808/526-1410. www.hankscafehonolulu.com. Bus: 2. Map p 128.

★ Murphy's Bar & Grill DOWN-TOWN   One of Honolulu's most popular downtown ale houses and media haunts. Over a dozen beers on tap, including (of course) Murphy's and Guinness. *2 Merchant St. (at Nuuanu Ave.).* ☎ 808/531-0422. www.gomurphys.com. Bus: 19 or 20. Map p 128.

Clubs

Bar 39 CHINATOWN   If you are looking for a brew, their claim to fame is the 110 beers available, plus wine, cocktails, and even pizzas. You must be 21 to enter (strictly enforced). *3535 N. Hotel St. (between Smith St. and Nuuanu Ave.).* ☎ 808/537-3535. Bus: 13. Map p 128.

★★ Indigo's CHINATOWN   This popular nightspot serves sizzling food during the day, turns to cool jazz in the early evening, and progresses to late-night DJs spinning Top 40, disco, rock, funk, and more. *1121 Nuuanu Ave. (between Hotel and Pauahi sts.).* ☎ 808/521-2900.

Murphy's Bar & Grill.

Get Down with ARTafterDark

The last Friday of every month (except Nov and Dec), the place to be after the sun goes down is **ARTafterDark**, a *pau-hana* (after-work) mixer in the **Honolulu Academy of Arts**, at 900 S. Beretania St. Each gathering has a theme combining art with food, music, and dancing. In addition to the exhibits in the gallery, ARTafterDark features visual and live performances. Last year the themes ranged from "Plant Rice" (with rice and sake tastings, rice dishes, Asian beers, live Asian fusion music, and a tour of the *Art of Rice* exhibit) to "'80s Night," "Turkish Delights," "Cool Nights, Hot Jazz and Blues," and "Havana Heat."

Entry fee is $10; the party gets going about 6pm and lasts to 10pm, the crowd age ranges from 20s to 50s, the dress is everything from jeans and T-shirts to designer cocktail party attire. For more information, call ☎ **808/532-8700** (www.artafterdark.org).

www.indigo-hawaii.com. No cover. Bus: 13. Map p 128.

★ **Pipeline** KAKAAKO This huge club/concert venue has dancing, darts, pool, and a sports bar with larger-than-life TV screens. Patrons here tend to be younger (you can get in at 18 years old) and are dressed to go clubbing. *805 Pohukaina St. (between Koula and Kamani sts.).* ☎ *808/589-1999. www.pipelinecafe hawaii.com. Cover $1–$3; concerts around $15. Map p 128.*

Rumours Nightclub ALA MOANA The disco of choice for those who remember Paul McCartney as something other than Stella's

Rumours Nightclub.

father, with "themes" that change monthly. A spacious dance floor, a good sound system, and Top-40 music draw a mix of generations. *Lobby, Ala Moana Hotel, 410 Atkinson Dr. (next to Ala Moana Shopping Center).* ☎ *808/955-4811. Cover $5–$12. Bus: 19 or 20. Map p 128.*

Thirtyninehotel CHINATOWN Live jazz and visiting and resident DJs rock all night (but during the day, it morphs into an art gallery). The door is unmarked, with only the address to tell you where you are. Enter and walk up the stairs to the second floor. *39 N. Hotel St. (between Smith St. and Nuuanu Ave.).* ☎ *808/599-2552. www.thirty ninehotel.com. Cover $8. Bus: 13. Map p 128.*

Film
★ **Honolulu Academy of Arts Theatre** KAKAAKO This is the film-as-art center of Honolulu, offering special screenings, guest appearances, and cultural performances, as well as noteworthy programs in the visual arts. *900 S. Beretania St. (at Ward Ave.).*

Brothers Cazimero playing at Chai's.

☎ *808/532-8703. www.honolulu academy.org. Ticket prices vary. Bus: 2 or 13. Map p 128.*

★★ The Movie Museum

KAIMUKI   Film buffs and esoteric movie lovers can enjoy special screenings as they recline comfortably on brown-vinyl stuffed recliners, or rent from a collection of 3,000 vintage and hard-to-find films. *3566 Harding Ave. (between 11th and 12th aves.).* ☎ *808/735-8771. Tickets $5. Bus: 22, transfer to 14. Map p 128.*

Hawaiian Music
★★ Banyan Veranda

WAIKIKI   Enjoy a romantic evening sitting on the back porch of this historic hotel, overlooking an islet-size canopy of banyan trees, as you watch the sun set and sip a liquid libation to the sounds of live Hawaiian music playing softly in the background. You'll be in good company; Robert Louis Stevenson once loved to linger here. *Moana Surfrider, 2365 Kalakaua Ave. (between Duke's Lane and Kaiulani Ave.).* ☎ *808/922-3111. www.moana-surfrider.com. 2-drink minimum. Bus: 19 or 20. Map p 127.*

★ Chai's Island Bistro ALOHA

TOWER   **Brothers Cazimero** remain one of Hawaii's most gifted duos (Robert on bass, Roland on 12-string guitar), appearing every Wednesday at 7pm at this leading venue for Hawaiian entertainment. Also at Chai's: Robert Cazimero plays by himself on the piano on Tuesday at 7pm, and **Jerry Santos** performs on Monday at 7pm. *Aloha Tower Marketplace, 1 Aloha Tower Dr., on the waterfront between piers 8 and 11, Honolulu Harbor (at Bishop St.).* ☎ *808/585-0011. www.chaisisland bistro.com. No cover. 2-drink minimum. Bus: 19 or 20. Map p 128.*

Don Ho's Island Grill ALOHA

TOWER   Hawaii's best-known musician helped design this relaxed island bar/eatery, where live music is always on tap. Aloha Tower Marketplace. *1 Aloha Tower Dr., on the waterfront between piers 8 and 11, Honolulu Harbor (at Bishop St.).* ☎ *808/528-0807. www.donho.com/ grill/aboutus.htm. No cover. Bus:19 or 20. Map p 128.*

★★ Duke's Canoe Club

WAIKIKI   The outside Barefoot Bar is perfect for sipping a tropical drink, watching the waves and sunset, and listening to music. It can get crowded, so get there early. Hawaii sunset music is usually from 4 to 6pm on weekends, and there's live entertainment nightly from 10pm to midnight. *Outrigger Waikiki on the Beach Hotel, 2335 Kalakaua Ave. (between Duke's Lane and Kaiulani Ave.).* ☎ *808/922-2268. www. dukeswaikiki.com. No cover. No minimum. Bus: 19 or 20. Map p 91.*

★★★ House Without a Key

WAIKIKI   This is my favorite place to relax at sunset. Watch the breathtaking Kanoelehua Miller dance hula to the riffs of Hawaiian steel-pedal guitar under a century-old kiawe tree with the sunset and ocean glowing behind her—a romantic, evocative, nostalgic scene. It doesn't hurt, either, that the Halekulani happens to make the best mai tais in the world. This place has the after-dinner hours covered, too, with light jazz by local artists from 10:15pm to midnight nightly. *Halekulani Hotel, 2199 Kalia Rd. (at Lewers St.).* ☎ *808/923-2311. www. halekulani.com. No cover. Bus: 19 or 20. Map p 127.*

Mai Tai Bar WAIKIKI

This circular bar, right down at beach level, features live Hawaiian music from 4:30 to 10:30pm nightly. *Royal Hawaiian Hotel, 2259 Kalakaua Ave. (at Seaside Ave.).* ☎ *808/923-7311. www. royal-hawaiian.com. 1-drink minimum. Bus: 19 or 20. Map p 127.*

★ Moana Terrace Bar WAIKIKI

Hawaii's queen of falsetto, **Genoa Keawe,** can be heard from 5:30 to 8:30pm every Thursday. The rest of the week, except Monday, other contemporary Hawaiian musicians fill in. *Waikiki Beach Marriott, 2552 Kalakaua Ave. (between Ohua and Paoakalani aves.).* ☎ *808/922-6611. www.marriottwaikiki.com. No cover. Bus: 19 or 20. Map p 128.*

★ Paradise Lounge

WAIKIKI   Impromptu hula and spirited music from the family and friends of the performers are an island tradition. *Hilton Hawaiian Village, 2005 Kalia Rd. (at Ala Moana Blvd.).* ☎ *808/949-4321. www.hilton hawaiianvillage.com. 2-drink minimum. Bus: 19 or 20. Map p 127.*

Luau

Royal Hawaiian Hotel WAIKIKI Waıkıkı's only oceanfront luau features a variety of traditional Hawaiian as well as continental American dishes: roasted kalua pig, mahimahi, teriyaki steak, poi, sweet potatoes, rice, vegetables, haupia (coconut pudding), and a selection of desserts. Entertainment includes songs and dances from Hawaii and other Polynesian island nations. *Royal Hawaiian Hotel, 2259 Kalakaua Ave. (at Seaside Ave.).* ☎ *888/808-4668. www.honuhawaiiactivities.com. Mon 5:30pm. Adults $152, children 5–12 $76. AE, DISC, MC, V. Bus: 19 or 20. Map p 127.*

Society of Seven.

Hawaii Opera Theatre's performance of Madame Butterfly.

Shows

★ kids "Creation—A Polynesian Odyssey" WAIKIKI Don't miss this theatrical journey of fire dancing, special effects, illusions, hula, and Polynesian dances from Hawaii and the South Pacific. *Sheraton Princess Kaiulani, 2nd-floor Ainahau Showroom, 120 Kaiulani Ave. (at Kalakaua Ave.).* ☎ 808/931-4660. *Shows 7:20pm Tues and Thurs–Sun. $70–$115 w/dinner; $38 for just cocktails. Bus: 19 or 20. Map p 127.*

★ kids "The Magic of Polynesia" WAIKIKI This is not your typical dinner theater. This stage show combines magic, illusions, and Polynesian dance, song, and chant with International Magician Society's Merlin award winning master illusionist John Hirokawa. Amazing magic with a pinch of pyrotechnics, lasers, and other special effects thrown in. *Ohana Waikiki Beachcomber, 2300 Kalakaua Ave. (at Duke's Lane).* ☎ 808/971-4321. *www.robertshawaii.com. 8pm show nightly. $85 w/dinner; $52 w/cocktails. Bus: 19 or 20. Map p 127.*

★ Society of Seven WAIKIKI This nightclub act (a blend of skits, Broadway hits, popular music, and costumed musical acts) is into its third decade, no small feat. *Outrigger Waikiki on the Beach, 2335 Kalakaua Ave. (between Duke's Lane and Kaiulani Ave.).* ☎ 808/922-6408.

8:30pm shows Tues–Sun. $72 w/dinner; $47 w/cocktails. Bus: 19 or 20. Map p 127.

Symphony, Opera & Dance Performances

★★ Neal Blaisdell Center KAKAAKO Hawaii's premier performance center for the best in entertaining. This arena/concert hall/exhibition building can be divided into an intimate 2,175-seat concert hall or an 8,805-seat arena, serving everyone from symphonygoers to punk rockers. Playing here from September to May is the **Honolulu Symphony Orchestra** (☎ 808/524-0815; www.honolulusymphony.com). As we went to press, the Symphony was having some economic problems, which has resulted in canceling some shows and laying off some performers. Hopefully this problem will have been remedied by the time you read this. From January to March, the highly successful **Hawaii Opera Theatre** takes to the stage with hits like *La Bohème, Carmen, Turandot, Romeo and Juliet, Rigoletto,* and *Aïda.* Also performing at this concert hall are Hawaii's four ballet companies: **Hawaii Ballet Theatre, Ballet Hawaii, Hawaii State Ballet,** and **Honolulu Dance Theatre.** *Neal Blaisdell Center, 777 Ward Ave. (between Kapiolani Ave. and King St.).* ☎ 808/591-2211. *www.blaisdell center.com. Bus: 19 or 20. Map p 128.*

Comedy Tonight

Local comics tend to move around a lot, so the best way to see comedy is to check their websites. The best in comedy acts are **Andy Bumatai** (www.andybumatai.com), **Augie T** (www.augie tulba.com), and **Frank Delima** (www.frankdelima.com), who perform "local" stand-up sketches that will have you not only understanding local residents, but also screaming with laughter.

★★ kids **Waikiki Shell** WAIKIKI
This outdoor venue in the middle of Kapiolani Park allows concertgoers to watch the sunset and see the stars come out before the concert begins. A range of performers, from Hawaiian to jazz musicians, have graced this stage. *2805 Monsarrat Ave. (between Kalakaua and Paki aves.). ☎ 808/527-5400. www.waikikishell. com. Bus: 19 or 20. Map p 127.*

Theater

★ **Diamond Head Theatre** DIAMOND HEAD   Hawaii's oldest theater (since 1915), this community theater presents a sort of "Broadway of the Pacific," producing a variety of performances from musicals to comedies to classical dramas. *520 Makapu'u Ave. (at Alohea Ave.). ☎ 808/733-0274. www.diamondheadtheatre.com. Tickets $12–$42. Bus: 58. Map p 128.*

★★★ **Hawaii Theatre** CHINATOWN   Audiences here have enjoyed performances ranging from the big off-Broadway percussion hit *Stomp* to the talent of *Tap Dogs*, Momix, the Jim Nabors Christmas show, the Hawaii International Jazz Festival, the American Repertory Dance Company, barbershop quartets, and John Ka'imikaua's *halau* (hula school). The neoclassical Beaux Arts landmark features a 1922 dome, 1,400 plush seats, a hydraulically elevated organ, and gilt galore. *1130*

Bethel St. (between Hotel and Pauahi sts.). ☎ 808/528-0506. www.hawaii theatre.com. Ticket prices vary. Bus: 2 or 13. Map p 128.

★★ **Kumu Kahua Theatre** DOWNTOWN   For an intimate glimpse at island life, take in a show at Kumu Kahua. This tiny theater (100 seats) produces plays dealing with today's cultural experience in Hawaii, often written by residents. *46 Merchant St. ☎ 808/536-4222. www.kumukahua.org. Tickets $13–$20. Map p 128.*

Manoa Valley Theatre MANOA Honolulu's equivalent of off-Broadway, with performances of well-known shows—anything from *Urinetown* to *Who's Afraid of Virginia Woolf*. *2833 E. Manoa Rd. (between Keama Place and Huapala St.). ☎ 808/988-6131. www.manoa valleytheatre.com. Tickets $15–$30. Map p 128.* ●

A detail of the Hawaii Theatre's architecture.

The **North Shore**

① U.S. Army Schofield Barracks
   & Tropic Lightning Museum
② Kukaniloko Birthing Stones
③ Dole Pineapple Plantation
④ Haleiwa
⑤ Matsumoto Shave Ice
⑥ North Shore Surf and Cultural Museum
⑦ Waimea Bay
⑧ Waimea Valley
⑨ Pupukea Beach
⑩ Bonzai Beach
⑪ Sunset Beach
⑫ Turtle Bay Resort
⑬ Polynesian Cultural Center

Where to Stay
Ke Iki Beach Bungalows **17**
Turtle Bay Resort **16**

Where to Dine
Cafe Haleiwa **18**
Paradise Found Cafe **19**
Ola at Turtle Bay Resort **15**
21 Degrees North **14**

Previous page: Hiking near Haleiwa.

In Hawaii, half the fun is getting there. That's especially true of a drive up through the center of the island on to the famous North Shore. If you can afford the splurge, rent a bright, shiny convertible—the perfect car for Oahu, so you can tan as you go. Majestic sandalwood trees once stood in the central plains; the Hawaiian chiefs ordered them cut down, and now they're covered with tract homes, malls, and factory outlets. Beyond that is the North Shore and Hawaii's surf city: Haleiwa, a quaint turn-of-the-20th-century sugar-plantation town designated a historic site. A collection of faded clap-board stores with a picturesque harbor, Haleiwa has evolved into a surfer outpost and major roadside attraction with art galleries, restaurants, and shops that sell hand-decorated clothing, jewelry, and sports gear. START: **Waikiki. Trip Length: 95 miles (153km).**

Take H-1 West to H-2 North, which becomes Hwy. 99. Turn left on Kunia Rd., then right on Lyman Rd. (through the gate), right on Flagler Rd., and left on Waianae Ave. Museum is in Bldg. 361. Bus: 6, transfer to 52, transfer to 72.

1 kids **U.S. Army Schofield Barracks & Tropic Lightning Museum.** This is the largest cavalry post operated by the U.S. Army outside the continental United States. See p 49, bullet **6**.

Retrace your route back to Hwy. 99, make a right at the next intersection to stay on Hwy. 99, then another right at Whitemore Ave. The Stones are about a half-mile down this road on the left, before the intersection of Kamehameha Hwy. (Hwy. 80). Bus: 52.

2 Kukaniloko Birthing Stones. This is the most sacred site in central Oahu. Two rows of 18 lava rocks once flanked a central birthing stone, where women of ancient Hawaii gave birth to potential *alii* (royalty). Used by Oahu's *alii* for generations of births, many of the *pohaku* (rocks) have bowl-like shapes. Some think the site also may have served ancient astronomers—like a Hawaiian Stonehenge. Look for the two interpretive signs, one explaining why this was chosen as a birth site and the other telling how the stones were used to aid in the birth process. ⏱ *30 min. Whitemore Ave. (between hwys. 99 and 80).*

Make a left on Kamehameha Hwy. (Hwy. 80), then a right at the intersection to Kamehamaha Hwy. (Hwy. 99). Bus: 52.

The Kukaniloko Birthing Stones lie within a grove of trees in a pineapple field.

❸ kids Dole Pineapple Plantation. Make this a quick rest stop or spend a couple hours exploring the gardens and wandering through the maze. *See p 60, bullet* **❻**.

Continue on Kamehameha Hwy. Bus: 52.

❹ ★★★ kids Haleiwa. Only 34 miles (55km) from Waikiki is Haleiwa, the funky ex-sugar-plantation town that's the world capital of big-wave surfing. This beach town really comes alive in winter, when waves rise up, light rain falls, and temperatures dip into the 70s; then, it seems, every surfer in the world is here to see and be seen. Officially designated a historic cultural and scenic district, Haleiwa thrives in a time warp recalling the turn of the 20th century, when it was founded by sugar baron Benjamin Dillingham. He opened a Victorian hotel overlooking Kaiaka Bay and named it Haleiwa, or "house of the Iwa," the tropical seabird often seen here. The hotel is gone, but Haleiwa, which was rediscovered in the late 1960s by hippies, resonates with rare rustic charm. Tofu, not taro, is a staple in the local diet. Arts and crafts, boutiques, and burger stands line both sides of the town. There's also a busy fishing harbor full of charter boats. ⏱ *2–3 hr.*

❺ ★★ kids Matsumoto Shave Ice. Since 1951, this small, humble shop operated by the Matsumoto family has served a popular rendition of the Hawaii-style snow cone (for a real exotic treat try the azuki beans—sweet red beans—in the shave ice). *See p 16, bullet* **❶❶**.

❻ kids North Shore Surf and Cultural Museum. Oahu's only surf museum tells the history of this Hawaiian sport of kings. The collection of memorabilia traces the evolution of surfboards from an enormous, weathered redwood board made in the 1930s to the modern-day equivalent—a light, sleek, racy, foam-and-fiberglass board. Other items include classic 1950s surf-meet posters, 1960s surf-music album covers, old beach-movie posters, historic photographs, and trophies won by surfing's greatest. ⏱ *30 min. North Shore Marketplace, 66–250 Kamehameha Hwy. (behind Kentucky Fried Chicken), Haleiwa.* ☎ *808/637-8888. www.captainrick.com/surf_museum.htm. Free admission. Tues–Sun noon–6pm (hours may change if the surf is up).*

Continue on Kamehameha Hwy. Bus: 52.

❼ ★★ kids Waimea Bay. From November to March, monstrous waves—some 30 feet (9m) tall—roll into Waimea. When they break on the shore, the ground actually shakes. The best surfers in the world paddle out to challenge these freight trains—it's amazing to see how small they appear in the lip of the giant waves. *See p 162.*

Turn toward the mountain on Waimea Valley Rd.

❽ ★ kids Waimea Valley. The 150-acre (61-hectare) Arboretum

Signs mark the entrance to the North Shore Surf and Cultural Museum.

Waimea Bay.

and Botanical Garden contains more than 5,000 species of tropical plants. Walk through the gardens (take the paved paths or dirt trails) and wind up at 45-foot-high (14m) Waimea Falls—bring your bathing suit and you can dive into the cold, murky water. The public is invited to hike the trails and spend a day in this quiet oasis. There are several free walking tours at 10, 11am, 1, and 2pm. Plus cultural activities like lei-making, kappa demonstrations, hula lessons, Hawaiian games and crafts, and music and storytelling. *See p 61, bullet* **8**.

Continue on Kamehameha Hwy. and spend some time at one of the following three beaches. Bus: 52.

9 ★ **kids** **Pupukea Beach.** This 80-acre (32-hectare) beach park, excellent for snorkeling and diving, is a Marine Life Conservation District with strict rules about taking marine life, sand, coral, shells, and rocks. *See p 159.*

Continue on Kamehameha Hwy.; access is via Ehukai Beach Park, off Kamehameha Hwy. on Ke Nui Rd. in Pupukea. Bus: 52.

10 ★ **kids** **Banzai Beach.** In the winter, this is a very popular beach with surfers, surf fans, curious residents, and visitors; it's less crowded in the summer months. *See p 155.*

Continue on Kamehameha Hwy. Bus: 52.

11 ★★ **kids** **Sunset Beach.** If it's winter, just people-watch on this sandy beach, as the waves are huge here. But during the summer it's safe to go swimming. *See p 161.*

Continue on Kamehameha Hwy. Bus: 52.

12 ★★★ **kids** **Turtle Bay Resort.** The resort is spectacular—an hour's drive from Waikiki, but eons away in its country feeling. Sitting on 808 acres (327 hectares), this place is loaded with activities and 5 miles (8km) of shoreline with secluded white-sand coves. Even if you don't stay here, check out the beach activities, golf, horseback riding, tennis, and spa. 🕐 *Depends on your activity. 57–091 Kamehameha Hwy., Kahuku.* ☎ *808/293-6000. www.turtlebayresort.com.*

Continue on Kamehameha Hwy. Bus: 55.

13 ★ **kids** **Polynesian Cultural Center.** Visit all the islands of the Pacific in a single day at the Polynesian Cultural Center. *See p 17, bullet* **13**.

Continue on Kamehameha Hwy. Turn right on Likelike Hwy. Take the Kalihi St./H-1 exit and continue on H-1 to Waikiki. Bus: 55, transfer to City Express B.

The North Shore's Best Spa

The Zen-like **Spa Luana**, at the Turtle Bay Resort, has a thatched-hut treatment room right on the water, plus a meditation waiting area, an outdoor workout area, and a complete fitness center. Best of all, you can book a room on the second floor and use the private elevator reserved for guests getting spa treatments.

Where to **Stay**

★ **kids** **Ke Iki Beach Bungalows** BONSAI BEACH   This collection of studio, one-, and two-bedroom cottages, located on a 200-foot (61m) stretch of beautiful white-sand beach, is affordable and perfect for families (plus all units have full kitchens and their own barbecue areas). *59–579 Ke Iki Rd. (off Kamehameha Hwy.).* ☎ *866/638-8229 or 808/638-8829. www. keikibeach.com. 11 units. Studio $145–$160; 1-bedroom $195–$215; 2-bedroom $175–$230. AE, MC, V. Bus: 52.*

★★★ **kids** **Turtle Bay Resort** KAHUKU   Located in the "country" on 5 miles (8km) of shoreline with secluded white-sand coves, this is the place to stay to get away from everything. The resort offers lots of activities, and all rooms have ocean views and balconies. It also boasts one of the best spas on the island. *57–091 Kamehameha Hwy. (at Kuhuku Dr.).* ☎ *800/203-3650 or 808/293-6000. www.turtlebayresort. com. 443 units. Doubles $186–$219; cottages from $381; suites from $270; villas from $1,090. AE, DC, DISC, MC, V. Bus: 52 or 55.*

Where to **Dine**

★ **kids** **Cafe Haleiwa** HALEIWA *BREAKFAST/MEXICAN*   Haleiwa's legendary breakfast joint is a big hit with surfers, urban gentry with weekend country homes, reclusive artists, and anyone who loves mahimahi plate lunches and heroic sandwiches in a Formica-casual setting. *66–460 Kamehameha Hwy.*

(near Paalaa Rd.). ☎ *808/637-5516. Main courses $7–$14. AE, MC, V. Breakfast & lunch daily.*

★★ **kids** **Ola at Turtle Bay Resort** KAHUKU *ISLAND-STYLE CUISINE & SEAFOOD*   The location (literally on the beach), the view (lapping waves), the romantic atmosphere (tiki torches at sunset), and

Turtle Bay Resort.

The Shrimp Trucks

The best, sweetest, juiciest shrimp you'll ever eat will be from a shrimp truck on Oahu's North Shore. Several trucks line up around the entry to Haleiwa, just off the Kamehameha Hwy., but my two favorites are **Giovanni's Original White Shrimp Truck** and **Holy Smokes: Hawaiian Meats and Seafood.**

Giovanni's Shrimp Truck.

Giovanni's (☎ **808/293-1839;** usually parked across the street from the Halewai Senior Housing) claims to be the first shrimp truck to serve the delicious aquaculture shrimp farmed in the surrounding area. The menu is simple: spicy, garlic, or lemon-and-butter shrimp for $12. The battered white truck has picnic tables under the awning outside, so you can munch away right there.

Holy Smokes (no phone; parked in the same area) has a bit more of an extensive menu; in addition to the famous shrimp, they have pork spareribs ($10), smoked chicken ($9), and a steak plate ($12).

The trucks are usually in place before noon and stay until about sunset.

the food (slow-poached salmon; fishermen's stew with lobster, shrimp, scallops, and fresh fish; and a kiawe-smoked beef tenderloin) make this open-air eatery one of the best on the North Shore. Also a great option for families. *Turtle Bay Resort, 57–091 Kamehameha Hwy. (at Kuhuku Dr.).* ☎ *808/293-0801. Entrees $10–$24 lunch, $19–$60 dinner. AE, DC, DISC, MC, V. Lunch & dinner daily. Bus: 52 or 55.*

kids Paradise Found Cafe

HALEIWA *VEGETARIAN* This tiny hole in the wall offers organic, healthy breakfast and lunch to eat in or take out. *66–443 Kamehameha Hwy. (near Paalaa Rd.).*

☎ *808/637-4540. All items less than $12. No credit cards. Breakfast & lunch daily.*

★★★ kids 21 Degrees North

KAHUKU *PACIFIC RIM CUISINE* The signature restaurant at Turtle Bay Resort boasts floor-to-ceiling windows overlooking the North Shore's famous rolling surf. The contemporary island cuisine is just as inspiring as the view, with items such as crab-crusted Hawaiian sea bass, salmon with Molokai mashed sweet potatoes, and roasted Peking duck. *57–091 Kamehameha Hwy. (at Kuhuku Dr.).* ☎ *808/293-8811. Entrees $28–$50. AE, DC, DISC, MC, V. Dinner Tues–Sat. Bus: 52 or 55.*

Southern Oahu & the Windward Coast

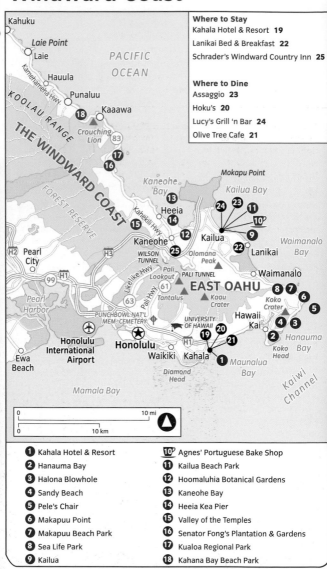

Where to Stay

Kahala Hotel & Resort **19**

Lanikai Bed & Breakfast **22**

Schrader's Windward Country Inn **25**

Where to Dine

Assaggio **23**

Hoku's **20**

Lucy's Grill 'n Bar **24**

Olive Tree Cafe **21**

❶ Kahala Hotel & Resort	❿ Agnes' Portuguese Bake Shop
❷ Hanauma Bay	⓫ Kailua Beach Park
❸ Halona Blowhole	⓬ Hoomaluhia Botanical Gardens
❹ Sandy Beach	⓭ Kaneohe Bay
❺ Pele's Chair	⓮ Heeia Kea Pier
❻ Makapuu Point	⓯ Valley of the Temples
❼ Makapuu Beach Park	⓰ Senator Fong's Plantation & Gardens
❽ Sea Life Park	⓱ Kualoa Regional Park
❾ Kailua	⓲ Kahana Bay Beach Park

From the high-rises of Waikiki, venture to a very different Oahu, the arid south shore and lush windward coast. The landscape on the south side is like a moonscape, with prickly cactuses onshore and, in winter, spouting whales cavorting in the water. Hawaiians call this area *Ka Iwi,* which means "the bone"—no doubt because of all the bone-cracking shore breaks along this popular bodyboarding coastline. The South gives way to the lush Windward side, where lots of rain keeps the vegetation green and growing, and a string of white-sand cove beaches promises a great outing. START: Waikiki. LENGTH: 85 miles (137km).

From Waikiki, take Kalakaua Ave. to Poni Moi Rd. and turn left. Go right on Diamond Head Rd., which becomes Kahala Ave.; go to the end of the street. Bus: 14.

1 ★★ **kids** **Kahala Hotel & Resort.** Stop by and check out this lush, tropical resort where the grounds include an 800-foot (244m) crescent-shaped beach and a 26,000-square-foot (2,415-sq.-m) lagoon (home to two bottlenose dolphins, sea turtles, and tropical fish), plus great dining and a fabulous spa. ⏲ *1 hr. 5000 Kahala Ave. (next to the Waialae Country Club).* ☎ *800/367-2525 or 808/739-8888.*

Backtrack on Kahala Ave., then turn right on Kealaolu Ave. Take a slight right at Waialae Ave., which becomes Kalanianaole Hwy., then go right at Hanauma Bay. Bus: Walk about 1 mile (1.6km) to Kilauea Ave. and Makaiwa St. to catch bus 22.

2 ★★★ **kids** **Hanauma Bay.** This marine preserve is a great place to stop for a swim; you'll find the friendliest fish on the island here. The beach park is closed on Tuesdays. *See p 155.*

Continue about a mile down Kalanianaole Hwy. (Hwy. 72) to around mile marker 11. Bus: 58.

3 **Halona Blowhole.** I'll give you two reasons to pull over at this scenic lookout: You get to watch the ocean waves forced through a hole

Hanauma Bay.

Pele's Chair.

in the rocks shoot up 30 feet (9m) in the air, and there's a great view of Sandy Beach and across the 26-mile (42km) gulf to neighboring Molokai, with the faint triangular shadow of Lanai on the far horizon. Be sure to obey all the signs warning you to stay away from the blowhole. ⏱ *15 min. Kalanianaole Hwy. (Hwy. 72) to around mile marker 11.*

Continue about ½ mile (.8km) down Kalanianaole Hwy. Bus: 58.

❹ ★ **Sandy Beach.** This is Oahu's most dangerous beach—it's the only one with an ambulance always standing by to whisk injured wave catchers to the hospital. Bodyboarders just love it. I suggest you just sit on the sand and watch. *See p 160.*

Continue on Kalanianaole Hwy. Bus: 58.

❺ **Pele's Chair.** Just after you leave Sandy's, look out to sea for this famous formation, which from a distance looks like a mighty throne; it's believed to be the fire goddess's last resting place on Oahu before she flew off to continue her work on other islands.

Continue on Kalanianaole Hwy. Bus: 58.

❻ **Makapuu Point.** As you round the bend, ahead lies a 647-foot-high (197m) hill, with a lighthouse that once signaled safe passage for steamship passengers arriving from San Francisco. Today it lights the south coast for passing tankers, fishing boats, and sailors. You can take a short hike up here for a spectacular vista.

Continue on Kalanianaole Hwy. Bus: 58.

❼ **Makapuu Beach Park.** In summer, the ocean here is as gentle as a Jacuzzi, and swimming and diving are perfect; come winter, however, Makapuu is hit with big, pounding waves that are ideal for expert bodysurfers, but too dangerous for regular swimmers. *See p 158.*

Across Kalanianaole Hwy. Bus: 58.

❽ ★ **kids Sea Life Park.** This 62-acre (25-hectare) ocean theme park is one of the island's top attractions, with marine animal shows, exhibits, and displays. Don't miss the Hawaiian reef tank full of tropical fish; a "touch" pool, where you can touch a real sea cucumber; and a bird sanctuary, where you can see birds like the red-footed booby and the frigate bird. ⏱ *2–4 hr. 41–202 Kalanianaole Hwy. (at Makapuu Point).* ☎ *808/259-7933 www.sea lifeparkhawaii.com. Admission $31 adults, $21 children 4–12, plus $5 for parking. Daily 10:30am–5pm.*

Continue on Kalanianaole Hwy., right at Kailua Dr. Bus: 58, transfer to 57.

9 Kailua. This is Hawaii's biggest beach town, with more than 50,000 residents and two special beaches, Kailua and Lanikai, begging for visitors. Funky little Kailua is lined with million-dollar houses next to tar paper shacks, antiques shops, and bed-and-breakfasts.

From Kailua Dr. left on Hoolai St. Bus: 56.

10 ★ kids Agnes' Portuguese Bake Shop. Take a break at this old-fashioned tea shop with the best baked goods in Kailua. My faves are the chocolate brownie and the homemade bread pudding. *40 Hoolai St.* ☎ *808/262-5367. $$.*

Dolphin encounter at Sea Life Park.

Left on Kailua Dr., which becomes Kuulei Rd., then left on Kalaheo Ave., which becomes Kawailoa Rd. No bus service.

11 ★★ kids Kailua Beach Park. Windward Oahu's premier beach is a 2-mile-long (3.2km), wide golden strand with dunes, palm trees, panoramic views, and offshore islets that are home to seabirds and every type of ocean activity you can think of. *See p 156.*

Kailua Beach Park.

Oahu's Best Spa

The Kahala Hotel & Resort has taken the concept of spa as a journey into relaxation to a new level with **Spa Suites at the Kahala** (☎ **808/739-8938**). The former garden guest rooms have been converted into individual personal spa treatment rooms, each with a glass-enclosed shower, private changing area, infinity-edge deep-soaking Jacuzzi tub, and personal relaxation area. No detail is overlooked, from the warm foot bath when you arrive to the refreshing hot tea served on your personal enclosed garden lanai after your relaxation treatment.

Retrace your route back to Kalaheo Ave., then turn left on Kuulei Rd., right on Oneawa St., and left at Mokapu Blvd., which becomes Mokapu Saddle Rd. Make a slight left on Kaneohe Bay Dr., left on Kamehameha Hwy., and right on Luluku Rd. Bus: 70, transfer to 57, transfer to 65, and walk 1 mile.

12 ★ **kids Hoomaluhia Botanical Gardens.** If you have had enough time at the beach and exposure to the sun, stop by this 400-acre (162-hectare) botanical garden, the perfect place for a picnic or hike. *See p 61, bullet* **10**.

Retrace your route back to Kamehameha Hwy., turn right, and immediately get on H-3 East. Take the Kaneohe Bay Dr. Exit. Drive down Kaneohe Bay Dr., then turn right on Kamehameha Hwy. No bus service.

13 Kaneohe Bay. Take an incredibly scenic drive around Kaneohe Bay, which is spiked with islets and lined with gold-sand beach parks. The bay has a barrier reef and four tiny islets, one of which is known as Moku o loe, or Coconut Island. Don't be surprised if it looks familiar—it appeared in *Gilligan's Island*. 🕐 *15 min.*

Turn right out on Heeia Kea Pier off Kamehameha Hwy.

14 Heeia Kea Pier. This old fishing pier jutting out into Kaneohe Bay is a great place to view the bay. Take a snorkel cruise here, or sail out to a sandbar in the middle of the bay for an incredible view of Oahu. 🕐 *30 min., longer if you snorkel or sail.*

Retrace your route on Kamehameha Hwy., then turn right at Haiku Rd. Take a right at Kahekili Hwy. (Hwy. 83), then a left at Avenue of the Temples. Bus: 65.

15 Valley of the Temples. This famous site is stalked by wild peacocks and about 700 curious people a day, who pay to see the 9-foot (2.7m) meditation Buddha, 2 acres (.8 hectares) of ponds full of more than 10,000 Japanese koi carp, and a replica of Japan's 900-year-old Byodo-In Temple. A 3-ton (2,722kg) brass temple bell brings good luck to those who can ring it. 🕐 *1 hr. 47–200 Kahekili Hwy. (across the street from Temple Valley Shopping Center).* ☎ *808/239-8811. Admission $3 adults, $2 children 11 and under & seniors 65 and over. Daily 9am–5pm.*

The Byodo-In Temple.

Continue on Kahekili Hwy., which becomes Kamehameha Hwy., then turn left on Pulama Rd. Bus: 65, transfer to 55, then walk about 1 mile (1.6km) uphill.

16 kids Senator Fong's Plantation & Gardens. You can ride an open-air tram through five gardens on former U.S. Senator Hiram Fong's 725-acre (293-hectare) private estate, which includes 75 edible nuts and fruits. *See p 61, bullet* **9**.

Turn left on Kamehameha Hwy. for 1 mile (1.6km). Bus: 55.

17 ★★ kids Kualoa Regional Park. This 150-acre (61-hectare) coconut palm–fringed peninsula is the biggest beach park on the windward side and one of Hawaii's most scenic. The long, narrow, white-sand beach is perfect for swimming, walking, beachcombing, kite flying, or just sunbathing. *See p 157.*

Continue on Kamehameha Hwy. about 10 miles (16km). Bus: 55.

18 ★★ kids Kahana Bay Beach Park. This white-sand, crescent-shaped beach has a picture-perfect

backdrop: a huge, jungle-cloaked valley with dramatic, jagged cliffs. The bay's calm water and shallow, sandy bottom make it a safe swimming area for children. *See p 156.*

Retrace your route on Kamehameha Hwy. to Kahekili Hwy. Turn right on Likelike Hwy. Take the Kahilli St./H-1 Exit. Merge onto H-1 and continue into Waikiki. Bus: 55, transfer to City Express B.

Kualoa Park.

Where to **Stay**

★★ **kids** **Kahala Hotel & Resort**
KAHALA   Located in one of Oahu's
most prestigious residential areas,
the Kahala offers elegant rooms and
the peace and serenity of a neigh-
bor-island resort, with the conve-
niences of Waikiki just a 10-minute
drive away. The lush, tropical
grounds include an 800-foot (244m)
crescent-shaped beach and a
26,000-square-foot (2,415-sq.-m)
lagoon that's home to sea turtles,
tropical fish, and two bottle-nosed
dolphins. Activities range from
Hawaiian cultural programs to daily
dolphin-education talks by a trainer
from Sea Life Park. *5000 Kahala Ave.
(next to the Waialae Country Club).*
☎ *800/367-2525 or 808/739-8888.
www.kahalaresort.com. 343 units.
Doubles $515–$1,055. AE, DC, DISC,
MC, V.*

★ **Lanikai Tree House & Garden
Studio** LANIKAI   Choose from a
1,000-square-foot (93-sq.-m) two-
bedroom apartment or a
540-square-foot (50-sq.-m) honey-
mooner's studio in this B&B tucked
away in the swank beach community. They also have a booking
agency to help you with other B&B
and vacation rentals nearby. *1277
Mokulua Dr. (between Onekea and
Aala drives).* ☎ *800/258-7895 or
808/261-1059. www.lanikaibb.com. 2
units. Doubles $160–$175.*

Kahala Resort.

kids **Schrader's Windward
Country Inn** KANEOHE   Despite
the name, the ambience here is
more motel than "country inn," but
Schrader's offers a great buy for
families. Nestled in the tranquil,
tropical setting on Kaneohe Bay, the
complex is made up of aging cot-
tage-style motels and a collection of
older homes, all with cooking facilities. *Tip:* When booking, ask for a
unit with a lanai; that way you'll end
up with at least a partial view of the
bay. *47–039 Lihikai Dr. (off Kamehameha Hwy.).* ☎ *800/735-5071 or
808/239-5711. www.schradersinn.
com. 20 units. 1-bedroom $72–$143;
2-bedroom for 4 $127–$215; 3-bed-
room for 6 $226–$358; 4-bedroom
for 8 $446–$501; all rates with
breakfast. AE, DC, DISC, MC, V.*

Schrader's Windward Country Inn.

Hawaiian Seafood Primer

The seafood in Hawaii has been described as the best in the world. And why not? Without a doubt, the islands' surrounding waters and a growing aquaculture industry contribute to the high quality of the seafood here.

Although some menus include the Western description for the fresh fish used, most often the local nomenclature is listed. To help familiarize you with the menu language of Hawaii, here's a basic glossary of island fish:

ahi   yellowfin or big-eye tuna, important for its use in sashimi and poke at sushi bars and in Hawaii Regional Cuisine

aku   skipjack tuna, heavily used in home cooking and poke

ehu   red snapper, delicate and sumptuous, yet lesser known than opakapaka

hapuupuu   grouper, a sea bass whose use is expanding

hebi   spearfish, mildly flavored, and frequently featured as the "catch of the day" in upscale restaurants

kajiki   Pacific blue marlin, also called *au,* with a firm flesh and high fat content that make it a plausible substitute for tuna

mahimahi   dolphin fish (the game fish, not the mammal) or dorado, a classic sweet, white-fleshed fish

monchong   big-scale or sickle pomfret, an exotic, tasty fish, scarce but gaining a higher profile on Hawaiian Island menus

nairagi   striped marlin, also called *au;* good as sashimi and in poke, and often substituted for ahi in raw-fish products

onaga   ruby snapper, a luxury fish, versatile, moist, and flaky

ono   wahoo, firmer and drier than the snappers, often served grilled and in sandwiches

opah   moonfish, rich and fatty, and versatile—cooked, raw, smoked, and broiled

opakapaka   pink snapper, light, flaky, and luxurious, suited for sashimi, poaching, sautéing, and baking

papio   jack trevally, light, firm, and flavorful

shutome   broadbill swordfish, of beeflike texture and rich flavor

tombo   albacore tuna, with a high fat content, suitable for grilling

uhu   parrotfish, most often encountered steamed, Chinese style

uku   gray snapper of clear, pale-pink flesh, delicately flavored and moist

ulua   large jack trevally, firm fleshed and versatile

Where to **Dine**

★ **Assaggio** KAILUA *ITALIAN*
Assaggio's affordable prices, attentive service, and winning menu
items won this neighborhood bistro
many loyal fans. You can choose lin-
guine, fettuccine, or ziti with 10 different sauces in small or regular
portions, or any of the extensive list
of seafood or chicken dishes. *354
Uluniu St. (at Aulike St.).* ☎ *808/261-
2772. Entrees $9–$11 lunch, $16–$20
dinner. AE, DC, DISC, MC, V. Lunch
Mon–Fri, dinner daily.*

★★★ **Hoku's** KAHALA *HAWAIIAN
REGIONAL*   Elegant without being
stuffy, and creative without being
overwrought, the upscale dining
room of the Kahala Hotel & Resort
combines European finesse with an
island touch, with dishes like
steamed whole fresh fish, pan-
seared foie gras, rack of lamb, ahi
steak, and the full range of East-
West specialties. Sunday brunch is
not to be missed. *Kahala Hotel,
5000 Kahala Ave. (end of street).*
☎ *808/739-8780. Entrees $30–$84.
AE, DC, DISC, MC, V. Dinner daily;
brunch Sun.*

Assaggio.

Salmon at Hoku's.

★★ kids **Lucy's Grill 'n Bar.**
KAILUA *HAWAII REGIONAL CUISINE*
This is one of Kailua's most popular
restaurants, not just because of the
open-air bar and the outdoor lanai
seating, but also because of the terrific food. I recommend the Szech-
uan-spiced jumbo tiger prawns
with black-bean cream and penne
pasta, or the lemon grass–crusted
scallops with yellow Thai curry. *33
Aulike St. (at Kuulei Rd.).* ☎ *808/
230-8188. Entrees $12–$30. MC, V.
Dinner daily.*

★★ kids **Olive Tree Cafe.**
KAHALA *GREEK/EASTERN MEDITER-
RANEAN*   This is Honolulu's best
restaurant for a meal under $20, a
totally hip hole-in-the-wall eatery
with divine Greek fare. There are
umbrella tables outside and a few
seats indoors, and you order and
pay at the counter. Winners include
mussel ceviche; creamy, tender
chicken saffron; and the generous
Greek salad. *4614 Kilauea Ave.,
across from Kahala Mall.*
☎ *808/737-0303. Entrees $10–$15.
No credit cards. Dinner daily.* ●

6 The Best Beaches

Oahu's Best **Beaches**

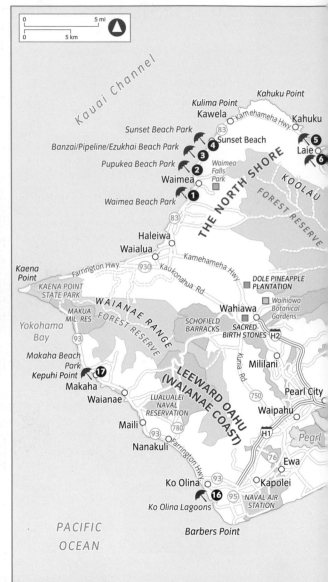

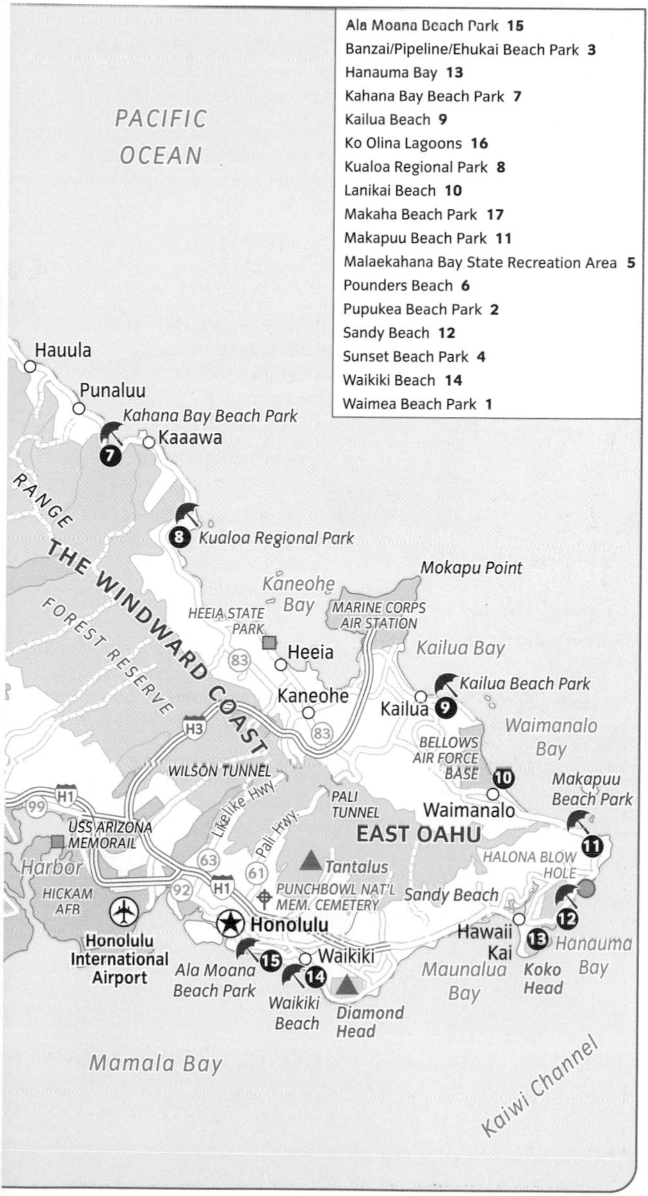

PACIFIC
OCEAN

Ala Moana Beach Park **15**
Banzai/Pipeline/Ehukai Beach Park **3**
Hanauma Bay **13**
Kahana Bay Beach Park **7**
Kailua Beach **9**
Ko Olina Lagoons **16**
Kualoa Regional Park **8**
Lanikai Beach **10**
Makaha Beach Park **17**
Makapuu Beach Park **11**
Malaekahana Bay State Recreation Area **5**
Pounders Beach **6**
Pupukea Beach Park **2**
Sandy Beach **12**
Sunset Beach Park **4**
Waikiki Beach **14**
Waimea Beach Park **1**

Hauula
Punaluu
Kahana Bay Beach Park
Kaaawa
7

Kualoa Regional Park
8

THE WINDWARD COAST
RANGE
FOREST RESERVE

Kāneohe Bay
HEEIA STATE PARK
MARINE CORPS AIR STATION
Mokapu Point

Heeia
Kaneohe
(83)
Kailua Bay
Kailua Beach Park
Kailua
9

H3
WILSON TUNNEL
BELLOWS AIR FORCE BASE
Waimanalo Bay

PALI TUNNEL
Likelike Hwy.
Pali Hwy.
10
Waimanalo
EAST OAHU
Makapuu Beach Park
11

H1
99
USS ARIZONA MEMORIAL
63
61
Tantalus
PUNCHBOWL NAT'L MEM. CEMETERY
HALONA BLOW HOLE
Harbor
HICKAM AFB
92
H1
Sandy Beach
12

Honolulu
Hawaii Kai
13 Hanauma Bay
Honolulu International Airport
Ala Moana Beach Park
15
Waikiki
14
Maunalua Bay
Koko Head
Waikiki Beach
Diamond Head
Koko Head

Mamala Bay

Kaiwi Channel

Beaches Best Bets

Best for a **Picnic**
★★ Ala Moana Beach Park, *1200 Ala Moana Blvd. (p 155)*

Best Place to **"Shoot the Tube"**
★ Banzai/Pipeline/Ehukai Beach Park, *59–337 Ka Nui Rd. (p 155)*

Best **Snorkeling**
★★★ Hanauma Bay, *7455 Koko Kalanianaole Hwy. (p 155)*

Best Place to **Kayak**
★★ Kahana Bay Beach Park, *52–222 Kamehameha Hwy. (p 156)*

Best **Windsurfing**
★★★ Kailua Beach, *450 Kawailoa Rd. (p 156)*

Best for **Kids**
Ko Olina Lagoons, *Aliinui Dr. (p 156)*

Best **Scenic Beach Park**
★★ Kualoa Regional Park, *49–600 Kamehameha Hwy. (p 157)*

Best for **Swimming**
★★ Lanikai Beach, *Mokulua Dr. (p 158)*

Best for **Expert Body Surfing**
★ Makapuu Beach Park, *41–095 Kalanianaole Hwy. (p 158)*

Best **Secluded Beach**
★★★ Malaekahana Bay State Recreation Area, *Kamehameha Hwy. (p 158)*

Best **Diving**
★ Pupukea Beach Park, *59–727 Kamehameha Hwy. (p 159)*

Best Beach for **Watching Bodyboarders**
★ Sandy Beach, *8800 Kalanianaole Hwy. (p 160)*

Best for **People-Watching**
★★ Sunset Beach Park, *59–100 Kamehameha Hwy. (p 161)*

Best for **Sunbathing & Partying**
★★★ Waikiki Beach, *from Ala Wai Yacht Harbor to Diamond Head Park (p 161)*

Best for **Big Waves**
★★ Waimea Bay Beach Park, *51–031 Kamehameha Hwy. (p 162)*

Lanikai Beach.

Oahu Beaches **A to Z**

★★ kids Ala Moana Beach Park HONOLULU

The gold-sand Ala Moana ("by the sea") stretches for more than a mile along Honolulu's coast between downtown and Waikiki. This 76-acre (31-hectare) midtown beach park, with spreading lawns shaded by banyans and palms, is one of the island's most popular playgrounds, with its own lagoon, yacht harbor, tennis courts, music pavilion, bathhouses, picnic tables, and plenty of wide-open green spaces. The water is calm almost year-round, protected by black lava rocks set offshore. There's a large parking lot as well as metered street parking. *1200 Ala Moana Blvd. (between Kamakee St. and Atkinson Dr.).*

★ Banzai/Pipeline/Ehukai Beach Park NORTH SHORE

There are three separate areas here, but because the sandy beach is continuous, most people think of it as one beach park. Located near Pupukea, **Ehukai Beach Park** is 1 acre (.4 hectare) of grass with a parking lot, great for winter surfing and summer swimming. **Pipeline** is about 100 yards (91m) to the left of Ehukai. When the winter surf rolls in and hits the shallow coral shelf, the waves that quickly form are steep—so steep, in fact, that the crest of the wave falls forward, forming a near-perfect tube, or "pipeline." Just west of Pipeline is the area surfers call **"Banzai Beach."** The Japanese word *banzai* means "10,000 years"; it's given as a toast or as a battle charge, meaning "go for it." In the late 1950s, filmmaker Bruce Brown was shooting one of the first surf movies ever made, *Surf Safari,* when he saw a bodysurfer ride a huge wave. Brown yelled: "Banzai!" and the name stuck. In the winter,

Ala Moana Beach Park.

this is a very popular beach with surfers and surf fans. *Access is via Ehukai Beach Park, 59–337 Ka Nui Rd. (off Kamehameha Hwy.), Pupukea. TheBus: 52.*

A Word of Warning

Wherever you are on Oahu, remember that you're in an urban area. Never leave valuables in your car. Thefts do occur at Oahu's beaches, and locked cars are not a deterrent.

★★★ kids Hanauma Bay KOKO HEAD

This small, curved, 2,000-foot (610m) gold-sand beach is packed elbow-to-elbow with people year-round. The bay's shallow shoreline water and abundant marine life draw snorkelers, but this good-looking beach is also popular for sunbathing and

You'll see Oahu's biggest waves off the North Shore in winter.

people-watching. The deeper water outside the bay is great for scuba diving. Hanauma Bay is a conservation district; don't touch any marine life or feed the fish. Facilities include parking, restrooms, a pavilion, a grass volleyball court, lifeguards, barbecues, picnic tables, and food concessions. Alcohol is prohibited in the park; no smoking past the visitor center. Expect to pay $1 per vehicle to park and a $3-per-person entrance fee (children 12 and under are free). Avoid the crowds by going early on a weekday morning; once the parking lot's full, you're out of luck. *7455 Koko Kalanianaole Hwy. (at Hanauma Bay Rd.). Closed Tues. Take TheBus to escape the parking problem: The Hanauma Bay Shuttle runs from Waikiki to Hanauma Bay every half-hour 8:45am–1pm; you can catch it at the Ala Moana Hotel, the Ilikai Hotel, or any city bus stop. It returns every hour noon–4:30pm.*

★★ **kids** **Kahana Bay Beach Park** WINDWARD　This white-sand, crescent-shaped beach is backed by a huge, jungle-cloaked valley with dramatic, jagged cliffs and is protected by ironwood and kamani trees. The bay's calm water and shallow, sandy bottom make it a safe swimming area for children. The surrounding park has picnic areas, camping, and hiking trails. The wide sand-bottom channel that runs through the park and out to Kahana Bay is one of the largest on Oahu—it's perfect for kayakers. *52–222 Kamehameha Hwy., Kahana. TheBus: 55.*

★★★ **kids** **Kailua Beach** WINDWARD　Windward Oahu's premier beach is a 2-mile-long (3.2km), wide golden strand with dunes, palm trees, panoramic views, and offshore islets that are home to seabirds. The swimming is excellent, and the warm, azure waters are usually decorated with bright sails; this is Oahu's premier windsurfing beach as well. It's also a favorite spot to sail catamarans, bodysurf the gentle waves, or paddle a kayak. Water conditions are quite safe, especially at the mouth of Kaelepulu Stream, where toddlers play in the freshwater shallows at the middle of the beach park. Facilities include lifeguards, picnic tables, barbecues, restrooms, a volleyball court, a public boat ramp, and free parking. *450 Kawailoa Rd., Kailua. TheBus: 56 or 57, transfer to 70.*

Ko Olina Lagoons LEEWARD　The developer of the 640-acre (259-hectare) Ko Olina Resort has

Staying Safe in the Water

According to the latest statistics from the Hawaii State Department of Health, in 2009 the number of drownings of nonresident Hawaiians was 33, most of them in the ocean. Below are some tips to keep in mind when swimming in Hawaii's gorgeous waters:

- Never swim alone.
- Always supervise children in the water.
- Always swim at beaches with lifeguards.
- Know your limits—don't swim out farther than you think you can.
- Read the posted warning signs before you enter the water.
- Call a lifeguard or 911 if you see someone in distress.

created four white-sand lagoons to make the rocky shoreline more attractive and accessible. The lagoons offer calm, shallow waters and a powdery white-sand beach bordered by a broad, grassy lawn. No lifeguards are present, but the generally tranquil waters are great for swimming, are perfect for kids, and offer some snorkeling opportunities around the boulders at the entrance to the lagoons. Two lagoons have restrooms, and there's plenty of public parking. *Off Aliinui Dr. (between Olani and Mauloa pls.), Ko Olina Resort.*

★★ **kids** Kualoa Regional Park
WINDWARD   This 150-acre (61-hectare) coconut palm–fringed peninsula is the biggest beach park on the windward side and one of Hawaii's most scenic. The park has a broad, grassy lawn and a long, narrow, white-sand beach ideal for swimming, walking, beachcombing, kite flying, or sunbathing. The waters are shallow and safe for swimming year-round, and at low tide, you can swim or wade out to the islet of Mokolii (popularly known as Chinaman's Hat), which has a small sandy beach and is a bird

Kailua Beach.

preserve. Lifeguards are on duty, and picnic and camping areas are available. *49–600 Kamehameha Hwy., Kualoa. TheBus: 55.*

★★ Lanikai Beach WINDWARD

One of Hawaii's best spots for swimming, gold-sand Lanikai's crystal-clear lagoon is like a giant saltwater swimming pool. The beach is a mile (1.6km) long and thin in places, but the sand is soft and onshore trade winds make this an excellent place for sailing and windsurfing. Kayakers often paddle out to the two tiny offshore Mokulua islands, which are seabird sanctuaries. Sun worshipers: Arrive in the morning; the Koolau Mountains block the afternoon rays. *Mokulua Dr., Kailua. TheBus: 56 or 57, transfer to 70.*

Makaha Beach Park LEEWARD

When surf's up here, it's spectacular: Monstrous waves pound the beach from October to April. Nearly a mile (1.6km) long, this half-moon gold-sand beach is tucked between 231-foot (70m) Lahilahi Point, which locals call Black Rock, and Kepuhi Point, a toe of the Waianae mountain range. Summer is the best time for swimming. Children hug the shore on the north side of the beach, near the lifeguard stand,

while surfers dodge the rocks and divers seek an offshore channel full of big fish. Facilities include restrooms, lifeguards, and parking. *84–369 Farrington Hwy. (near Kili Dr.), Waianae. TheBus: 51.*

★ Makapuu Beach Park WINDWARD

Hawaii's most famous bodysurfing beach is a beautiful 1,000-foot-long (305m) gold-sand beach cupped in the stark black Koolau cliffs. In summer, the ocean here is as gentle as a Jacuzzi, and swimming and diving are perfect; come winter, however, Makapuu is hit with big, pounding waves that are ideal for expert bodysurfers, but too dangerous for regular swimmers. Small boards—no longer than 3 feet (.9m), and no skeg (bottom fin)—are permitted; regular board surfing is banned. Facilities include restrooms, lifeguards, barbecue grills, picnic tables, and parking. *41–095 Kalanianaole Hwy. (across the street from Sea Life Park), Waimanalo. TheBus: 57 or 58.*

★★★ kids Malaekahana Bay State Recreation Area NORTH SHORE

This almost mile-long white-sand crescent lives up to just about everyone's image of the perfect Hawaiian beach: excellent for

Kualoa Regional Park.

Makapuu Beach Park.

swimming and at low tide you can wade offshore to Goat Island, a sanctuary for seabirds and turtles. Facilities include restrooms, barbecue grills, picnic tables, outdoor showers, and parking. *Kamehameha Hwy. 83 (2 miles/3.2km north of the Polynesian Cultural Center). TheBus: 52.*

Pounders Beach NORTH SHORE This wide beach, extending a quarter-mile (.4km) between two points, has easy access from the highway and is very popular on weekends. At the west end of the beach, the waters usually are calm and safe for swimming (during May–Sept). However, at the opposite end, near the limestone cliffs, there's a shore break that can be dangerous for inexperienced bodysurfers; there the bottom drops off abruptly, causing strong rip currents. Go on a weekday morning to have the beach to yourself. *Kamehameha Hwy. (about ½ mile/.8km south of Polynesian Cultural Center), Laie. TheBus: 55.*

★ **Pupukea Beach Park** NORTH SHORE This 80-acre (32-hectare) beach park, very popular for snorkeling and diving, is a Marine Life Conservation District. Locals divide the area into two: **Shark's Cove** (which is *not* named for an abundance of sharks), great for snorkeling and, outside the cove, good

diving; and at the southern end **Three Tables** (named for the three flat sections of reef visible at low tide), also great for snorkeling where the water is about 15 feet (4.6m) deep, and diving outside the tables, where the water is 30 to 45 feet (9.1–14m) deep. It's packed May to October, when swimming, diving, and snorkeling are best; the water is usually calm but watch out for surges. In the winter, when currents form and waves roll in, this

Three Tables beach at Pupukea Beach Park.

Don't Get Burned: Smart Tanning Tips

Hawaii's Caucasian population has the highest incidence of malignant melanoma (deadly skin cancer) in the world. And nobody is completely safe from the sun's harmful rays: All skin types and races can burn. To ensure that your vacation won't be ruined by a painful sunburn, here are some helpful tips:

- **Wear a strong sunscreen at all times.** Use a sunscreen with an SPF of 15 or higher; people with light complexions should use SPF 30. Apply it liberally and reapply every 2 hours.
- **Wrinkle prevention.** Wrinkles, sagging skin, and other signs of premature aging can be caused by ultraviolet A (UVA) rays. Some sunscreens block out only ultraviolet B (UVB) rays. Look for a sunscreen that blocks both. Zinc oxide, benzophenone, oxybenzone, sulisobenzone, titanium dioxide, or avobenzone (also known as Parsol 1789) all protect against UVA rays.
- **Wear a hat and sunglasses.** The hat should have a brim all the way around to cover not only your face but also the sensitive back of your neck. Make sure your sunglasses have UV filters.
- **Protect children from the sun.** Infants under 6 months should not be in the sun at all. Older babies need zinc oxide to protect their fragile skin, and all children should be slathered with sunscreen frequently.
- **If it's too late.** The best remedy for a sunburn is to stay out of the sun until all the redness is gone. Aloe vera, cool compresses, cold baths, and anesthetic benzocaine also help with the pain of sunburn.

area is very dangerous, even in the tide pools, and also much less crowded. No lifeguards. *59–727 Kamehameha Hwy. (Pupukea Rd.), Pupukea. TheBus: 52.*

★ **Sandy Beach** KOKO HEAD Sandy Beach is one of the best bodysurfing beaches on Oahu. It's also one of the most dangerous. The 1,200-foot-long (366m) gold-sand beach is pounded by wild waves and haunted by a dangerous shore break and strong backwash; the experienced bodysurfers make wave riding look easy, but it's best just to watch the daredevils risking their necks. Weak swimmers and children should definitely stay out of the water here—Sandy Beach's heroic lifeguards make more rescues in a year than those at any other beach on Oahu. Lifeguards post flags to alert beachgoers to the day's surf: Green means safe, yellow means caution, and red indicates very dangerous water conditions; always check the flags before you dive in. Facilities include restrooms and parking. Go weekdays to avoid the crowds, weekends to catch the bodysurfers in action. *8800 Kalanianaole Hwy. (about 2 miles/3.2km east of Hanauma Bay). TheBus: 22.*

★★ **Sunset Beach Park** NORTH
SHORE   Surfers around the world
know this famous site for its spectacular winter surf—the huge thun-
dering waves can reach 15 to 20
feet (4.5–6m). During the winter surf
season (Sept–Apr), swimming is
very dangerous here, due to the
alongshore currents and powerful
rip currents. The only safe time to
swim is during the calm summer
months. A great place to people-
watch is on the wide sandy beach,
but don't go too near the water
when the lifeguards have posted
the red warning flags. *59–100 Kamehameha Hwy. (near Paumalu Pl.).
TheBus: 52.*

★★★ **kids** **Waikiki Beach**
WAIKIKI   No beach anywhere is so
widely known or so universally
sought after as this narrow, 1½-mile-
long (2.4km) crescent of imported
sand (from Molokai) at the foot of a
string of high-rise hotels. Home to
the world's longest-running beach
party, Waikiki attracts nearly five
million visitors a year from every
corner of the planet. Waikiki is actually a string of beaches that extends
from **Sans Souci State Recreational Area,** near Diamond Head
to the east, to **Duke Kahanamoku**

Sunset Beach Park.

Beach, in front of the Hilton Hawaiian Village Beach Resort & Spa, to
the west. Great stretches along
Waikiki include **Kuhio Beach,** next
to the Moana Surfrider, which provides the quickest access to the
Waikiki shoreline; the stretch in
front of the Royal Hawaiian Hotel
known as **Grey's Beach,** which is
canted so it catches the rays perfectly; and **Sans Souci,** the small,
popular beach in front of the New
Otani Kaimana Beach Hotel that's
locally known as "Dig Me" Beach
because of all the gorgeous bods
who strut their stuff here. Waikiki is
fabulous for swimming, board and
bodysurfing, outrigger canoeing,
diving, sailing, snorkeling, and pole
fishing. Every imaginable type of

Sandy Beach.

Surf end of the beach (at Kapiolani Park, between the zoo and the aquarium). *Stretching from Ala Wai Yacht Harbor to Diamond Head Park. TheBus: 19 or 20.*

★★ Waimea Bay Beach Park

NORTH SHORE   This deep, sandy bowl has gentle summer waves that are excellent for swimming, snorkeling, and bodysurfing. To one side of the bay is a huge rock that local kids like to climb up and dive from. The scene is much different in winter, when waves pound the narrow bay, sometimes rising to 50 feet (15m) high. When the surf's really up, very strong currents and shore breaks sweep the bay—and it seems like everyone on Oahu drives out to Waimea to get a look at the monster waves and those who ride them. Weekends are great for watching the surfers; to avoid the crowds, go on weekdays. Facilities include lifeguards, restrooms, showers, parking, and nearby restaurants and shops in Haleiwa town. *51–031 Kamehameha Hwy., Waimea. TheBus: 52.* ●

Waimea Bay Beach Park.

marine equipment is available for rent here. Facilities include showers, lifeguards, restrooms, grills, picnic tables, and pavilions at the **Queen's**

Waikiki Beach.

Oahu's Best Hiking & Camping

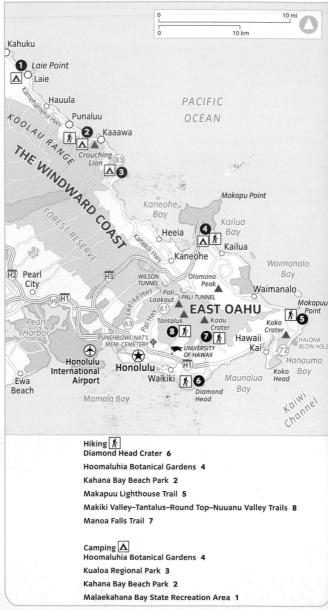

Hiking 🚶

Diamond Head Crater 6

Hoomaluhia Botanical Gardens 4

Kahana Bay Beach Park 2

Makapuu Lighthouse Trail 5

Makiki Valley–Tantalus–Round Top–Nuuanu Valley Trails 8

Manoa Falls Trail 7

Camping ⛺

Hoomaluhia Botanical Gardens 4

Kualoa Regional Park 3

Kahana Bay Beach Park 2

Malaekahana Bay State Recreation Area 1

Previous page: Windsurfer.

On Oahu you can camp by the ocean, hike in a tropical rainforest, and take in scenic views that will imprint themselves on your memory forever. Just a couple of warnings: If you plan to camp, you must bring your own gear—no one on Oahu rents it. If you plan to go hiking, take a fully charged cellphone, in case of emergency.

★★★ kids Diamond Head Crater

Hiking   This is a moderate (but steep) walk to the summit of the 750-foot (229m) volcanic cone, Hawaii's most famous landmark, with a reward of a 360-degree view of the island. The 1.4-mile (2.3km) round-trip takes about 1½ hours and the entry fee is $1. Wear decent shoes (rubber-soled tennies are fine) and take a flashlight (you'll walk through several dark tunnels), binoculars, water, a hat to protect you from the sun, and a camera. You might want to put all your gear in a pack to leave your hands free for the climb. Go early, preferably just after the 6:30am opening, before the midday sun starts beating down. *Monsarrat and 18th aves. Bus: 58.*

Safety Tip

When planning sunset activities, be aware that Hawaii, like other places close to the Equator, has a very short (5–10 min.) twilight period after the sun sets. After that, it's dark. If you hike out to watch the sunset, be sure you can make it back quickly, or take a flashlight.

★ kids Hoomaluhia Botanical Gardens

Hiking & Camping   This relatively unknown windward-side camping area, outside Kaneohe, is a real find. *Hoomaluhia* means "peace and tranquillity," an apt description for this 400-acre (162-hectare) lush botanical garden. Standing among the rare plants, with craggy cliffs in the background, it's hard to believe you're just a half-hour from downtown Honolulu. A 32-acre (13-hectare) lake sits in the middle of the scenic park (no swimming or boating is allowed), and there are numerous hiking trails. The Visitors Center can suggest a host of activities, ranging from guided walks to demonstrations of ancient Hawaiian

The climb up Diamond Head is steep, but anyone reasonably fit can do it.

plant use. Facilities include a tent-camp area, restrooms, cold showers, dishwashing stations, picnic tables, grills, and water. Permits are free, but you have to get here on a Friday no later than 3pm, as the office is not open on weekends. Stays are limited to Friday, Saturday, and Sunday nights only. *Hoomaluhia Botanical Gardens, 45–680 Luluku Rd. (at Kamehameha Hwy.), Kaneohe.* ☎ *808/233-7323. Bus: 55.*

★★ kids Kahana Bay Beach Park

Camping Under Tahiti-like cliffs, with a beautiful, gold-sand crescent beach framed by pine needle casuarina trees, Kahana Bay Beach Park is a place of serene beauty. You can swim, bodysurf, fish, hike, and picnic, or just sit and listen to the trade winds whistle through the beach pines. Both tent and vehicle camping are allowed at this oceanside oasis. Facilities include restrooms, picnic tables, drinking water, public phones, and a boat-launching ramp.

Hiking Spectacular views of this verdant valley and a few swimming holes are the rewards of a 4.5-mile (7.2km) loop trail above the beach. The downside to this 2- to 3-hour, somewhat ardent adventure are mosquitoes (clouds of them) and some thrashing about in dense forest where a bit of navigation is required along the not-always-marked trail. The trail starts behind the Visitor's Center at the Kahana Valley State Park. *52–222 Kamehameha Hwy. (between Kaaawa and Kahana). Bus: 55.*

★★ kids Kualoa Regional Park

Camping Located on a peninsula in Kaneohe Bay, this park has a spectacular setting right on a gold-sand beach, with a great view of Mokolii Island. Facilities include restrooms, showers, picnic tables, drinking fountains, and a public phone. *49–600 Kamehameha Hwy., across from Mokolii Island (between Waikane and Kaaawa). Bus: 55.*

★ kids Makapuu Lighthouse Trail

Hiking It's a little precarious at times, but anyone in reasonably good shape can handle this 45-minute (one-way) hike, which winds around the 646-foot-high (197m) sea bluff to the Lighthouse. The rewards are the views: the entire Windward Coast, across the azure Pacific and out to Manana (Rabbit) Island. *Kalanianaole Hwy. (½ mile/.8km down the road from the Hawaii Kai Golf Course), past Sandy Beach. Bus: 57 or 58.*

Water Safety

Water might be everywhere in Hawaii, but it more than likely isn't safe to drink. Most stream water is contaminated with bacterium

Kahana Valley.

The Makapuu Lighthouse.

leptospirosis, which produces flulike symptoms and can be fatal. Make sure that your drinking water is safe by vigorously boiling it, or if boiling is not an option, use tablets with hydroperiodide; portable water filters will not screen out bacterium leptospirosis.

★★ Makiki Valley–Tantalus–Round Top–Nuuanu Valley Trails

Hiking This is the starting place for some of Oahu's best hiking trails—miles of trails converge through the area. The draws here are the breathtaking views, historic remains, and incredible vegetation.

Stop at the Hawaii Nature Center, by the trail head, for information and maps. *2131 Makiki Heights Dr.* ☎ *808/955-0100. Mon–Fri 8am–4:30pm. Bus: 4.*

★★★ kids Malaekahana Bay State Recreation Area

Camping This beautiful beach camping site has a mile-long (1.6km) gold-sand beach. Facilities include picnic tables, restrooms, showers, sinks, drinking water, and a phone. *Kamehameha Hwy. between Laie and Kahuku. Bus: 55.*

★★ kids Manoa Falls Trail

Hiking This easy, .75-mile (1.2km) hike (one-way) is terrific for families; it takes less than an hour to reach idyllic Manoa Falls. The often-muddy trail follows Waihi Stream and meanders through the forest reserve past guavas, mountain apples, and wild ginger. The forest is moist and humid and is inhabited by giant bloodthirsty mosquitoes, so bring repellent. If it has rained recently, stay on the trail and step carefully, as it can be very slippery. The trail head is marked by a footbridge. *End of Manoa Rd., past Lyon Arboretum. Bus: 5.*

Camping Permits

You must get a permit for all camping in all parks on Oahu. For Honolulu County Parks (like Kualoa Regional Park), contact Honolulu Department of Parks and Recreation, 650 King St., Honolulu, HI 96713 (☎ 808/523-4525; www.co.honolulu.hi.us), for information and permits. For state parks (like Kahana Bay Beach Park and Malaekahana Bay State Recreation Area), there's an $18 fee for camping (per campsite per night), and you must get a permit. Permits are limited to 5 nights; contact any state parks office, including the Department of Land and Natural Resources, State Parks Division, P.O. Box 621, Honolulu, HI 96809 (☎ 808/587-0300; www.hawaiistateparks.org/parks/oahu). County and state parks do not allow camping Wednesday or Thursday.

Oahu's Best **Golf Courses**

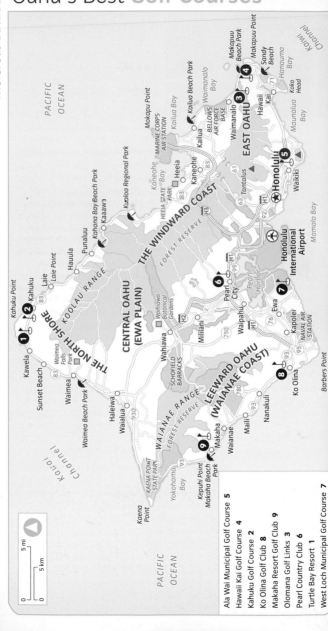

Oahu has nearly three dozen golf courses, ranging from bare-bones municipal courses to exclusive country club courses with membership fees running to six figures a year. Below are the best of a great bunch. As you play Oahu's courses, you'll come to know that the windward courses play much differently than the leeward courses. On the windward side, the prevailing winds blow from the ocean to shore, and the grain direction of the greens tends to run the same way—from the ocean to the mountains. Leeward golf courses have the opposite tendency: The winds usually blow from the mountains to the ocean, with the grain direction of the greens corresponding.

Ala Wai Municipal Golf Course

The *Guinness Book of World Records* lists this as the busiest golf course in the world; duffers play some 500 rounds a day on this 18-hole municipal course, within walking distance of Waikiki's hotels. It is a challenge to get a tee time (you can book only 3 days in advance). Ala Wai has a flat layout and is less windy than most Oahu courses, but pay attention; some holes are not as easy as you may think. *404 Kapahulu Ave., Waikiki.* ☎ *808/733-7387 (golf course), or 808/296-2000 tee time reservations. www.co.honolulu.hi.us/des/golf/alawai.htm. Greens fees: $44; twilight rate $23. Bus: 19, 20, or 22.*

Hawaii Kai Golf Course

This is actually two golf courses in one. The par-72, 6,222-yard (5,689m) Hawaii Kai Championship Golf Course is moderately challenging, with scenic vistas. The course is forgiving to high-handicap golfers, although it does have a few surprises. The par-3 Hawaii Kai Executive Golf Course is fun for beginners and those just getting back in the game after a few years. The course has lots of hills and valleys, with no water hazards and only a few sand traps. *8902 Kalanianaole Hwy., Honolulu.* ☎ *808/395-2358. www.hawaiikaigolf.com. Greens fees: Champion Course $100 Mon–Fri, $110 Sat–Sun, twilight rates $70; Executive Course $39 Mon–Fri, $44 Sat–Sun. Check the website for discounts. Bus: 58.*

Kahuku Golf Course

This 9-hole budget golf course is a bit funky: no club rentals, no clubhouse, and no facilities other than a few pull carts that disappear with the first handful of golfers. But a round at this scenic oceanside course amid the tranquillity of the North Shore is quite an experience. Duffers will love the ease of this

Ko Olina Golf Club.

recreational course, and weight watchers will be happy to walk the gently sloping greens. Don't forget to bring your camera for the views. No reservations are taken; tee times are first-come, first-served, and with plenty of retirees happy to sit and wait, the competition is fierce for early tee times. Bring your own clubs and call ahead to check the weather. *56–501 Kamehameha Hwy., Kahuku.* ☎ *808/293-5842. Greens fees: $12 for 9 holes. Bus: 55.*

★★★ Ko Olina Golf Club

The Ted Robinson–designed course (6,867-yard/6,279m, par 72) has rolling fairways and elevated tee and water features. The signature hole—the 12th, a par 3—has an elevated tee that sits on a rock garden with a cascading waterfall. At the 18th hole, you'll see and hear water all around you—seven pools begin on the right side of the fairway and slope down to a lake. Book in advance; this course is crowded all the time. Facilities include a driving range, locker rooms, a Jacuzzi, steam rooms, and a restaurant and bar. Lessons are available. *92–1220 Aliinui Dr., Kapolei.* ☎ *808/676-5309. www.koolinagolf. com. Greens fees: $179 ($159 for Ihilani Resort guests); twilight rates $109 (after 1pm in winter and 2:30pm in summer). Men and women are asked to wear a collared shirt. No bus service.*

★★ Makaha Resort Golf Club

This challenging course sits some 45 miles (72km) west of Honolulu, in Makaha Valley. Designed by William Bell, the par-72, 7,091-yard (6,484m) course meanders toward the ocean before turning and heading into the valley. Sheer volcanic walls tower 1,500 feet (457m) above the course, which is surrounded by swaying palm trees and neon-bright bougainvillea; an occasional peacock will even strut across the fairways. The beauty here could make it difficult to keep your mind on the game if it weren't for the course's many challenges: eight water hazards, 107 bunkers, and frequent brisk winds. This course is packed on weekends, so it's best to try weekdays. Facilities include a pro shop, bag storage, and a snack shop. *84–627 Makaha Valley Rd., Waianae.* ☎ *808/695-7111 or 808/695-5239. www.makahavalley cc.com. Greens fees: $160 (check the website for specials). Bus: 51.*

Olomana Golf Links

Low-handicap golfers may not find this gorgeous course difficult, but the striking views of the craggy Koolau mountain ridge alone are worth the fees. The par-72, 6,326-yard (5,784m) course is popular with locals and visitors alike. The course starts off a bit hilly on the front 9 but flattens out by the back 9,

Olomana Golf Links.

where there are some tricky water hazards. This course is very, very green; the rain gods bless it regularly with brief passing showers. You can spot the regular players here—they all carry umbrellas, wait patiently for the squalls to pass, and then resume play. Facilities include a driving range, practice greens, club rental, pro shop, and restaurant. *41–1801 Kalanianaole Hwy., Waimanalo.* ☎ *808/259-7926. ww.olomanagolflinks.com. Greens fees: $95; twilight fees $80. Bus: 57.*

Pearl Country Club Looking for a challenge? You'll find one at this popular public course, located just above Pearl City in Aiea. Sure, the 6,230-yard (5,697m), par-72 course looks harmless enough, and the views of Pearl Harbor and the USS *Arizona* Memorial are gorgeous, but around the 5th hole, you'll start to see what you're in for: water hazards, forest, and doglegs that allow only a small margin of error between the tee and the steep out-of-bounds hillside. Oahu residents can't get enough of it, so don't even try to get a tee time on weekends. Facilities include a driving range, practice greens, club rental, pro shop, and restaurant. *98–535 Kaonohi St., Aiea.* ☎ *808/487-3802. www.pearlcc.com. Greens fees: $110 Mon–Fri, $120 Sat–Sun; after 4pm 9 holes are $45 weekdays, $50 weekends. Bus: 32 (stops at Pearlridge Shopping Center at Kaonohi and Moanalua sts.; you'll have to walk about ⅓ mile/.8km uphill from here).*

★★ Turtle Bay Resort This North Shore resort is home to two of Hawaii's top golf courses: the 18-hole Arnold Palmer Course (formerly the Links at Kuilima) was designed by Arnold Palmer and Ed Seay, and the par-71, 6,200-yard (5,669m) George Fazio Course. Palmer's is the most challenging, with the front 9 playing like a British Isles

Turtle Bay Resort.

course (rolling terrain, only a few trees, and lots of wind). The back 9 has narrower, tree-lined fairways and water. Fazio is a more forgiving course, without all the water hazards and bunkers of the Palmer course. Facilities include a pro shop, driving range, putting and chipping green, and snack bar. Weekdays are best for tee times. *57–049 Kamehamcha Hwy., Kahuku.* ☎ *808/293-8574 or 808/293-9094. www.turtlebayresort. com. Greens fees: Palmer Course $175, $110 after 2pm; Fazio Course $125 before noon, $110 noon–2pm, $75 after 2pm (and here's the deal: after 3pm you can walk the course for $15!). Bus: 52 or 55.*

West Loch Municipal Golf Course This par-72, 6,615-yard (6,049m) course located just 30 minutes from Waikiki, in Ewa Beach, offers golfers a challenge at bargain rates. The difficulties on this unusual municipal course, designed by Robin Nelson and Rodney Wright, are water (lots of hazards), constant trade winds, and narrow fairways. To help you out, the course features a "water" driving range (with a lake) to practice your drives. Facilities include a driving range, practice greens, a pro shop, and a restaurant. *91–1126 Okupe St., Ewa Beach.* ☎ *808/675-6076. Greens fees: $46. Book a week in advance. Bus: 50.*

Adventures **on Land**

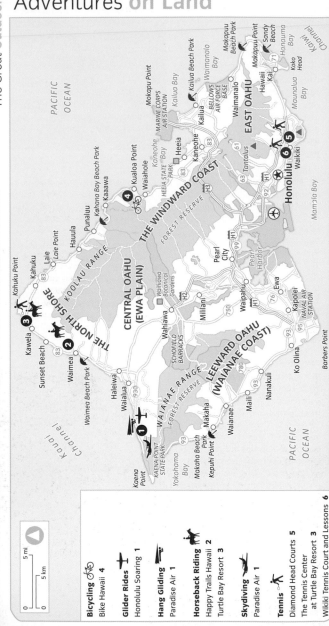

PACIFIC
OCEAN

Makapuu
Beach Park

Makapuu Point

Kaiwi Channel

Sandy
Beach

Honauma
Bay

Koko
Head

EAST OAHU

Hawaii
Kai

Makapuu Point

Maunalua
Bay

Waikiki

Honolulu

Kaneohe Bay

Kailua Beach Park

Mokapu Point

MARINE CORPS
AIR STATION

Kailua Bay

Heeia

BELLOWS
AIR FORCE
BASE

Waimanalo
Bay

Waimanalo

Kailua

Kaneohe

HEEIA STATE
PARK

Tantalus

Kualoa Point

Waiahole

Kahana Bay Beach Park

Kaaawa

THE WINDWARD COAST

KOOLAU RANGE

FOREST RESERVE

H3

Punaluu

Hauula

Laie Point

Laie

Kahuku

Kahuku Point

THE NORTH SHORE

Kawela

Sunset Beach

Waimea

Haleiwa

Waialua

Waimea Beach Park

Kauai Channel

Pearl City

Pearl Harbor

CENTRAL OAHU (EWA PLAIN)

Waihiawa Botanical Gardens

Wahiawa

SCHOFIELD BARRACKS

Mililani

Waipahu

Ewa

NAVAL AIR STATION

Kapolei

Ko Olina

Borbers Point

Mamala Bay

LEEWARD OAHU (WAIANAE COAST)

WAIANAE RANGE

FOREST RESERVE

Nanakuli

Maili

Waianae

Makaha

Makaha Beach Park

Kepuhi Point

Yokohama Bay

KAENA POINT STATE PARK

Kaena Point

PACIFIC
OCEAN

0   5 mi
0   5 km

Bicycling 🚲
Bike Hawaii **4**

Glider Rides ✈
Honolulu Soaring **1**

Hang Gliding ✈
Paradise Air **1**

Horseback Riding 🐎
Happy Trails Hawaii **2**
Turtle Bay Resort **3**

Skydiving ✈
Paradise Air **1**

Tennis 🎾
Diamond Head Courts **5**
The Tennis Center
at Turtle Bay Resort **3**
Wikiki Tennis Court and Lessons **6**

onolulu isn't just sparkling ocean water and rainbow-colored fish; it's also the land of adventure—you can cycle back through history to an ancient, terraced taro field, soar through the air in a glider, gallop along a deserted sandy beach, or even leap from a plane and float to earth under a parachute.

Bicycling

Get off the street and get dirty with an off-road, guided mountain bike tour from **Bike Hawaii,** through the 1,000-acre (405-hectare) Kaaawa Valley on Oahu's northeast shore. The tour is the same site as the annual 24 Hours of Hell Mountain Bike Race; you'll follow dirt roads and single-track through verdant tropical landscape, dotted with mountain streams. Stops on the 6-mile (9.7km), 2-hour ride include an ancient Hawaiian house site in the midst of a terraced taro field, an old military bunker converted into a movie museum for films shot within this historical valley (*Jurassic Park, Godzilla, Mighty Joe Young, Windtalkers*), and views of sheer valley walls, panoramic ocean vistas, and lush Hawaiian vegetation. ☎ *877/MTV-RIDE (688-7433) or*

808/734-4214. www.bikehawaii.com. Adults $110, children 13 and under $80 (includes mountain bike, van transportation, helmet, lunch, snacks, water bottle and guide).

Glider Rides

Imagine soaring through silence on gossamer wings, a panoramic view of Oahu below you. A glider ride is an unforgettable experience, and it's available from **Honolulu Soaring,** at Dillingham Air Field, in Mokuleia, on Oahu's North Shore. The glider is towed behind a plane; at the proper altitude, the tow is dropped, and you (and the glider pilot) are left to soar in the thermals. *Dillingham Air Field, Mokuleia.* ☎ *808/677-3404. www.honolulusoaring.com. From $79 for 10 min.*

Soar silently over the North Shore's breathtaking landscape in a glider.

You can explore Oahu by bike on your own or with a tour.

Hang Gliding

See things from a bird's-eye view as you and your instructor float high above Oahu on a tandem hang glider with **Paradise Air.** *Dillingham Air Field. Mokuleia.* 📞 *808/497-6033. www.paradiseairhawaii.com. Ground school plus 30 min. in the air $150.*

Horseback Riding

★ kids **Happy Trails Hawaii** NORTH SHORE   This small operation welcomes families (kids as young as 6 are okay) on these guided trail rides on a hilltop above Pupukea Beach and overlooking Waimea Valley, on the North Shore. *59–231 Pupukea Rd.* 📞 *808/638-RIDE (7433). www.happytrails hawaii.com. From $75 for 1½-hr. rides.*

★ **Turtle Bay Resort** NORTH SHORE   You can gallop along a deserted North Shore beach with spectacular ocean views and through a forest of ironwood trees, or take a romantic evening ride at

Biking on Your Own

Bicycling is a great way to see Oahu, and most streets here have bike lanes. For information on bikeways and maps, contact the **Honolulu City and County Bicycle Coordinator** (📞 **808/527-5044;** www.honolulu.gov/dts/bikepage.htm).

If you're in Waikiki, you can rent a bike for as little as $10 for a half-day and $20 for 24 hours at **Big Kahuna Rentals,** 407 Seaside Ave. (📞 **808/924-2736;** www.bigkahunarentals.com). On the North Shore, for a full-suspension mountain bike, try **Raging Isle,** 66–250 Kamehameha Hwy., Haleiwa (📞 **808/637-7707;** www.ragingisle.com), which rents bikes for $40 for 24 hours.

One of my favorite ways to tour Waikiki is on a Segway Personal Transporter, one of those two-wheeled machines that look like an old push lawn mower (big wheels and a long handle). It takes only a few minutes to get the hang of this contraption (which works through a series of high-tech stabilization mechanisms that read the motion of your body to turn or go forward or backward), and it's a lot of fun (think back to the first time you rode your bicycle—the incredible freedom of zipping through space without walking). **Glide Ride Tours and Rentals,** located in the Hawaii Tapa Tower of the Hilton Hawaiian Village Beach Resort & Spa, 2005 Kalia Rd. (☎ 808/941-3151; www.segwayofhawaii.com), offers instruction and several tours ranging from a 40-minute introductory tour for $89 per person to a 2½-hour tour of Waikiki, Kapiolani Park, and Diamond Head for $110 per person.

sunset with your sweetheart. *57–091 Kamehameha Hwy., Kahuku.* ☎ *808/293-8811. www.turtlebay resort.com. Bus: 52 or 55. Beach ride (45 min.) $65 ages 7 and up (children must be at least 4 ft. 4 in./1.3m tall); sunset ride $105.*

Sky Diving
SkyDive Hawaii offers a once-in-a-lifetime experience: Leap from a plane and float to earth in a tandem jump (you're strapped to an expert who wears a chute big enough for the both of you). *68–760 Farrington Hwy., Wahiawa.* ☎ *800/766-0446. www.hawaiiskydiving.net. From $190.*

Tennis
Free Tennis Courts Oahu has 181 free public tennis courts. The courts are available on a first-come, first-served basis; playing time is limited to 45 minutes if others are waiting. The closest courts to Waikiki are the **Diamond Head Courts.** *3908 Paki Ave. (across from Kapiolani Park).* ☎ *808/971-7150.*

The Tennis Center at Turtle Bay Resort
Turtle Bay has eight Plexipave courts, two of which are lit for night play. Instruction, rental equipment, player matchup, and even a ball machine are available here. You must reserve the night courts in advance; they're very popular. *57–091 Kamehameha Hwy., Kahuku.* ☎ *808/293-6024. www. turtlebayresort.com. Bus: 52 or 55. Court time $10 per person (complimentary for guests); equipment rental $8; lessons $35 for 30 min., $60 for 1 hr.*

Waikiki Tennis Courts and Lessons
If you are staying in Waikiki, one of the most accessible courts is tucked away at the entrance to Waikiki, just across the bridge over Ala Wai Canal at **Aqua Marina Hotel.** *1700 Ala Moana Blvd.* ☎ *808/551-9438. Bus: 19 or 20. Daily 9am–9pm. Court rental $25 per person per hour; racket rental $5 per day; private lessons $60 per hour, semiprivate $75 per hour for 2 or more.*

's Best **Snorkeling**

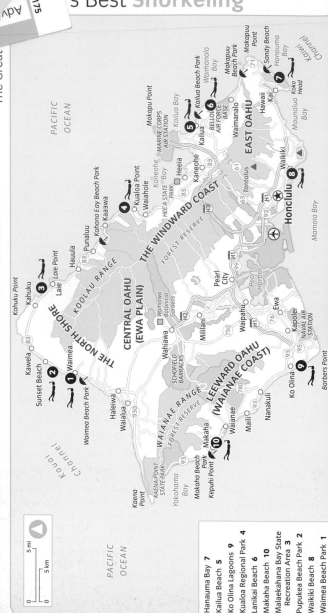

Snorkeling is a huge attraction on Oahu—just relax as you float over underwater worlds populated with colorful clouds of tropical fish. If you've never snorkeled before, most resorts and excursion boats offer instruction, but it's plenty easy to figure it out for yourself. All you need are a mask, a snorkel, fins, and some basic swimming skills. In many places all you have to do is wade into the water and look down. Below are Oahu's best snorkeling beaches.

★★★ **kids Hanauma Bay** KOKO HEAD   Oahu's most popular snorkeling spot is a curved, 2,000-foot (610m) gold-sand beach packed elbow-to-elbow with people year-round. Part of an old crater that fell into the sea, the bay's shallow shoreline water and abundant marine life are the main attractions to snorkelers. A shallow reef outside the bay protects it from the surf, keeping the waters very calm. Hanauma Bay is a conservation district; you may look at but not touch or take any marine life here. Feeding the fish is also prohibited. *7455 Koko Kalanianaole Hwy. (at Hanauma Bay Rd.). Or take TheBus to escape the parking problem: The Hanauma Bay Shuttle runs from Waikiki to Hanauma Bay every ½-hr. 8:45am–1pm.*

★★★ **kids Kailua Beach** WIND-WARD   Stretched out between two points, this 2-mile-long (3.2km) golden strand (with dunes, palm trees, panoramic views,

and offshore islets) offers great snorkeling (along with a host of other ocean activities) with safe water conditions most of the year. *450 Kawailoa Rd., Kailua. Bus: 56 or 57, transfer to 70.*

Ko Olina Lagoons LEEWARD When the developer of the 640-acre (259-hectare) Ko Olina Resort blasted four white-sand lagoons out of the shoreline to make the rocky shoreline more attractive and accessible, he created a great snorkeling area around the boulders at the entrance to each lagoon. The man-made lagoons offer calm, shallow waters and a powdery white-sand beach bordered by a broad, grassy lawn. No lifeguards are present, but the generally tranquil waters are safe. *Off Aliinui Dr. (between Olani and Mauloa pl.), Ko Olina Resort. No bus.*

★★ **kids Kualoa Regional Park** WINDWARD   This 150-acre (61-hectare) coconut palm–fringed peninsula is the biggest beach park

Snorkeling with a sea turtle in Hanauma Bay.

Kualoa Park.

on the windward side and one of Hawaii's most scenic. The sandy waters offshore are safe and have snorkeling areas. Just 500 yards (457m) offshore is the tiny islet Mokolii Island (popularly known as Chinaman's Hat), which has a small sandy beach and is a bird preserve—so don't spook the red-footed boobies. *49–600 Kamehameha Hwy., Kualoa. Bus: 55.*

★★ **Lanikai Beach** WINDWARD   One of Hawaii's best spots for snorkeling is off the gold-sand Lanikai's crystal-clear lagoon (there are so many fish it feels like a giant saltwater aquarium). The reef extends out for about ½ mile (.8km), with snorkeling along the entire length. *Mokulua Dr., Kailua. Bus: 56 or 57, transfer to 70.*

★ **Makaha Beach** LEEWARD   During the summer, the waters here are clear and filled with a range of sea life (from green sea turtles to schools of tropical fish to an occasional manta ray). Plus the underwater landscape has arches and tunnels just 40 feet (12m) down, great habitats for reef fish. *84–369 Farrington Hwy., Makaha. Bus: City Express B, transfer to Country Express C.*

★★★ kids **Malaekahana Bay State Recreation Area** NORTH SHORE   This almost mile-long (1.6km) white-sand crescent lives up to just about everyone's image of

Where to Rent Beach Equipment

If you want to rent beach toys (snorkeling equipment, boogie boards, surfboards, kayaks, and more), check out the following rental shops: **Snorkel Bob's,** on the way to Hanauma Bay at 700 Kapahulu Ave. (at Date St.), Honolulu (☎ **808/735-7944;** www. snorkelbob.com); and **Aloha Beach Service,** in the Moana Surfrider, 2365 Kalakaua Ave. (☎ **808/922-3111,** ext. 2341), in Waikiki. On Oahu's windward side, try **Kailua Sailboards & Kayaks,** 130 Kailua Rd., a block from the Kailua Beach Park (☎ **808/262-2555;** www.kailuasailboards.com). On the North Shore, get equipment from **Surf-N-Sea,** 62–595 Kamehameha Hwy., Haleiwa (☎ **808/637-9887;** www.surfnsea.com).

the perfect Hawaiian beach. I head for the rocky areas around either of the two points (Makahoa Point and Kalanai Point) that define this bay. *Kamehamehu Hwy. (2 miles/3.2km north of the Polynesian Cultural Center). Bus: 52.*

★ **Pupukea Beach Park** NORTH SHORE   This North Shore beach is great for snorkeling (May–Oct) not only because of the lush marine life, but also because it is a Marine Life Conservation District (sort of like an underwater park), which means that it's illegal to take anything from this park (fish, marine critters, even coral); thus the fish are not only plentiful but also very friendly. As you face the ocean, the northern end is known as Shark's Cove. (Don't let the name deter you from snorkeling here. Just as there are birds in the sky, there are sharks in the ocean. This can be a great snorkeling spot—if the waves are flat.) The southern end is called Three Tables (from the shore you can see the three flat "tables" and fairly shallow water. Snorkeling is great in both areas. In the winter, when the big waves roll into the North Shore, this area can be very dangerous. *59–727 Kamehameha Hwy. (Pupukea Rd.), Pupukea. Bus: 52.*

★★★ **kids Waikiki Beach** WAIKIKI   This famous 1½-mile-long (2.4km) crescent of imported sand

The shallow waters at Pupukea are ideal for first-time snorkelers.

(from Molokai) has great snorkeling spots along nearly the entire length of the beach, but my favorite snorkeling spot is Queen's Beach or Queen's Surf Beach, between the Natatorium and the Waikiki Aquarium. It's less crowded here, the waters are calm, and the fish are plentiful. I usually get in the water behind the Waikiki Aquarium and snorkel up to the Natatorium and back. *Stretching from Ala Wai Yacht Harbor to Diamond Head Park. Bus: 19 or 20.*

★★ **Waimea Beach Park** NORTH SHORE   In summer, this deep, sandy bowl has gentle waves that allow access to great snorkeling around the rocks and reef. Snorkeling isn't an option in the winter, when huge waves pummel the shoreline. *51–031 Kamehameha Hwy., Waimea. Bus: 52.*

Snorkeling with butterflyfish at Hanauma Bay.

Adventures **in the Ocean**

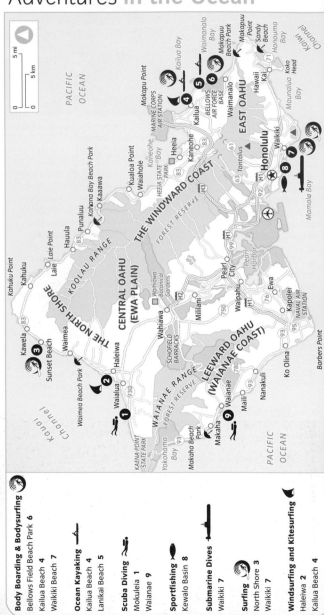

Body Boarding & Bodysurfing
Bellows Field Beach Park 6
Kailua Beach 4
Waikiki Beach 7

Ocean Kayaking
Kailua Beach 4
Lanikai Beach 5

Scuba Diving
Mokuleia 1
Waianae 9

Sportfishing
Kewalo Basin 8

Submarine Dives
Waikiki 7

Surfing
North Shore 3
Waikiki 7

Windsurfing and Kitesurfing
Haleiwa 2
Kailua Beach 4

To really appreciate Oahu, you need to get off the land. Strap on some scuba gear and plunge beneath the ocean, skip across the water in a sailing charter, go sportfishing and battle a 1,000-pound (454kg) marlin, glide over the water in the kayak, or ride the waves bodysurfing, board surfing, or windsurfing. Whatever ocean adventure thrills you, you will find it here.

Bodyboarding (Boogie Boarding) & Bodysurfing

Riding the waves without a board, becoming one with the rolling water, is a way of life in Hawaii. Some bodysurfers just rely on their hands to ride the waves; others use hand boards or a boogie board or bodyboard. Both bodysurfing and bodyboarding require a pair of open-heeled swim fins to help propel you through the water. Good places to learn to bodyboard are in the small waves of **Waikiki Beach** and **Kailua Beach** (both reviewed in chapter 6), and Bellows Field Beach Park, off Kalanianaole Hwy. 72 (Hughs Rd.), in Waimanalo (bus 57), which is open to the public on weekends (noon Fri to midnight Sun and holidays).

Ocean Kayaking

Gliding silently over the water, propelled by a paddle, seeing Oahu from the sea the way the early Hawaiians did—that's what ocean kayaking is all about. Early mornings are always best, because the wind comes up around 11am, making seas choppy and paddling difficult. For a wonderful adventure, rent a kayak, arrive at **Lanikai Beach** just as the sun is appearing, and paddle across the emerald lagoon to the pyramid-shaped islands called Mokulua—it's an experience you won't forget. A second favorite kayak launching area is **Kailua Beach.** Kayak equipment rental starts at $12 an hour for a single kayak, and $25 an hour for a double kayak. See the box "Where to Rent Beach Equipment" on p 178.

★★ kids **Kailua Sailboards & Kayaks** First-time kayakers can learn a lot on the "excursion" tour, designed for the novice. The fee covers lunch, all equipment, lessons, transportation from Waikiki

A bodyboarder takes on some North Shore waves.

Sailing & Snorkeling Tours

A funny thing happens to people when they come to Hawaii: Maybe it's the salt air, the warm tropical nights, or the blue Hawaiian moonlight, but otherwise-rational people who have never set foot on a boat in their life suddenly want to go out to sea. You can opt for a "booze cruise," jammed with loud, rum-soaked strangers, or you can sail on one of these special yachts, all of which will take you out whale-watching in season (roughly Jan–Apr).

With ★ **Captain Bob's Adventure Cruises** (☎ 808/942-5077) you can see the majestic Windward Coast the way it should be seen—from Kaneohe Bay. The 42-foot (13m) catamaran skims across the almost always calm water above the shallow coral reef, lands at the disappearing sandbar Ahu o Laka, and takes you past two small islands to snorkel among abundant tropical fish and, sometimes, turtles. The trip costs $88 adults, $73 children 3 to 14 (free for kids 2 and under).

The 140-foot-long (43m) ★★ *Navatek I* (☎ 808/973-1311) isn't even called a boat; it's actually a SWATH (Small Waterplane Area Twin Hull) vessel, which guarantees that you'll be "seasick free." It's the smoothest ride in Waikiki. In fact, *Navatek I* is the only dinner-cruise ship to receive U.S. Coast Guard certification to travel beyond Diamond Head. They offer both lunch ($63 adults, $56 kids 2–11) and sunset dinner cruises ($80–$112 adults, $74–$95 kids 2–11), and during the whale season (roughly Jan–Apr), you get whales to boot. Both cruises include live Hawaiian music. The cruise leaves from Aloha Tower Marketplace, Pier 6.

Picture this: floating in the calm waters off the Waianae coast, where your 42-foot (13m) sailing catamaran has just dropped you off. You watch turtles swimming in the reef below, and in the distance, a pod of spinner dolphins appears. In the winter, you may spot humpback whales on the morning cruise, which also includes continental breakfast and other refreshments and snorkel gear, instruction, and a floatation device. Sound good? Call **Wild Side Tours** (☎ 808/306-7273; www.sailhawaii.com). Tours leave from the Waianae Boat Harbor. The morning sail/snorkel tour costs $115 (ages 6 and up; not recommended for younger children).

hotels, and 2 hours of kayaking in Kailua Bay. *130 Kailua Rd.* ☎ *808/262-2555. www.kailuasail boards.com. Excursion tour $95 adults, $81 kids 8–12.*

Scuba Diving

Oahu is a wonderful place to scuba dive, especially for those interested in wreck diving. One of the more famous wrecks in Hawaii is the

Mahi, a 185-foot (56m) former mine-sweeper easily accessible just south of Waianae. Abundant marine life makes this a great place to shoot photos—schools of lemon butterfly fish and taape (blue-lined snapper) are so comfortable with divers and photographers that they practically pose. Eagle rays, green sea turtles, manta rays, and white-tipped sharks occasionally cruise by as well, and eels peer out from the wreck.

For nonwreck diving, one of the best dive spots in summer is Kahuna Canyon, a massive amphitheater located near Mokuleia. Walls rising from the ocean floor create the illusion of an underwater Grand Canyon. Inside the amphitheater, crabs, octopuses, slippers, and spiny lobsters abound (be aware that taking them in summer is illegal), and giant trevally, parrotfish, and unicorn fish congregate as well. Outside the amphitheater, you're likely to see an occasional shark in the distance.

Because Oahu's greatest dives are offshore, your best bet is to book a two-tank dive from a dive boat. Hawaii's oldest and largest outfitter is **Aaron's Dive Shop,** 307 Hahani St., Kailua (☎ **808/262-2333;** www.hawaii-scuba.com). A two-tank boat dive costs $115 (you provide your own gear), $125 (they provide rental gear), including transportation from the Kailua shop. **Dive Oahu,** 1085 Ala Moana Blvd., Waikiki (☎ **808/922-3483;** www.diveoahu.com), has two-tank boat dives for $129. **Surf-N-Sea,** 62–595 Kamehameha Hwy., Haleiwa (☎ **808/637-9887;** www.surfnsea.com), has two-tank boat dives for $140.

Diving Tips

A great resource for diving on your own is the University of Hawaii Sea Grant's Dive Hawaii

Kayaking on the windward coast.

Guide (www.hawaiiscubadiving.com), which describes nearly every dive site on the various Hawaiian islands, including Oahu.

Sportfishing

Marlin (as big as 1,200 lb./544kg), tuna, ono, and mahimahi await the baited hook in Hawaii's coastal and channel waters. No license is required; just book a sportfishing vessel out of Kewalo Basin, on Ala Moana Boulevard (at Ward Ave.), the main location for charter fishing boats on Oahu, located between the Honolulu International Airport and Waikiki. When the fish are biting, the captains display the catch of the day in the afternoon. Or contact **Sportfish Hawaii.** This sportfishing booking agency helps match you with the best fishing boat; every vessel they book has been inspected and must meet rigorous criteria to guarantee that you will have a great time. ☎ *877/388-1376* or *808/396-2607. www.sportfishhawaii.com. $812–$1,300 for a full-day exclusive charter (you, plus 5 friends, get the entire boat to yourself); $717 for a ½-day exclusive; or from $191 for a*

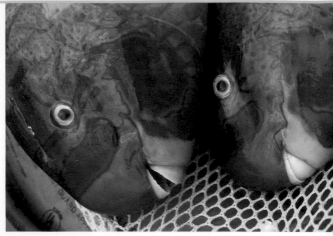

Spectacled parrotfish.

full-day share charter (you share the boat with 5 other people).

Submarine Dives

Here's your chance to play Jules Verne and experience the underwater world from the comfort of a submarine. ★★ *Atlantis* **Submarine** will take you on an adventure below the surface in high-tech comfort, narrating your tour as you watch tropical fish and sunken ships just outside the sub; if swimming's not your thing, this is a great way to see Hawaii's spectacular sea life. ***Warning:*** *Skip this if you suffer from claustrophobia.* ***Shuttle boats to the sub leave from Hilton Hawaiian Village Pier.*** ☎ *800/548-6262 or 808/ 973-9811. www.atlantissubmarines. com. $106 for adults, $48 for kids 12 and under (children must be at least 3 ft./.9m tall). Tip: Book online for discount rates of $96 for adults and $44 for kids.*

Surfing

The ancient Hawaiian sport of *hee nalu* (wave sliding) is probably the sport most people picture when

they think of the islands. In summer, when the water's warm and there's a soft breeze in the air, the south swell comes up. It's surf season in Waikiki, the best place on Oahu to learn how to surf. For lessons in Waikiki, go early to **Aloha Beach Service,** next to the Moana Surfrider, 2365 Kalakaua Ave. (☎ **808/922-3111**). Lessons are $30 an hour, and rentals are $10 to $15 for the first hour, $5 for every hour after that. On the North Shore, contact the **Hans Hedemann Surf School** at the Turtle Bay Resort (☎ **808/924-7778;** www.hhsurf. com); Hedemann has been a champion surfer for some 34 years. Lessons start at $75 a hour.

Surf's Up!

To find out where the waves are, call the Surf News Network Surfline (☎ 808/596-SURF [7873]) to get the latest surf conditions.

Windsurfing & Kitesurfing

Windward Oahu's Kailua Beach is the home of champion and pioneer

Sea Life Primer

You're likely to spot one or more of the following fish while underwater:

Angelfish can be distinguished by the spine, located low on the gill plate. These fish are very shy; several species live in colonies close to coral.

Blennies are small, elongated fish, ranging from 2 to 10 inches (5–25cm) long, with the majority in the 3- to 4-inch (7.6–10cm) range. Blennies are so small that they can live in tide pools; you might have a hard time spotting one.

Butterflyfish, among the most colorful of the reef fish, are usually seen in pairs (scientists believe they mate for life) and appear to spend most of their day feeding. Most butterflyfish have a dark band through the eye and a spot near the tail resembling an eye, meant to confuse their predators (moray eels love to lunch on them).

Moray and **conger eels** are the most common eels seen in Hawaii. Morays are usually docile except when provoked or when there's food around. Although morays may look menacing, conger eels look downright happy, with big lips and pectoral fins (situated so that they look like big ears) that give them the appearance of a perpetually smiling face.

Parrotfish, one of the largest and most colorful of the reef fish, can grow up to 40 inches (102cm) long. They're easy to spot—their front teeth are fused together, protruding like buck teeth that allow them to feed by scraping algae from rocks and coral. Native parrotfish species include yellowbar, regal, and spectacled.

Scorpion fish are what scientists call "ambush predators." They hide under camouflaged exteriors and ambush their prey. Several kinds sport a venomous dorsal spine. These fish don't have a gas bladder, so when they stop swimming, they sink—that's why you usually find them "resting" on ledges and on the ocean bottom. They're not aggressive, but be very careful where you put your hands and feet in the water so as to avoid those venomous spines.

Surgeonfish, sometimes called *tang,* get their name from the scalpel-like spines located on each side of the body near the base of the tail. Several surgeonfish, such as the brightly colored yellow tang, are boldly colored; others are adorned in more conservative shades of gray, brown, or black.

Wrasses are a very diverse family of fish, ranging in length from 2 to 15 inches (5–38cm). Wrasses can change gender from female to male. Some have brilliant coloration that changes as they age.

Experiencing *Jaws:*
Up Close & Personal

You're 4 miles (over 6km) out from land, surrounded by open ocean. Suddenly from out of the blue depths a shape emerges: the sleek, pale shadow of a 6-foot-long (nearly 2m) gray reef shark, followed quickly by a couple of 10-foot-long (3m) Galapagos sharks. Within a couple of heartbeats, you are surrounded by sharks on all sides. Do you panic? No—you paid $120 to be in the midst of these jaws of the deep. And, of course, you have a 6×6×10-foot (1.8×1.8×3m) aluminum shark cage separating you from all those teeth. If this sounds like your idea of a good time, call **North Shore Shark Adventures** (☎ 808/256-2769; www.hawaiishark adventures.com). The shark cage, connected to the boat with wire line, holds up to four snorkelers (it's comfortable with two but pretty snug at full capacity). You can stay on the boat and view the sharks from a more respectable distance for just $60.

windsurfer Robbie Naish; it's also the best place to learn to windsurf. The oldest and most established windsurfing business in Hawaii is **Naish Hawaii/Naish Windsurfing Hawaii,** 155-A Hamakua Dr., Kailua (☎ **800/767-6068** or 808/262-6068; www.naish.com). Private lessons start at $75 for a 60-minute session.

Kite-surfing lessons are also available from **Kailua Sailboards & Kayaks,** 130 Kailua Rd. (☎ **808/ 262-2555;** www.kailuasailboards. com). Group lessons cost $129 per person for 2 hours (including all gear and lunch). These companies also rent equipment. ●

Waikiki is the ideal place to learn to hang ten.

The
Savvy Traveler

Before You Go

Government Tourist Offices

The **Hawaii Visitors and Convention Bureau (HVCB)** has an office at 2270 Kalakaua Ave., Seventh Floor, Honolulu, HI 96815 (☎ **800/ GO-HAWAII** [464-2924] or 808/923-1811; www.gohawaii.com). The **Oahu Visitors Bureau** is at 735 Bishop St., Ste. 1872, Honolulu, HI 96813 (☎ **877/525-OAHU** [6248] or 808/524-0722; www.visit-oahu.com).

The Best Time to Go

Most visitors don't come to Honolulu when the weather's best in the islands; rather, they come when it's at its worst everywhere else. Thus, the **high season**—when prices are up and resorts are booked to capacity—generally runs from mid-December to March or mid-April (depending on when Easter falls). The last 2 weeks of December in particular are the prime time for travel. If you're planning a holiday trip, make your reservations as early as possible, count on holiday crowds, and expect to pay top dollar for accommodations, car rentals, and airfare. Whale-watching season begins in January and continues through the rest of winter, sometimes lasting into May.

The **off seasons,** when the best bargain rates are available, are spring (mid-Apr to mid-June) and fall (Sept to mid-Dec)—a paradox, since these are the best seasons in terms of reliably great weather. If you're looking to save money, or if you just want to avoid the crowds, this is the time to visit. Hotel rates tend to be significantly lower during these off seasons. Airfares also tend to be lower—again, sometimes substantially—and good packages and special deals are often available.

Previous page: Waikiki Trolley.

Note: If you plan to come to Honolulu between the last week in April and the first week in May, be sure to book your accommodations, air reservations, and car rental in advance. In Japan the last week of April is called **Golden Week,** because three Japanese holidays take place one after the other. The islands are especially busy with Japanese tourists during this time.

Due to the large number of families traveling in **summer** (June–Aug), you won't get the fantastic bargains of spring and fall. However, you'll still do much better on packages, airfare, and accommodations than you will in the winter months.

Festivals & Special Events

WINTER. At the **Triple Crown of Surfing,** the world's top professional surfers compete in events for more than $1 million in prize money. Competition takes place on the North Shore whenever the surf's up from late November to December. Call ☎ **808/739-3965** (www.triple crownofsurfing.com). The second Sunday in December is the **Honolulu Marathon,** one of the largest marathons in the world, with more than 30,000 competitors. Call ☎ **808/ 734-7200** (www.honolulu marathon.org). In late January or early February (depending on the lunar calendar), the red carpet is rolled out for **Chinese New Year** with a traditional lion dance, fireworks, food booths, and a host of activities. Call ☎ **808/533-3181.** Depending on surf conditions, February or March brings the **Buffalo's Big Board Classic** at Makaha Beach. You'll see traditional Hawaiian surfing, long boarding, and canoe surfing. Call ☎ **808/951-7877.**

SPRING. The **Annual Easter Sunrise Service** is celebrated with the century-old sunrise services at the National Cemetery of the Pacific, Punchbowl Crater, Honolulu. Call ☎ **808/566-1430.** May 1 means Lei Day in Hawaii and the largest celebration is the **Annual Lei Day Concert** with the Brothers Cazimero at the Waikiki Shell. Call ☎ **808/597-1888,** ext. 232. Mid-May brings the **World Fire-Knife Dance Championships and Samoan Festival,** Polynesian Cultural Center, Laie, where junior and adult fire-knife dancers from around the world converge for one of the most amazing performances you'll ever see. Authentic Samoan food and cultural festivities round out the fun. Call ☎ **808/293-3333** (www.polynesian culturalcenter.com).

SUMMER. In June, the **King Kamehameha Celebration,** a state holiday, features a massive floral parade, *hoolaulea* (party), and much more. Call ☎ **808/586-0333** (http://hawaii.gov/dags/king_kamehameha_commission). The third weekend in June brings the **King Kamehameha Hula Competition** to the Neal Blaisdell Center; it's one of the top hula competitions in the world, with dancers from as far away as Japan. Call ☎ **808/586-0333** (www.hawaii.gov). In late July, head for the annual **Ukulele Festival,** Kapiolani Park Bandstand, Waikiki, a free concert with a ukulele orchestra of some 600 students (ages 4–92). Hawaii's top musicians all pitch in. Call ☎ **808/732-3739** (www.roysakuma.net). Late July is the annual **Queen Liliuokalani Keiki Hula Competition** at the Neal Blaisdell Center, Honolulu. More than 500 *keiki* (children) representing 22 *halau* (hula schools) from the islands compete in this dancefest. Call ☎ **808/521-6905.** In August, the **Hawaii International Jazz Festival,** The Hawaii Theatre, Honolulu, includes evening concerts and daily jam sessions plus scholarship giveaways, the University of Southern California jazz band, and many popular jazz and blues artists. Call ☎ **808/941-9974.**

Useful Websites

- **www.gohawaii.com**: An excellent, all-around guide to activities, tours, lodging, and events by the members of the Hawaii Visitors and Convention Bureau.
- **www.planet-hawaii.com**: Click on "Island" for an island-by-island guide to activities, lodging, shopping, culture, the surf report, and weather.
- **www.visit-oahu.com**: Oahu chapter of the state visitors bureau lists activities, dining, lodging, parks, shopping, and more.
- **www.hawaiian105.com**: Hawaiian music radio station.
- **www.staradvertiser.com**: Honolulu's daily newspaper with a section on entertainment.
- **www.honoluluweekly.com**: The alternative weekly newspaper, a good source to find out entertainment listings.
- **www.weather.com**: Up-to-the-minute worldwide weather reports.

HONOLULU'S AVERAGE TEMPERATURES & RAINFALL

	JAN	FEB	MAR	APR	MAY	JUNE
High (F/C)	80/27	81/27	82/28	83/28	85/29	87/31
Low (F/C)	66/19	65/18	67/19	68/20	70/21	72/22
Water Temp (F/C)	75/24	75/24	76/24	77/25	79/26	81/27
Rain (IN/CM)	3.5/9	2.5/6.5	2.5/6.5	1.5/4	1/2.5	0.5/1.5

	JULY	AUG	SEPT	OCT	NOV	DEC
High (F/C)	88/31	89/32	89/32	87/31	84/29	82/28
Low (F/C)	74/23	75/24	74/23	73/23	71/22	68/20
Water Temp (F/C)	81/27	81/27	81/27	81/27	79/26	76/24
Rain (IN/CM)	0.5/1.5	0.5/1.5	1/2.5	2.5/6.5	3/7.5	4/10

FALL. In September and October are the statewide **Aloha Festivals,** with parades and other events celebrating Hawaiian culture and friendliness throughout the state. Call ☎ **808/589-1771** (www.aloha festivals.com) for a schedule of events. The annual **Hawaii International Film Festival** takes place the first 2 weeks in November. This cinema festival with a cross-cultural spin features filmmakers from Asia, the Pacific Islands, and the United States. Call ☎ **808/550-8457** (www.hiff.org).

The Weather

Because Honolulu lies at the edge of the tropical zone, it technically has only two seasons, both of them warm. The dry season corresponds to summer, and the rainy season generally runs during the winter, from November to March. It rains every day somewhere in the islands at any time of the year, but the rainy season can cause "gray" weather and spoil your tanning opportunities. Honolulu and Waikiki generally may have a brief rain shower, followed by bright sunshine and maybe a rainbow. The **year-round temperature** usually varies no more than about 10°, but it depends on where you are. Honolulu's **leeward** sides (the west and south,

where Waikiki and Honolulu are located) are usually hot and dry, whereas the **windward** sides (east and north) are generally cooler and moist. If you want arid, sunbaked, desert-like weather, go leeward. If you want lush, often wet, junglelike weather, go windward. If you want to know how to pack just before you go, check CNN's online 5-day forecast at www.cnn.com/weather. You can also get the local weather by calling ☎ **808/871-5111.**

Restaurant & Activity Reservations

I can't say it enough: Book well in advance if you're determined to eat at a particular spot or participate in a certain activity. For popular restaurants, if you didn't call in advance, try asking for early or late hours—often tables are available before 6:30pm and after 9pm. You could also call the day before or first thing in the morning, when you may be able to take advantage of a cancellation.

Cell (Mobile) Phones

In general it's a good bet that your phone will work in Honolulu, although coverage may not be as good as in your hometown. You'll be appalled at the poor reach of our GSM (Global System for Mobiles) wireless network, which is used by much of the rest of the world. (To see where GSM phones work in the U.S., check out www.t-mobile.com/coverage/national_popup.asp). And you may not be able to send SMS (text messages) overseas. Assume nothing—call your wireless provider and get the full scoop. In a worst-case scenario, you can always rent a phone from InTouch USA (☎ 800/872-7626; www.intouch global.com), but be beware that you'll pay $1 a minute or more for airtime.

Getting **There**

By Plane
Fly directly to Honolulu. **United Airlines** (☎ 800/225-5825; www.ual.com) offers the most frequent service from the U.S. mainland. **Alaska Airlines/Horizon Air** (☎ 800/252-7522; www.alaskaair.com) has flights from Seattle and Anchorage. **American Airlines** (☎ 800/433-7300; www.aa.com) offers flights from Dallas, Chicago, San Francisco, San Jose, Los Angeles, and St. Louis. **ATA,** code sharing with **Southwest Airlines** (800/435-9792; www.southwest.com), has direct flights from Oakland, Los Angeles, Orange County, Las Vegas, and Phoenix. **Continental Airlines** (☎ 800/231-0856; www.continental.com) offers the only daily nonstop from the New York area (Newark) to Honolulu. **Delta Air Lines** (☎ 800/221-1212; www.delta.com) flies nonstop from the West Coast and from Houston and Cincinnati. **Hawaiian Airlines** (☎ 800/367-5320; www.hawaiian air.com) offers nonstop flights to Honolulu from several West Coast cities (including new service from San Diego). Airlines serving Honolulu from places other than the U.S. mainland include **Air Canada** (☎ 800/776-3000; www.aircanada.ca); **Air New Zealand** (☎ 0800/737-000 in Auckland, 643/379-5200 in Christchurch, 800/926-7255 in the U.S.; www.airnewzealand.com); **Air Pacific Airways** (☎ 808/833 5582 in the US; www.airpacific.com); **Continental Air Micronesia** (☎ 800/231-0856; www.continental.com); **Qantas** (☎ 008/177-767 in Australia, 800/227-4500 in the U.S.; www.qantas.com.au); **Japan Air Lines** (☎ 03/5489-1111 in Tokyo, 800/525-3663 in the U.S.; www.jal.com); **Jetstar** (☎ 866/397-8170; www.jetstar.com) from Sydney; **All Nippon Airways (ANA;** ☎ 03/5489-1212 in Tokyo, 800/235-9262 in the U.S.; www.fly-ana.com); **China Airlines** (☎ 02/715-1212 in Taipei, 800/227-5118 in the U.S.; www.china-airlines.com); **Air Pacific,** serving Fiji, Australia, New Zealand, and the South Pacific (☎ 800/227-4446; www.airpacific.com); **Korean Air** (☎ 02/656-2000 in Seoul, 800/223-1155 on the East Coast, 800/421-8200 on the West Coast, 800/438-5000 from Hawaii; www.koreanair.com); and **Philippine Airlines** (☎ 631/816-6691 in Manila, 800/435-9725 in the U.S.; www.philippineair.com).

Getting Around
Really, the only way to get around Honolulu and the entire island is to rent a car. There is bus service, but you must be able to put all your luggage under the seat (no surfboards or golf clubs), plus the bus service is set up for local residents and many visitor attractions do not have direct routes from Waikiki. The best way to get a good deal on a car rental is to

book online. Surprisingly, Honolulu has one of the least expensive car-rental rates in the country—about $47 a day (including all state tax and fees); the national average is about $56. Cars are usually plentiful, except on holiday weekends, which in Hawaii also means King Kamehameha Day (June 10 or the closest weekend), Prince Kuhio Day (Mar 26), and Admission Day (third weekend in Aug). All the major car-rental agencies have offices in Honolulu: **Alamo** (☎ 800/327-9633; www.goalamo.com), **Avis** (☎ 800/321-3712; www.avis.com), **Budget** (☎ 800/572-0700; www.budget.com), **Dollar** (☎ 800/800-4000; www.dollarcar.com), **Enterprise** (☎ 800/325-8007; www.enterprise.com), **Hertz** (☎ 800/654-3011; www.hertz.com), **National** (☎ 800/227-7368; www.nationalcar.com), and **Thrifty** (☎ 800/367-2277; www.thrifty.com). It's almost always cheaper to rent a car at the airport than in Waikiki or through your hotel (unless there's one already included in your package deal).

To rent a car in Hawaii, you must be at least 25 years old and have a valid driver's license and a credit card. Hawaii is a no-fault state, which means that if you don't have collision-damage insurance, you are required to pay for all damages before you leave the state, whether or not the accident was your fault. Your personal car insurance back home may provide rental-car coverage; read your policy or call your insurer before you leave home. Bring your insurance identification card if you decline the optional insurance, which usually costs from $12 to $20 a day, and obtain the name of your company's local claim representative before you go. Some credit card companies also provide collision-damage insurance for their customers; check with yours before you rent.

Fast **Facts**

ATMS Hawaii pioneered the use of **ATMs** nearly 3 decades ago, and now they're everywhere. You'll find them at most banks, in supermarkets, at Long's Drugs, and in most resorts and shopping centers. **Cirrus** (☎ 800/424-7787; www.mastercard.com) and **PLUS** (☎ 800/843-7587; www.visa.com) are the two most popular networks; check the back of your ATM card to see which network your bank belongs to (most banks belong to both these days).

BABYSITTING The first place to check is with your hotel. Many hotels have babysitting services or will provide you with lists of reliable sitters. If this doesn't pan out, call **People Attentive to Children** (PATCH; ☎ **808/839-1988;** www.patchhawaii.org), which will refer you to individuals who have taken their training courses on child-care.

BANKING HOURS Bank hours are Monday through Thursday from 8:30am to 3pm, Friday from 8:30am to 6pm; some banks are open on Saturday.

BED & BREAKFAST, CONDOMINIUM & VACATION HOMES RENTALS The top reservations service for bed-and-breakfasts is **Hawaii's Best Bed & Breakfasts** (☎ **800/262-9912;** www.bestbnb.com). For condos, I recommend **Hawaii Condo Exchange** (☎ **800/442-0404;** www.hawaiicondoexchange.com); for vacation rentals, contact **Hawai-**

ian Beach Rentals (☎ **808/ 262-69368;** www.hawaiianbeach rentals.com)

BUSINESS HOURS Most offices are open from 8am to 5pm. Most shopping centers are open Monday through Friday from 10am to 9pm, Saturday from 10am to 5:30pm, and Sunday from 10am to 5 or 6pm.

CLIMATE See "The Weather" on p 190.

CONSULATES & EMBASSIES Honolulu has the following consulates: **Australia,** 1000 Bishop St., Penthouse Suite, Honolulu, HI 96813 (☎ 808/ 524-5050); **Federated States of Micronesia,** 3049 Ualena St., Ste. 908, Honolulu, HI 96819 (☎ 808/ 836-4775); **Japan,** 1742 Nuuanu Ave., Honolulu, HI 96817 (☎ 808/ 543-3111); and **Republic of the Marshall Islands,** 1888 Lusitana St., Ste. 301, Honolulu, HI 96813 (☎ 808/545-7767).

CUSTOMS Depending on the city of your departure, some countries (like Canada) clear customs at the city of their departure, while other countries clear customs in Honolulu.

DENTISTS If you have dental problems, a nationwide referral service known as 1-800-DENTIST (☎ **800/ 336-8478**) will provide the name of a nearby dentist or clinic.

Emergency dental care is available from Dr. Ronald Kashiwada, 3049 Ualena St., Ste. 716, Honolulu (☎ **808/836-3348**); Dr. Dino Dee, 1441 Kapiolani Blvd., Ste. 1112, Honolulu (☎ **808/942-8877**); and Dr. Herman Zampetti, 1441 Kapiolani Blvd., Ste. 518, Honolulu (☎ **808/941-6222**).

DINING With a few exceptions at the high end of the scale, dining attire is fairly casual. It's a good idea to make reservations in advance if you plan on eating between 7 and 9pm.

DOCTORS **Doctors On Call** offers daily, 24-hour office visits and house calls, as well as 24-hr. courtesy pickup service; 2335 Kalakaua Ave., #207, Honolulu (☎ **808/971-6000** [English] or ☎ 808/923-9966 [Japanese]). They also have offices in the following Waikiki hotels: **Hilton Hawaiian Village,** 2005 Kalia Rd., Rainbow Bazaar, upper level (☎ **808/973-5252;** daily 8am–5pm); and the **Sheraton Princess,** 120 Kaiulani Ave. (☎ **808/971-6000**).

ELECTRICITY Like Canada, the United States uses 110–120 volts AC (60 cycles), compared to 220–240 volts AC (50 cycles) in most of Europe, Australia, and New Zealand. If your small appliances use 220 to 240 volts, you'll need a 110-volt transformer and a plug adapter with two flat parallel pins to operate them here. Downward converters that change 220–240 volts to 110–120 volts are difficult to find in the United States, so bring one with you.

EMBASSIES See "Consulates & Embassies," above.

EMERGENCIES Dial ☎ **911** for the police, an ambulance, or the fire department. For the **Poison Control Center,** call ☎ **800/362-3585.**

EVENT LISTINGS The best sources for listings are the Friday edition of the local daily newspaper, *Honolulu Star-Advertiser* (www.honolulu star-advertiser.com); the weekly alternative newspaper, *Honolulu Weekly* (www.honoluluweekly. com); and the weekly shopper, *Mid-Week* (www.midweek.com). There are also several tourist publications, such as *This Week on Oahu* (www.thisweek.com).

GLBT TRAVELERS The International Gay & Lesbian Travel Association (IGLTA; ☎ 800/448-8550 or 954/776-2626; www.iglta.org) is the trade association for the gay and lesbian travel industry, and offers an online directory of gay- and lesbian-friendly travel businesses. For information on gay-friendly business, accommodations, and gay-owned and gay-friendly lodgings, contact **Pacific Ocean Holidays,** P.O. Box 88245, Honolulu, HI 96830 (☎ **800/735-6600;** www.gayhawaii.com). **The Aloha Pride Center,** P.O. Box 22718, Honolulu, HI 96823 (mailing address), or 2424 S. Beretania St. (between Isenberg and University), Honolulu (☎ **808/951-7000;** www.alohapridecenter.org), is a referral center for nearly every kind of gay-related service you can think of, including the latest happenings on Oahu. Open Monday through Friday from 10am to 6pm, Saturday from noon to 4pm. Check out their quarterly community newspaper, *Outlook,* which covers local issues concerning the islands' gay community.

INTERNET CENTERS Every major hotel and even many small B&Bs have Internet access. Many of them offer high-speed wireless; check ahead of time, because the charges can be exorbitant. The best Internet deal in Hawaii is the service at the **public libraries** (to find the closest location near you, check www.publiclibraries.com/hawaii.htm), which offer free access if you have a library card. You can purchase a 3-month visitor card for $10. **Shaka-Net,** Hawaii's largest wireless Internet service provider, has completed the first phase of its free Wireless Waikiki network. Phase I covers a significant portion of Waikiki and includes an estimated 1,000 hotel rooms, portions of the Honolulu Zoo, Kapiolani Park, Queens Beach,

Kuhio Beach, and the adjacent shoreline. The boundaries of Phase I are roughly Kalakaua Avenue from Liliuokalani Avenue to Queen's Beach in the Diamond Head direction, and Liliuokalani Avenue/Kuhio Avenue on the Ewa side, down Kuhio Avenue across Kapiolani Park to Monsarrat Avenue.

LOST PROPERTY Check **Travelers Aid International,** Waikiki Shopping Plaza, 2250 Kalakauā Ave., Ste. 403–3, Waikiki (☎ **808/926-8274;** www.visitoralohasocietyofhawaii.org).

MAIL & POSTAGE To find the nearest post office, call ☎ **800/ASK-USPS** (275-8777) or log on to www.usps.gov. In Waikiki, the post office is located at 330 Saratoga Rd. (☎ **808/973-7515**). Mail can be sent to you, in your name, c/o General Delivery, at the post office. Most post offices will hold your mail for up to 1 month. At press time, domestic postage rates were 28¢ for a postcard and 44¢ for a letter. For international mail, a first-class letter of up to 1 ounce costs 63¢ and a first-class postcard costs 55¢.

PASSPORTS Always keep a photocopy of your passport with you when you're traveling. If your passport is lost or stolen, having a copy significantly facilitates the reissuing process at your consulate. Keep your passport and other valuables in your room's safe or in the hotel safe.

PHARMACIES There are no 24-hour pharmacies in Honolulu or Waikiki. Pharmacies I recommend are **Longs Drugs:** in Waikiki at 1450 Ala Moana Blvd. at Atkins Drive (☎ 808/941-4433); in Honolulu at 330 Pali Hwy. near Vineyard Boulevard (☎ 808/536-7302); or at 4211 Waialae Ave. near Hunakai Street (☎ 808/732-0781).

SAFETY Although Hawaii is generally a safe tourist destination, visitors have been crime victims, so stay alert. The most common crime against tourists is rental-car break-ins. Never leave any valuables in your car, not even in your trunk. Be especially careful in high-risk areas such as beaches and resorts. Never carry large amounts of cash with you. Stay in well-lighted areas after dark. Don't hike on deserted trails or swim in the ocean alone. If you are a victim of crime, contact The **Visitor Aloha Society of Hawaii (VASH),** Waikiki Shopping Plaza, 2250 Kalakaua Ave., Ste. 403–3 (☎ **808/926-8274;** www.visitor alohasocietyofhawaii.org).

SPECTATOR SPORTS You've got your choice of **golf tournaments** (☎ **808/792-9300**); **Hawaiian outrigger canoe races,** from May to September (☎ **808/383-7798;** www.y2kanu.com); and **surfing** (☎ **808/739-3965;** www.triple crownofsurfing.com).

TAXIS Taxis are abundant at the airport; an attendant will be happy to flag one down for you. Fares are standard for all taxi firms; from the airport, expect to pay about $28 to $35 to Waikiki and about $25 to downtown Honolulu (plus tip). For a flat fee of $25, ★ **Star Taxi** (☎ **800/671-2999** or 808/942-STAR [7827]; www.hawaiistartaxi.net) will take up to five passengers from the airport to Waikiki (with no extra charge for baggage); however, you must book in advance, and call Star again after you've arrived and before you pick up your luggage to make sure a cab will be outside waiting for you. All taxis in Honolulu take cash and traveler's checks, no credit cards.

TELEPHONE For directory assistance, dial ☎ **411;** for long-distance information, dial 1, then the appropriate area code and 555-1212. Pay phones cost 50¢ for local calls (all calls on the island of Oahu are local calls). The area code for all of Hawaii is 808. Calls to other islands are considered long distance, so you have to dial 1 + 808 + the 7-digit phone number.

TIPPING Tipping is ingrained in the American way of life. Here are some rules of thumb: In hotels, tip bellhops at least $1 per bag ($2–$3 if you have a lot of luggage) and tip the chamber staff $1 to $2 per person per day (more if you've left a disaster area for him or her to clean up, or if you're traveling with kids and/or pets). Tip the doorman or concierge only if he or she has provided you with some specific service (like calling a cab). In restaurants, bars, and nightclubs, tip service staff 15% to 20% of the check, and tip bartenders 10% to 15%. Tipping is not expected in cafeterias and fast-food restaurants. Tip cab drivers 15% of the fare and tip skycaps at airports at least $1 per bag ($2–$3 if you have a lot of luggage).

TOILETS Your best bet is Starbucks or a fast-food restaurant. You can also head to hotel lobbies and shopping centers. Parks have restrooms, but generally they are not very clean and are in need of major repairs.

TOURIST OFFICES See "Government Tourist Offices" on p 188.

TRAVELERS WITH DISABILITIES Travelers with disabilities are made to feel very welcome in Hawaii. Hotels are usually equipped with wheelchair-accessible rooms, and tour companies provide many special services. The only travel agency in Hawaii specializing in needs for travelers with disabilities is **Access Aloha Travel** (☎ **800/480-1143;** www.accessalohatravel.com), which can book anything, including rental vans, accommodations, tours, cruises, airfare, and just about anything else you can think of.

Handicabs of the Pacific (☎ 808/524-3866) is a private company offering wheelchair taxi services in air-conditioned vehicles that are specially equipped with ramps and wheelchair lockdowns. Handicabs offers a range of taxi services (airport pickup to Waikiki hotels is $47 one-way for two). To rent wheelchair-accessible vans, contact **Accessible Vans of Hawaii**

(☎ **800/303-3750);** for hand-controlled cars contact **Avis** (☎ **800/ 331-1212;** www.avis.com) and **Hertz** (☎ **800/654-3131;** www.hertz.com). The number of hand-controlled cars in Hawaii is limited, so be sure to book well in advance. Vision-impaired travelers who use a Seeing Eye dog need to present documentation that the dog is a trained Seeing Eye dog and has had rabies shots. For more information, contact the Animal Quarantine Facility (☎ **808/ 483-7171;** www.hawaii.gov).

Hawaii: **A Brief History**

AROUND 250–700 Paddling outrigger canoes, the first ancestors of today's Hawaiians followed the stars and birds across the sea to Hawaii, which they called "the land of raging fire."

AROUND 1300, the transoceanic voyages stopped for some reason, and Hawaii began to develop its own culture in earnest. The settlers built temples, fishponds, and aqueducts to irrigate taro plantations. Sailors became farmers and fishermen. Each island was a separate kingdom. The *alii* (royalty) created a caste system and established taboos. Violators were strangled. High priests asked the gods Lono and Ku for divine guidance. Ritual human sacrifices were common.

1778 Captain James Cook, trying to find the mythical Northwest Passage to link the Pacific and Atlantic oceans, sailed into Waimea Bay on Kauai, where he was welcomed as the god Lono. Overnight, Stone Age Hawaii entered the age of iron. Nails were traded for fresh water, pigs, and the affections of Hawaiian women.

The sailors brought syphilis, measles, and other diseases to which the Hawaiians had no natural immunity, thereby unwittingly wreaking havoc on the native population.

FEB. 14, 1779 Cook and four of his crew were killed in Kealakekua Bay on the Big Island.

1782 Kamehameha I begins his campaign to unify the Hawaiian islands.

1804 King Kamehameha I conquers Oahu in a bloody battle fought the length of Nuuanu Valley, then moves his court from the island of Hawaii to Waikiki. Five years later, he relocates to what is now downtown Honolulu, next to Nimitz Highway at Queen and Bethel streets.

1810 Kamehameha I unites the Hawaiian Islands under a single leader.

1819 This year brings events that change the Hawaiian Islands forever: Kamehameha I dies, his son Liholiho is proclaimed Kamehameha II, and under the influence of Queen Kaahumanu, Kamehameha II orders the destruction of *heiau* (temples) and an end to the *kapu* (taboo) system, thus overthrowing the traditional Hawaiian religion. The first whaling ship, *Bellina,* drops anchor in Lahaina.

1823 The whalers meet their rivals for this hedonistic playground: the missionaries, who arrive from New England bent on converting the pagans. Intent on instilling their brand of rock-ribbed Christianity in the islanders, the missionaries clothe the natives, ban them from dancing the hula, and nearly dismantle their ancient culture. They try to keep the whalers and sailors out of the bawdy houses, where a flood of whiskey quenches fleet-size thirsts and where the virtue of native women is never safe.

1845 King Kamehameha III moves the capital of Hawaii from Lahaina to Honolulu, where more commerce can be accommodated due to the natural harbor there.

1848 The Great Mahele is signed by King Kamehameha III, which allows commoners and foreigners to own land outright or in "fee simple," a concept that continues today.

1850 Kamehameha III proclaims Honolulu the capital city of his kingdom. It is still the capital and dominant city of the nation's 50th state.

1882 America's only royal residence, Iolani Palace, is built on Oahu.

1885 The first contract laborers from Japan arrive to work on the sugar cane plantations.

JAN. 17, 1893 A group of American sugar planters and missionary descendants, with the support of U.S. Marines, imprison Queen Liliuokalani in her own palace in Honolulu and illegally overthrow the Hawaiian government.

1898 Hawaii is annexed to the United States.

1900 Hawaii becomes a United States territory. The Great Chinatown fire leaves 7,000 people homeless in Honolulu.

1922 Prince Jonah Kalanianaole Kuhio, the last powerful member of the royal Hawaiian family, dies.

1927 First nonstop air flight from the mainland to Honolulu.

DEC. 7, 1941 Japanese Zeros bomb American warships based at Pearl Harbor, plunging the United States into World War II.

MAR. 18, 1959 Hawaii becomes the last star on the Stars and Stripes, the 50th state of the Union. This year also sees the arrival of the first jet airliners, which bring 250,000 tourists to the fledgling state.

1967 The state of Hawaii hosts one million tourists this year.

1990s Hawaii's state economy goes into a tailspin following a series of events: First, the Gulf War severely curtails air travel to the island; then Hurricane Iniki slams into Kauai, crippling its infrastructure; and, finally, sugar cane companies across the state begin shutting down, laying off thousands of workers.

2008 One of the biggest booms to Hawaii's tourism comes from a son of Hawaii, Barack Obama, when he becomes the 44th president of the United States.

The Hawaiian **Language**

Almost everyone here speaks English. But many folks in Hawaii now speak Hawaiian as well. All visitors will hear the words *aloha* (hello/goodbye/love) and *mahalo* (thank you). If you've just arrived, you're a *malihini.* Someone who's been here a long time is a *kamaaina.* When you finish a job or your meal, you are *pau* (finished). On Friday it's *pau hana,* work finished. You eat *pupu* (Hawaii's version of hors d'oeuvres) when you go *pau hana.*

The Hawaiian alphabet, created by the New England missionaries, has only 12 letters: the five regular vowels (a, e, i, o, and u) and seven consonants (h, k, l, m, n, p, and w). The vowels are pronounced in the Roman fashion, that is, *ah, ay, ee, oh,* and *oo* (as in "too")—not *ay, ee, eye, oh,* and *you,* as in English. For example, *huhu* is pronounced *who-who.* Most vowels are sounded separately, though some are pronounced together, as in Kalakaua: *Kah-lah-cow-ah.*

Useful Words & Phrases

Here are some basic Hawaiian words that you'll often hear in Hawaii and see throughout this book. For a more complete list of Hawaiian words, point your Web browser to www.hisurf.com/hawaiian/dictionary.html.

alii Hawaiian royalty
aloha greeting or farewell
halau school
hale house or building
heiau Hawaiian temple or place of worship
kahuna priest or expert
kamaaina old-timer
kapa tapa, bark cloth
kapu taboo, forbidden
keiki child
lanai porch or veranda
lomilomi massage
mahalo thank you
makai a direction, toward the sea
mana spirit power
mauka a direction, toward the mountains
muumuu loose-fitting gown or dress
ono delicious
pali cliff
paniolo Hawaiian cowboy(s)
wiki quick

Eating in **Honolulu**

In the mid-1980s, Hawaii Regional Cuisine (HRC) ignited a culinary revolution. Waves of new Asian residents have planted the food traditions of their homelands in the fertile soil of Hawaii, resulting in unforgettable taste treats true to their Thai, Vietnamese, Japanese, Chinese, and Indo-Pacific roots. Traditions are mixed and matched—and when combined with the fresh harvests from sea and land for which Hawaii is known, these ethnic and culinary traditions take on renewed vigor and a cross-cultural, yet uniquely Hawaiian, quality.

At the other end of the spectrum is the vast and endearing world of "local food." By that I mean plate lunches and poke, shave ice and saimin, bento lunches and *manapua*—cultural hybrids all. A **plate lunch,** usually ordered from a lunch wagon, consists of fried mahimahi (or teriyaki beef or shoyu chicken), "two scoops rice," macaroni salad, and a few leaves of green—typically julienned cabbage. Heavy gravy is often the condiment of choice, accompanied by a soft drink in a paper cup or straight out of the can. Another favorite is **saimin**—the local version of noodles in broth topped with scrambled eggs, green onions, and sometimes pork.

The **bento,** another popular quick meal available throughout Hawaii, is a compact, boxed assortment of picnic fare usually consisting of neatly arranged sections of rice, pickled vegetables, and fried chicken, beef, or pork. From the plantations come **manapua,** a bready, doughy sphere filled with tasty fillings of sweetened pork or sweet beans. The daintier Chinese delicacy **dim sum** is made of translucent wrappers filled with fresh seafood, pork hash, and vegetables, served for breakfast and lunch. For dessert or a snack, the prevailing choice is **shave ice,** the island version of a snow cone.

Recommended **Reading**

Fiction

The first book people think about is James A. Michener's *Hawaii* (Fawcett Crest, 1974). This epic novel manages to put the Island's history into chronological order, but remember, it is still fiction, and very sanitized fiction too. For a more contemporary look at life in Hawaii today, one of the best novels is *Shark Dialogue,* by Kiana Davenport (Plume, 1995). The novel tells the story of Pono, the larger-than-life matriarch, and her four daughters of mixed races. Lois-Ann Yamanaka uses a very "local" voice and stark depictions of life in the islands in her fabulous novels *Wild Meat and the Bully Burgers* (Farrar, Straus, Giroux, 1996), *Blu's Hanging* (Avon, 1997), and *Heads by Harry* (Avon, 1999).

Nonfiction

Mark Twain's writing on Hawaii in the 1860s offers a wonderful introduction to Hawaii's history. One of his best books is *Mark Twain in Hawaii: Roughing It in the Sandwich Islands* (Mutual Publishing, 1990). Another great depiction of the Hawaii of 1889 is *Travels in Hawaii* (University of Hawaii Press, 1973), by Robert Louis Stevenson. For contemporary voices on Hawaii's unique culture, one of the best books to get is *Voices of Wisdom: Hawaiian Elders Speak,* by M. J. Harden (Aka Press, 1999). Some 24 different *kahuna* (experts) in their fields were interviewed about their talent, skill, or artistic practice.

The recently rereleased *Native Planters in Old Hawaii: Their Life, Lore and Environment* (Bishop Museum Press, Honolulu, 2004) was originally published in 1972 but is still one of the most important ethnographic works on traditional Hawaiian culture, portraying the lives of the common folk and their relationship with the land before the arrival of Westerners.

History

There are many great books on Hawaii's history, but one of the best places to start is with the formation of the Hawaiian islands, vividly described in David E. Eyre's *By Wind, By Wave: An Introduction to Hawaii's Natural History* (Bess Press, 2000). In addition to chronicling the natural history of Hawaii, Eyre describes the complex interrelationships among the plants, animals, ocean, and people that are necessary.

For a history of "precontact" Hawaii (before Westerners arrived), David Malo's *Hawaiian Antiquities* (Bishop Museum Press, 1976) is the preeminent source. Malo was born around 1793 and wrote about the Hawaiian lifestyle at that time, as well as the beliefs and religion of his people. It's an excellent reference book, but not a fast read. For more readable books on old Hawaii, try *Stories of Old Hawaii* (Bess Press, 1997), by Roy Kakulu Alameide, on myths and legends; *Hawaiian Folk Tales* (Mutual Publishing, 1998), by Thomas G. Thrum; and *The Legends and Myths of Hawaii* (Charles E. Tuttle Company, 1992), by His Hawaiian Majesty King David Kalakaua.

The best story of the 1893 overthrow of the Hawaiian monarchy is told by Queen Liliuokalani, in her book *Hawaii's Story by Hawaii's Queen Liliuokalani* (Mutual Publishing, 1990). When it was written, it was an international plea for justice for her people, but it is a poignant read even today. It's also a "must read" for people interested in current events and the recent rally in the 50th state for sovereignty. Two contemporary books on the question of Hawaii's sovereignty are Tom Coffman's *Nation Within—The Story of America's Annexation of the Nation of Hawaii* (Epicenter, 1998), and *Hawaiian Sovereignty: Do the*

Facts Matter? (Goodale, 2000), by Thurston Twigg-Smith, which explores the opposite view. Twigg-Smith, former publisher of the statewide newspaper *The Honolulu Advertiser,* is the grandson of Lorrin A. Thurston, one of the architects of the 1893 overthrow of the monarchy. His so-called "politically incorrect" views present a different look on this hotly debated topic.

For more recent history, Lawrence H. Fuchs's *Hawaii Pono* (Bess Press, 1991) is a carefully researched tome on the contributions of each of Hawaii's main immigrant communities (Chinese, Japanese, and Filipino) between 1893 and 1959.

An insightful look at history and its effect on the Hawaiian culture is *Waikiki, A History of Forgetting and Remembering,* by Andrea Feeser (University of Hawaii Press, 2006). A beautiful art book (designed by Gaye Chan), this is not your normal coffee-table book, but a different look at the cultural and environmental history of Waikiki. Using historical texts, photos, government documents, and interviews, this book lays out the story of how Waikiki went from a self-sufficient agricultural area to a tourism mecca.

Another great cultural book is Davianna Pomaikai McGreggor's *Na Kua'aina, Living Hawaiian Culture* (University of Hawaii Press, 2007). McGregor, a professor of ethnic studies at UH, examines how people lived in rural lands and how they kept the Hawaiian traditions alive.

Index

See also Accommodations and Restaurant indexes, below.

Restaurants

Photo **Credits**

p viii © Douglas Peebles/Jupiterimages; p 3 © Douglas Peebles/Jupiterimages; p 4 © David Fleetham/Mira.com/drr.net; p 5 © Ryan Siphers; p 6 © Photo Resource Hawaii/Danita Delimont.com; p 7 © David R. Frazier/DanitaDelimont.com; p 9 © Thorsten Indra/Alamy; p 10 top © Photo Resource Hawaii/DanitaDelimont.com/drr.net; p 10 bottom © Photo Resource Hawaii/DanitaDelimont.com/drr.net; p 11 © Karl Lehmann/Lonely Planet Images; p 13 top © James Montgomery/Jon Arnold Images/Alamy; p 13 bottom © Jonathan Blair/ Corbis; p 14 © Photo Resource Hawaii/DanitaDelimont.com; p 15 © SIME s.a.s./eStock Photo; p 16 top © Andrew Woodley/Alamy; p 16 bottom © Kord.com/AGE Fotostock; p 17 © John Borthwick/Lonely Planet Images; p 19 top © Andre Seale/Alamy; p 19 bottom © VisionsofParadise.com/Alamy; p 20 © P. Narayan/AGE Fotostock; p 21 © David L. Moore/ Alamy; p 22 © David Franzen Photography; p 23 top © Photo Resource Hawaii/Danita Delimont.com; p 23 bottom © David L. Moore/Alamy; p 24 top © Photo Resource Hawaii/ DanitaDelimont.com; p 24 bottom © Honolulu Academy of Arts, Hawaii, USA, Giraudon/The Bridgeman Art Library International; p 27 © David L. Moore/Alamy; p 28 © Ryan Siphers; p 29 top © Courtesy The Contemporary Museum; p 29 bottom © Bruce Behnke/Danita Delimont.com; p 30 © Ryan Siphers; p 31 © Richard Cummins/Lonely Planet Images; p 33 © Photo Resource Hawaii/DanitaDelimont.com/drr.net; p 34 © Ryan Siphers; p 35 © Douglas Peebles/Corbis; p 37 top © Photo Resource Hawaii/DanitaDelimont.com/drr.net; p 37 bottom © Photo Resource Hawaii/DanitaDelimont.com/drr.net; p 38 top © Ryan Siphers; p 38 bottom © David Franzen; p 39 © Courtesy Atlantis Adventures; p 41 © Photo Resource Hawaii/DanitaDelimont.com; p 42 © Kord.com/AGE Fotostock; p 43 top © nagelestock.com/ Alamy; p 43 bottom © Photo Resource Hawaii/DanitaDelimont.com; p 44 © Photo Resource Hawaii/DanitaDelimont.com; p 45 © Michele Burgess/Index Stock Imagery; p 47 © Corbis; p 48 © Walter Bibikow/AGE Fotostock; p 49 © Douglas Peebles/AGE Fotostock; p 49 © David J. & Janice L. Frent Collection/Corbis; p 51 © Bettmann/Corbis; p 52 top © David L. Moore/Alamy; p 52 bottom © Photo Resource Hawaii/DanitaDelimont.com/drr.net; p 53 © Courtesy Lodging: © Westin Moana Surfrider; p 54 © JTB/drr.net; p 55 top © Photo Resource Hawaii/DanitaDelimont.com/drr.net; p 55 bottom © David Franzen Photography; p 56 © Douglas Peebles/Jupiterimages; p 57 © Historical Picture Archive/Corbis; p 59 © VisionsofParadise.com/Alamy; p 60 top © Douglas Peebles Photography/Alamy; p 60 bottom © Ryan Siphers; p 61 © Mark Johnson/Mira.com/drr.net; p 63 © David L. Moore/ Alamy; p 65 © Dave Bartruff/Index Stock Imagery; p 66 © Photo Resource Hawaii/Danita Delimont.com/drr.net; p 67 © Photo Resource Hawaii/DanitaDelimont.com; p 68 top © Douglas Peebles Photography/Alamy; p 68 bottom © Douglas Peebles Photography/ Alamy; p 69 © Photo Resource Hawaii/DanitaDelimont.com; p 70 © Craig Ellenwood/Alamy; p 71 © Gisela Damm/eStock Photo; p 73 top © Photo Resource Hawaii/DanitaDelimont.com; p 73 bottom © John Oeth/Alamy; p 75 top © Ryan Siphers; p 75 bottom © John Elk III/Lonely Planet Images; p 77 © Marco Garcia; p 78 © Marco Garcia; p 79 © Marco Garcia; p 80 top © David Franzen/PhotoResourceHawaii/ DanitaDelimont.com; p 80 bottom © Marco Garcia; p 81 © Marco Garcia; p 83 top © Morvyn Rood/Alamy; p 83 bottom © David Franzen Photography; p 84 top © Douglas Peebles/Jupiterimages; p 84 bottom © John Elk III/Lonely Planet Images; p 85 top © Photo Resource Hawaii/DanitaDelimont.com; p 85 bottom © John Elk III/Lonely Planet Images; p 87 top © David L. Moore/Alamy; p 87 bottom © David Schrichte/Photo Resource Hawaii/Alamy; p 88 top © Bill Romerhaus/Index Stock Imagery; p 88 bottom © Nik Wheeler/Corbis; p 90 © David Franzen Photography; p 94 © Ryan Siphers; p 95 © David Franzen Photography; p 96 top © David Franzen Photography; p 96 bottom © David Franzen Photography; p 97 © Ryan Siphers; p 98 top © David Franzen Photography; p 98 bottom © David Franzen Photography; p 99 © Ryan Siphers; p 100 © Ryan Siphers; p 101 top © Ryan Siphers; p 101 bottom © Douglas Peebles Photography/Alamy; p 102 © Courtesy Halekulani; p 104 © Courtesy Doubletree Alana Waikiki; p 105 © Ryan Siphers; p 106 © Courtesy Lodging: © Westin Moana Surfrider; p 108 top © Photo Resource Hawaii/DanitaDelimont.com; p 108 bottom © Ryan Siphers; p 109 © Courtesy The Royal Hawaiian; p 110 © Tomas Del Amo/Alamy Images; p 111 © Courtesy Waikiki Parc Hotel; p 112 © Ryan Siphers; p 116 © Ryan Siphers; p 117 © Courtesy The Pegge Hopper Gallery; p 118 top © Ryan Siphers; p 118 bottom © Ryan Siphers; p 119 © David Franzen Photography; p 120 top © Ryan Siphers; p 120 bottom © Ryan Siphers; p 121 © Ryan Siphers; p 122 © Ryan Siphers; p 123 © Ryan Siphers; p 124 top © Ryan Siphers; p 124 bottom © David Franzen Photography; p 125 © Ryan Siphers; p 126 © Ryan Siphers; p 129 © Ryan Siphers; p 130 © David Franzen Photography; p 131 © Ryan Siphers; p 132 © Steve Lee Las Vegas; p 133 © Courtesy Hawaii Opera Theatre; p 134 © David Franzen Photography; p 135 © Photo Resource Hawaii/DanitaDelimont.com/drr.net; p 137 © Photo Resource